Helsinki
Stockholm
Moscow
Minsk
Warszawa
Praha
nna
Zagreb
Kiev
Tashkent
Alma Alta
blyana
Budapest
Sarjevo Bucarest
Tbilisi
Sofia
Dushanbe
Ulanbator
Belgrad
Baku
Pyongyang
Athn Ankara
Yerevan
Beijing
Seoul
Beirut
Ashkadabad
Tokyo
bahus
Damascus
Tehran
Jerusalem
Baghdad
Amman
Kuwait
Cairo
Islamabad
Kathmandu
Manamah
Riyadh Doha
New Delhi
Abu Dhabi
Masqat
Dhaka
Sana
Hanoi
Khartoum
Rangoon
Bangkok
Manila
Djibouti
Phnom Penh
Addis Ababa
Colombo
Kuala Lumpur
Muqdisha
Kampala
Singapore
Nairobi
Luanda
Dar-es-Salaam
Jakarta
Suva
Port Moresby
Lusaka
Mozambique
Noumea
Harare
Tananarive
dhoek
Gaborone
Canberra
Pretoria
Wellington

WORLD ARCHITECTURE 1900–2000:
A CRITICAL MOSAIC

VOLUME 10

SOUTHEAST ASIA AND OCEANIA

Prof. Kenneth Frampton
University of Columbia, New York, USA

William S. W. Lim
William Lim and Associates
Prof. Jennifer Taylor
Queensland University of Technology,
Brisbane, Australia

©1999 China Architecture & Building Press
Springer-Verlag/Wien
Printed by C & C Joint Printing Co (Guang Dong) Ltd.

Editor-in-Charge: Wang Boyang   Zhang Huizhen   Dong Suhua

Cover design: Tino Erben
Overall layout: Tino Erben and Huang Juzheng

Printed on acid-free and chlorine-free bleached paper

SPIN: 10718281
SPIN (complete series): 10718744

With 580 partly coloured Figures

CIP data applied for

ISBN 3-211-83293-9 Springer-Verlag Wien New York
ISBN 3-211-83283-1 (Complete Series) Springer-Verlag Wien New York

WORLD ARCHITECTURE 1900–2000: A CRITICAL MOSAIC

VOLUME 10

SOUTHEAST ASIA AND OCEANIA

General Editor: Kenneth Frampton
Volume Editors: William S.W. Lim
Jennifer Taylor

CHINA ARCHITECTURE & BUILDING PRESS

SpringerWienNewYork

WORLD ARCHITECTURE 1900–2000: A CRITICAL MOSAIC

General Editor: Kenneth Frampton
Associate General Editor: Zhang Qinnan

Volume X: Southeast Asia and Oceania
Volume Editors: William S.W. Lim and Jennifer Taylor
Chinese Volume Co–Editor: Zhang Qinnan

Nominators for this Volume (in alphabetical order):

For Southeast Asia:

Chen Voon Fee
Richard K. F. Ho
Sumet Jumsai
Duangrit Bunnag
Francisco "Bobby" Mañosa
Yuswadi Saliya
Brian Brace Taylor

For Oceania:

Philip James Goad
Andrew Metcalfe
Rahim B. Milani
Neville Quarry
Russell Walden
Julia Gatley

WORLD ARCHITECTURE 1900–2000: A CRITICAL MOSAIC

This book series is organized by the Architectural Society of China (ASC) and endorsed by the International Union of Architects (UIA) in coordination with the XX World Architects Congress convened in June 1999 in Beijing, China, and published by the China Architecture & Building Press (CABP) and Springer-Verlag.

CONTENTS

Complimentary Remarks by Sara Topelson de Grinberg, Past President of the International Union of Architects (UIA)   XI

Complimentary Remarks by Vassilis Sgoutas, President of the Internationa Union of Architects (UIA)   XII

Complimentary Remarks by Ye Rutang, President of the Architectural Society of China (ASC) –A Record of 20th Century World Architecture   XIII

General Introduction by Kenneth Frampton   XIV

Introductory Essay–From Nowhere to Somewhere and Beyond
on Southeast Asia by William S. W. Lim   XVII
on Oceania by Jennifer Taylor   XXX

Editors' Acknowledgments   XL

Selected Buildings   1

Southeast Asia

1900–1919

Vimanmek Palace, Bangkok, 1901, arch. Prince Narisaranuwatiwong   4
Istana Sri Menanti, Negeri Sembilan, Seremban, 1908, builders: Tukang Kahar & Tukang Taib   8
Pyre for Rama V, Bangkok, 1911, arch. Phraya Rajasongkram (Korn Hongsakul)   12
Ubudiah Mosque, Kuala Kangsar, Perak, 1917, arch. A. B. Hubback, PWD   14

1920–1939

Aula ITB (Institut Teknologi Bandung), Bandung, 1920, arch. Henry Maclaine Pont   18
Majestic Theater, Singapore, 1927, arch. unknown   22
stana Kenangan, Kuala Kangsar, Perak, 1931, builders: Haji Sopian and sons   24
Metropolitan Theater, Manila, 1931, arch. Juan M. Arellano   26
Clifford Pier, Singapore, 1931, arch. Public Works Department   30
Sultan Sulaiman Mosque, Klang, Selangor , 1932, arch. L. Kesteven   32
Singapore Railway Station and Hotel, Singapore, 1932, arch. Swan and Maclaren   34
The Municipal Office Building, Rangoon, 1933, arch. A.G. Bray and U Maung Tin   36
Villa Isola, Bandung, 1933, arch. Wolff Shoemaker   38
Grand Lycee Yersin, Dalat, 1935, arch. J. Lagisquet   42
The Central Market, Phnom Penh, 1937, arch. Jean Desbois and Louis Chauchon   46
Anglo–Oriental Building, Kuala Lumpur, 1937, arch. A. O. Coltman, Booty, Edwards & Partners   48

1940–1959

Tiong Bahru Flats, Singapore, 1941, arch. Singapore Improvement Trust (SIT)   52
Rachadamnern Boulevard Row House, Bangkok, 1946, arch. Chitrasen Abhaiwongse   54
Federal House, Kuala Lumpur, 1954, arch. B. M. Iversen   56
Asia Insurance Building, Singapore, 1954, arch. Ng Keng Siang   58
Lee Yian Lian Building, Kuala Lumpur, 1959, arch. E. S. Cooke   60

1960–1979

Parliament Building, Kuala Lumpur, 1963, arch. W. Ivor Shipley, J. K. R. **64**
Singapore Conference Hall and Trade Union House, Singapore, 1965, arch. Malayan Architects CoPartnership **66**
La Cité, Sihanouk, Phnom Penh, 1965, arch. Vladimir Bodiansky, Gerald Hanning with Vann Molyan **70**
State Mosque, Negeri Sembilan, Seremban, 1967, arch. Malayan Architects Co–Partnership **72**
Geology Building, University of Malaya, Kuala Lumpur, 1968, arch. Malayan Architects Co–Partnershipz **74**
Theater for the Performing Arts–Cultural Center of the Philippines, Manila, 1969, arch. Leandro Locsin and Associates **76**
Panabhandhu School, Classroom and Dormitory Building, Bangkok, 1970, arch. Ongard Architects **80**
British Council Building, Bangkok, 1970, arch. Sumet Jumsai & Associates **82**
People's Park Complex, Singapore, 1973, arch. Design Partnership **84**
Golden Mile Complex, Singapore, 1973, arch. Design Partnership **86**
National Arts Center of the Philippines, Mt. Makiling, Los Baños, 1976, arch. Leandro V. Locsin **88**
Science Museum, Bangkok, 1977, arch. Sumet Jumsai & Associates **90**

1980–1999

Bank of America Building, Bangkok, 1983, arch. Robert G. Boughey & Associates **94**
Walian House, Kuala Lumpur, 1984, arch. Jimmy Lim Cheok Siang **96**
Soekarno–Hatta International Airport, Jakarta, 1985, arch. Soejano & Rachman **100**
The Robot Building, Bangkok, 1986, arch. Sumet Jumsai & Associates **104**
Menara Maybank Tower, Kuala Lumpur, 1987, arch. Hijjas Kasturi Associates Sdn **108**
Central Market and Central Square, Kuala Lumpur, 1989, arch. William Lim Associates & Chen Voon Fee **110**
Reuter House, Singapore, 1990, arch. William Lim Associates & Chen Voon Fee **114**
Menara Mesiniaga, Subang Jaya, Selangor, 1992, arch. T. R. Hamzah and Yeang Sdn **116**
Eu House, Singapore, 1993, arch. Bedmar and Shi Designers Pte Ltd **120**
Bhd Chedi Bandung, Bandung, 1993, arch. Kerry Hill Architects **122**
The Datai, Langkawi Island, 1993, arch. Arkitek Jururancang (M) Sdn Bhd. & Kerry Hill Architects **124**
Floirendo Family Villas, Samal Island, Davao, 1993, arch. Francisco Mañosa and Partners **128**
Balina Serai, Indonesia, 1994, arch. Kerry Hill Architects **132**
Tan House, Bandung, 1994, arch. Tan Tjiang Ay **134**
Abelia Apartments, Singapore, 1994, arch. TangGuanBee Architects **136**
Boat Quay Conservation Area, Singapore, 1994, arch. various **138**

Oceania

1900–1919

Cathedral of the Blessed Sacrament, Christchurch, 1905, arch. Francis William Petre **142**
Main Reading Room, State Library of Victoria, Melbourne, 1911, arch. Bates, Peebles and Smart **144**
'Eryldene', Sydney, 1914, arch. William Hardy Wilson **146**
Tauroa Homestead, Hawkes Bay, 1916, arch. William Henry Gummer **150**
Newman College, University of Melbourne, Melbourne, 1917, arch. Walter Burley Griffin and Marion Mahony **152**
'Belvedere'(Stephens House), Sydney, 1919, arch. Alexander Stewart Jolly **154**

1920–1939

'Greenway', (Wilkinson House), Sydney, 1923, arch. Leslie Wilkinson **158**
Civic Theatre, Auckland, 1929, arch. Bohringer, Taylor and Johnson **160**

Macpherson Robertsonís Girls High School, Melbourne, 1934, arch. Seabrook & Fildes   **162**
Wellington Railway Station, Wellington,1937, arch. William Gray Young, Morton and Young   **164**

1940–1959

Berhampore Flats, Wellington, 1940, arch. Francis Gordon Wilson   **168**
Hamill House, Sydney, 1949, arch. Sydney Ancher   **170**
Rose Seidler House, Sydney, 1949, arch. Harry Seidler   **172**
Stanhill Flats, Melbourne, 1950, arch. Frederick Romberg   **174**
Grounds House, Melbourne, 1953, arch. Roy Grounds   **176**
Muller House, Sydney, 1955, arch. Peter Muller   **178**
Olympic Swimming Pool, Melbourne, 1956, arch. Borland, McIntyre, John and Phyllis Murphy   **180**
Boyd House, Melbourne, 1958, arch. Robin Boyd   **182**
CI House, Melbourne, 1959, arch. Bates, Smart and McCutcheon   **184**

1960–1979

War Memorial Hall, Wanganui, 1960, arch. Newman, Smith and Greenhough   **188**
Chapel of Futuna, Wellington, 1961, arch. John Scott   **190**
Rickard House, Sydney, 1961, arch. Bruce Rickard   **192**
Woolley House, Sydney, 1962, arch. Ken Woolley   **194**
C. B. Alexander College, Tocal, 1964, arch. Philip Cox and Ian McKay   **196**
Wentworth Memorial Church, Sydney, 1965, arch. Clarke Gazzard   **198**
Union College Hall of Residence, University of Queensland, Brisbane, 1965, arch. James Birrell   **200**
Athfield House, Wellington, 1965–, arch. Ian Athfield   **202**
Australia Square, Sydney, 1967, arch. Harry Seidler   **206**
Seidler House, Sydney, 1967, arch. Harry Seidler   **210**
Christchurch Town Hall, Christchurch, 1972, arch. Warren & Mahoney Architects Ltd   **212**
Sydney Opera House, Sydney, 1973, arch. Jorn Utzon and Hall, Todd and Littlemore   **214**
Cameron Offices, Canberra, 1976, arch. John Andrews   **218**
National Athletics Stadium, Canberra, 1977, arch. Philip Cox and Partners   **222**
Air Niugini Staff Housing, Korobosea, 1978, arch. Russell Hall with D. Collins of National Housing Commission   **224**

1980–1999

Jackson House, Shoreham, 1980, arch. Daryl Jackson   **228**
Nicholas and Carruthers Houes, Mt. Irvine, 1980, arch. Glenn Murcutt   **230**
Raun Raun Theatre, Goroka,1982, arch. Paul Frame and Rex Addison   **232**
Yulara Tourist Resort, Yulara, 1984, arch. Philip Cox and Partners   **234**
Papua New Guinea National Parliament Building, Waigani, 1984, arch. Cecil Hogan of PNG Department of Works and Supply and Peddle Thorp   **238**
Riverside Centre, Brisbane, 1986, arch. Harry Seidler   **242**
Parliament House of Australia, Canberra, 1988, arch. Mitchell/ Giurgola & Thorp   **246**
Sydney Football Stadium, Sydney, 1988, arch. Cox, Richardson & Taylor   **250**
Brambuk Living Cultural Centre, Halls Gap,1990, arch. Gregory Burgess   **252**
Beach House, St. Andrews Beach, 1991, arch Nonda Katsalidis   **254**
Parliament of Fiji, Suva, 1992, arch. Vitia Architects and the Fijian Government Architects   **256**
Great Southern Stand, Melbourne Cricket Ground, Melbourne, 1992, arch. Tompkins Shaw & Evans/ Daryl Jackson   **258**
Governor Phillip and Governor Macquarie Tower, Sydney, 1994, arch. Denton Corker Marshall   **260**
Headquarters for the South Pacific Commission, Noumea, 1994, arch. Architects Pacific   **262**

Melbourne Exhibition Centre, Melbourne, 1996, arch Denton Corker Marshall   **264**
Pugh House, Wellington, 1996, arch. Melling, Morse Architects   **266**
Jean–Marie Tjibaou Cultural Centre, Noumea, 1998, arch. Renzo Piano Workshop   **268**

Nominators' Statements   **272**

Southeast Asia   **273**
Chen Voon Fee   **273**
Richard K.F. Ho   **273**
Sumet Jumsai   **274**
Duangrit Bunnag   **274**
Franciso "Bobby " Mañosa   **275**
Yuswadi Saliya   **276**
Brian Brace Taylor   **276**

Oceania   **278**
Philip James Goad   **278**
Andrew Metcalf   **278**
Rahim B. Milani   **279**
Neville Quarry   **279**
Russell Walden   **280**
Julia Gatley   **280**

General Bibliography   **281**
Southeast Asia   **281**
Oceania   **282**

Index   **283**
Southeast Asia   **283**
Oceania   **286**

Complimentary Remarks

**Arch. Sara Topelson de Grinberg, Past President,
International Union of Architects (UIA)**

One of the main features of our century has been speed. Speed of communication, speed in technological development, speed in the transformation of the natural environment and speed in the evolution of philosophical thought. As many other disciplines, architecture has also been influenced by the constant will of change.

The first decades of the twentieth century saw the break with the past searching for an architecture that could represent the will of the *Zeitgeist*: the spirit of rationality, technology, pure form, movement. Many wrote about internationalism and admitted it as characteristic of the epoch. The cities around the world welcomed the new architecture introducing it into their local conditions. Man was in control of nature, he knew he had the means to transform his world, there were no limits that could stop him until he met the tragedy of war.

The Second World War brought new approaches to society. New forms were developed as a symbol of a new expressionism, whilst the reconstruction of the destroyed cities provoked the restatement of ideals. An extreme exaltation of technology became the image of future, new structural systems were employed that opened the way to fantasy. On the other hand, there were those who thought that a better future must be based on tradition. The optimistic approach of Modern movement was replaced by a more realistic *Weltanschauung,* less idealistic and more attached to the common citizen.

During the Sixties the Modern Movement was declared dead and Post–Modernism emerged. Modern urbanism was blamed for the destruction of human relationships and new theories based on the traditional block scheme were preferred. The recovery of historical typologies was one of the answers to the search of roots, either literal or interpreted. Surprising spaces, classical language, or community participation in design decisions were characteristic of the Post–Modern attitude.

But there were also other positions that looked forward evolving the language of its predecessor, the Modern Movement. Sculptural forms, megastructures and high–tech were the counter–position to historicism. While one looked for solutions in the past, the other tried to reach the future.

Critical positions such as deconstruction and critical regionalism are closing the century. The former, in an aggressive way, is giving another meaning to modern architectural language. The latter is trying to find a harmonic relationship between local culture and international influence.

We hope the collection of works presented in these volumes will give the interested reader a wide scope of the richness of twentieth century architecture around the world, from the different interpretations of a common language, the International Style, to unique regional examples.

Sara Topelson de Grinberg

Named Mexico Woman of the Year 1996, Mrs. Grinberg is Past President of the International Union of Architects.

During her career as a partner in the architectural firm of Grinberg & Topelson, she has developed projects in the fields of housing, industry, education, culture and low income housing in addition to her work in private practice, Sara has been a professor at the Universitad Anahuac teaching the history of architecture and conducting workshops in urban and architectural design for the past twenty five years.

In May 1998, she was honored by the French Ministry of Culture as Chevalier des Arts et des Lettres.

She is an academic Fellow at the Academia Mexicana de Arquitectura, an Honorary Fellow of the American Institute of Architects, the Royal Architectural Institute of Canada, the Association of Architects of Nicaragua and Venezuela, and has been recognized with the Academic Excellency Award at Universidad Anahuac.

Among her other awards are the 1996 Cruz Azul Prize for Accomplishment in the Profession and the 1996 Zazil Prize for Women Achievements in the Cultural and Scientific Area.

She is a graduate of the Faculty of Architecture at the National University of Mexico in UNAM.

Complimentary Remarks

Vassilis Sgoutas,
President
International Union of Architects

Vassilis Sgoutas

Born in Athens, Greece in 1934, he graduated from the University of Cape Town (UCT) in 1957 and entered private architectural practice in Athens, undertaking project designs covering public, industrial,commercial and hospital buildings as well as rehabilitation work and landscape architecture. He was President of the Greek Section (1951–1993), Vice President–Region II (1990–1993) of the UIA and has been its Secretary General since 1993. He is also Honorary Fellow of the Architectural Institutes of Australia (RAIA), Russia (UAR), Philippine (UAP) and Kazakhstan (UAK) and Member of EEC Helios Committee for the Handicapped (1989–1993) and Board Member of the Athens Forest Association and the Greek Spastics Society.

When the Architectural Society of China first came up with the idea of producing ten books on the architecture of this century that were to include no less than 1000 works, the undertaking seemed herculean. So it was. But it was also tantalizing. Against all odds, with faith, perseverance, knowledge and flair it has become reality. It is a truly impressive achievement.

With this series,world architecture has been highlighted in a way that transcends continents and cultures. Comparing the architecture built during the same period in geographically different regions of the world represents an education in itself. As the decades progress we witness a lessening influence of local tradition and a growing impact of supra–national architecture. Reaction to this leveling off of architecture has already resulted in a resurgence of local cultural identity. This is clearly apparent in some of the buildings depicted and gives hope that in the architecture of the future there will be a more balanced cohabitation between the reality of a globalized progressive architectural medium and the imperishable values of architectural heritage.

The buildings shown have given aesthetic training over the years to many people. With the help of these books they will continue to do so to a much larger audience. Of course many more than 1000 works could have been singled out. There exists such a great wealth of good individual buildings much as there is a dearth of collectively good architecture. This might well be a pointer for the future.

The fact that the UIA XX World Congress in Beijing is the launching pad of the XX Century World Architecture series is no coincidence. Beijing is the right place at the right time. Coming at the end of the century it sums up its architecture and at the same time initiates the new century with the Congress theme "Architecture of the 21st Century".

This book series on World Architecture is likely to become a reference document for scholars, students and architects alike. As such it will have served one of its objectives.

Another surely is public opinion. We hope that the impact of these books will go beyond our profession. Their presentation is such that they can reach out and speak to the layman as well. If this is achieved, and it can be, they will be contributing towards a public opinion that will eventually become more receptive to quality architecture. An architecturally educated public opinion is a sine qua non for a built environment that will live up to our planning and design standards.

Our thanks to the Architectural Society of China, to Kenneth Frampton, Zhang Qinnan and to all who contributed towards the World Architecture book series, a publication that has greatly enriched our knowledge of the architecture of this century.

In what we feet certain will be a successful journey ahead, the World Architecture book series will continue to receive the full support of the UIA. We are convinced that it will serve architecture well.

Complimentary Remarks

Ye Rutang,
President, Architectural Society of China (ASC)

A RECORD OF 20th CENTURY WORLD ARCHITECTURE

In connection with the XX World Architects Congress to be convened June, 1999, in Beijing, China, the Architectural Society of China (ASC), with the endorsement of the International Union of Architects (UIA), is honored to present to the architectural profession of the world this 10–volume series WORLD ARCHITECTURE 1900–2000: A CRITICAL MOSAIC as a historical record of the glorious achievements made by architects around the world.

We are further honored to invite the renowned architectural critic, Kenneth Frampton, Ware Professor of Architecture in the Columbia University to be the general editor of the series, and also distinguished scholars familiar with regional developments as volume editors. The whole series consists of 1000 significant buildings (or building complexes), selected through a nomination system by 5–9 invited critics per volume, split into five 20–year periods of this century.

As an architect, I am fully aware of the historical responsibility we are shouldering. Every architect is writing and interpreting history in his/her works, consciously or unconsciously reflecting the cultural features of his/her time, nation and region, and together they make the twentieth century architecture a historical record of the development of the world culture.

The twentieth century will be recognized as one of the important periods in human history. In sp. ~ of two tragic world wars and numerous local wars, mankind finally comes to recognize (or begins to recognize) the necessity of peaceful coexistence among different nations, races, cultures and beliefs, so as to work jointly for sustainable development of our planet.

Science and technology make amazing achievements in the twentieth century, leading countries from the industrial into the information age, and create the basis for new building types and flourishing of architectural schools, promoting a trend of globalization in the economic and cultural developments in individual countries. In the meantime, the advances in cultural and educational domains have nourished a more intensive concern and new interpretations on the cultural traditions and historical heritage in various countries. The developments of architectural cultures in all countries within this century have demonstrated that the global characteristics of science and technology can exist and grow in parallel with the national and regional cultural developments. A polymeric architectural culture will make our human habitat much more colorful and attractive.

We understand that the selected 1000 buildings is only a small part of the global achievements made by our profession, but we still believe that the collection made through the strenuous efforts of so many renowned scholars does present a valuable record that can reflect in the main the world architectural achievements in this century, and elevate our confidence in facing the challenges of the new century.

Ye Rutang

current President of the Architectural Society of China and also the First Vice Minister of Construction of the People's Republic of China, was born 1940 in Ningbo and completed his architectural education in 1965 from the Tsinghua Univerity in Beijing. He had been engaged in various architectural design works including housing, schools, theaters, hotels, hospitals and conference halls till 1985 when he was appointed the Minister of Urban and Rural Construction and Environmental Protection by the State Council. He devoted his energy to the reform of the Chinese architectural profession by introducing a comprehensive system from school accreditation to registration examination. He was also responsible for a new state regulation giving protection to a series of listed recent architectural works as heritage. Under his Presidency, the Architectural Society of China won the commissioning from the UIA to host the XXth World Architects Congress in Beijing in 1999, the first such Congress in Asia, and he was elected to the UIA Council in 1996. He has been awarded honorary membership or fellowship by the Hong Kong Institute of Architects, the Architectural Society of Japan and the American Institute of Architects, and won also a Presidential Medal from the AIA for his contributions to the architectural profession worldwide.

General Introduction– Sectorial Subdivision and the Nomination Method

Kenneth Frampton

Kenneth Frampton

Kenneth Frampton is Ware Professor of Architecture at Columbia University. He is the author of numerous books on architectural theory and history, among which are Modern Architecture, A Critical History (London: Thames and Hudson, 1980,1985, 1992) and Studies in Tectonic Culture, THe Poetics of Construction in Ninetheenth and Twentith Century Architecture, edited by John Cava (Cambridge: MIT press, second printing, 1996).

As we approach the millennium it is difficult to imagine anything more injudicious than to attempt a critical profile of architecture throughout the globe for the entire span of the twentieth century. This presumptuous undertaking was partially facilitated by dividing the world into ten areas of enormous size and variation; vast continental sectors that are heterogeneous and unequal not only in terms of their varied socio-economic and technological development across time but also in terms of their political histories.

Aside from celebrating the millenium, a single factor rose to the fore that seemed to justify this quixotic venture, namely, the emergence of the People's Republic of China as a rapidly modernizing nation, accompanied by indications that it would soon not only become the largest post–industrial society in the world, but also, in socio–technical terms, one of the most advanced. It was this emergent status that induced the China Building Press to issue this compendium on the occasion of the last twentieth century Congress of the Union Internationale des Architects (UIA) to be held in Beijing in June 1999.

While the motivations behind such centennial representations are invariably complex, the decision to assemble an anthology of canonical work on a global basis seems to have been motivated by two factors: first an obligation to bring China into the world debate on the future of architecture and second, a concomitant need to reactivate China's own architectural culture, after a century of rather varied and uncertain eclecticism, beginning with the arrival of foreign architects in Shanghai soon after the turn of the century.

After dividing the world into 10 continental sectors, the method adopted was to select 100 canonical buildings for each sector distributed evenly across the century. The normative aim in each sector was to select some 20 works every 20 period, thereby identifying 100 significant works for each sector and 1,000 works world wide for entire century. However, due to the uneven rate of modernization in the first quarter of the century, it was felt that up to half of the allocation for the first two decades should be evenly redistributed in some instances across the remaining 80 years of the century, thereby acknowledging differences in the initial rate of techno-economic development in different parts of the world as the (modern era(gradually came into being.

The ten continental sectors were divided up as follows: (1) North America (USA and Canada),(2) South America (Latin America), (3) Northern Central and Eastern Europe (the European Continent except for the Mediterranean and Russia), (4) The Mediterranean Basin (including the whole of North Africa but excluding Turkey), (5) The Near and Middle East, (6) Middle and Southern Africa, (7) Russia and the CIS, (8) South Asia, (9) East Asia (including China, Korea and Japan) and (10) Southeast Asia and Oceania (covering Australia, New Zealand, Tasmania and all other Pacific Islands).

Once this allocation had been agreed upon, an editor was appointed for each sector whose task was to monitor the process of selection and to write a comprehensive account of the architectural production of the sector in question. This essay was intended to serve as a critical gloss on the evolution of the architectural culture of the region as represented by the selection for each particular sector. Aside from providing this general overview, these essays were also expected to compensate for any imbalances that may have arisen as an inevitable consequence of pinion, oversight or happenstance, were not included in the final selection. The selection process itself was effected through a nomination procedure in which some five to eight nominators, architectural critics and historians, were asked to nominate 100 canonical works each sector. The results of this initial nomination were then tabulated by the sectorial editor and the final selection of buildings was derived from the number of votes cast for each work.

My own contribution was envisaged to an even broader degree not only for the artificiality of the global subdivisions but also for other anomalies that must inevitably arise with such a procedure. However, before proceeding further it is necessary to remark on the difference between a polemically modern work, conceived as part of the general modernizing process and a quasi-traditional work, that while cognizant of modernization, opts for some measure of the cultural continuity and resistance and in so doing may be regarded in some sense as being retarditaire. Thus one will find that the character and the mix of buildings selected for any given period will vary enormously from volume to volume, both in terms of their ideological content and the degree to which they express the techno-social potential of the epoch.

A further fluctuation that cuts across this play between tradition and innovation is the less easily explicable variation between different modes of architectural expression occurring at the same time and place not only in terms of their intensity but also with regard to their duration as a cultural force or movement. By way of illustrating this variation, one may remark on the continual evolution of the Prairie School in Chicago from the Great Fire of 1871 to Frank Lloyd Wright's Midway Gardens of 1915, after which the local movement loses its intensity and direction, as opposed to the much longer trajectory of domestic development in Southern California that passes as an unbroken progression of quality work, from Irving Gill's Dodge House, Los Angeles of 1910, through to the last of the Case Study Homes built in Los Angeles in the early 1960's. To a similar end we remark on a particular fertile period of architectural production taking place in Germany from around 1905 to 1933 or in Finland and Czechoslovakia, over the same period, although extending further as a wave of development up to the outbreak of the Second World War. One may also note that in the case of these last two countries, the cultivation of a radically modern architectural culture was somehow inseparable from the idea of the state as a progressive modernizing force. A similar ideological national-cultural trajectory may also be found in Scandinavia in general and in the Netherlands over the same period.

We may also observe how the related culture of structural engineering also varies in quality over place and time, attaining exceptional levels of technological prowess and plastic elegance in one country rather than another, even though the techniques in principle were universally available. Thus between 1918 and 1939 we may find a truly remarkable culture of structural engineering in France, Switzerland , Italy, Czechoslovakia and Spain, particularly in the field of reinforced concrete construction, whereas in the Anglo–American world over the same period where there was little development beyond the most pragmatic forms of construction. The only exception to this in Britain is the industrial buildings of the engineer E. Owen Williams, along with the pioneering work of the Danish immigrant Ove Arup, while within the United States, the exceptions in the field of concrete engineering are the magnificent hydraulic dams realized in the United States, particularly in association with the Tennessee Valley Authority and the remarkable Boulder Dam realized in Colorado.

There were, of course, great variations in the rate of techno–economic development throughout the world, wherein pre–industrial cultures and even pre–agricultural, nomadic, tribal cultures still survived in one way or another throughout the century and where organized building production as an industry together with the professional practice of architecture does not really emerge in many countries after the Second World War in 1945. This pre–architectural building culture, which Bernard Rudolfsky called *Architecture Without Architects* in his 1963 book of that title finds a perverse echo today in the so–called Third World where spontaneous migrations have accumulated around major cities, creating large urban conglomerations on appropriated land, without the provision of adequate infrastructures; that is to say without water, power or sewerage, services that are essential to healthy survival in such dense conditions. Along with this we have also to acknowledge the sobering fact that even in so called developed nations as the Unite States, something less than twenty percent of the annual built production comes to be designed by professional architects.

Introductory Essay
–Southeast Asia:
Nowhere to Somewhere and
Beyond

William S.W. Lim

Introduction

By the beginning of the 20th century, Southeast Asia had already become totally colonized. Political boundaries had been arbitrarily established by western powers without regard for historical, cultural and ethnic considerations. In the process, the region witnessed an enormous change from well established and relatively open societies with flexible inter–relations to a state of affairs dominated by exploitation, repression and subservience. Only Thailand, thanks to the rivalry between the French and the British and the Siamese adroitness in playing one power off against the other, retained her own identity and independence.

Port facilities, railway lines, roads and other supporting infrastructure such as telegraph and telephone, were developed in response to the rapid expansion of plantation economy and the introduction of agrarian capitalism. In the meantime, rapid urbanization took place in response to the growth of financial and commercial services needed for the new economy.

This increase in urban population was also accompanied by an accentuation of serious divisions along racial lines. Inequality of power and advantage was a notable feature in the colonial urban settlements. The colonial powers virtually controlled the modern economy, and dominated the major parts of large cities. Westerners lived in comfortable and often secluded choice locations. Iwan Sudradjat wrote in his critical assessment of the Dutch occupation: "architecture and urban design in the Indies became an integral part of the colonial domination, serving as one of the means to establish control, regulate activities and maintain a comprehensive order in the urban areas at both socio–political and aesthetic levels .... the Dutch colonial city in the early twentieth century Indies was a 'container' of cultural pluralism, where the privileged social groups tended to be advantaged in many respects, and subordinate groups normally suffered from poor life chances, low status and little political influence."[1]

During the colonial era, traditions in the ex–colonies were frozen in time. Worse, they were sometimes, modified or added to by deliberate intervention in order to satisfy the function, meaning or aesthetic expression of the colonial masters. Brenda Yeoh in her recent book: Contesting Space: Power Relations and the Urban Built Environment in Colonial Singapore: "Colonialism does not simply involve political and economic coercion but also ideological and cultural impositions .... The colonial encounter often takes on a ritualized form whose maintenance is dependent on the export of notions, systems and practices which displace indigenous forms or re–create them in the image of colonial power."[2]

In the decades after World War II, the states of Southeast Asia became independent after the departure of the colonial powers–some like Malaysia and Philippines, in relatively peaceful manner, while others only after tragic and brutal struggles. Vietnam, Laos and Cambodia were the unfortunate victims of the cold war. These countries were to witness half a century of great turmoil and ideological divisions. They have been engulfed by an extremely bloody form of warfare and destruction.

With the exception of minor territorial changes and the highly significant re-unification

Editor: William S. W. Lim

Born in 1932, Lim graduated from the Architectural Association (AA) and continued his graduate study at the Department of City and Regional Planning, Harvard University as a Fullbright Fellow. He is a citizen of the Republic of Singapore. His professional work involves architecture, planning and development economics. He is the principal partner of William Lim Associates Pte. The main focus of the firm is idea innovation and design excellence.

Lim writes and lectures on a wide range of subjects relating to the direction of architecture and issues of urbanism in Asia. He is the author of five books entitled: Equity and Urban Environment in the Third World–with special refernce to ASEAN countries and Singapore (1975); An Alternate Urban Strategy (1980); Cities for People: reflections of a South East Asian Architect (1990); Contemporary Vernacular: evoking traditions in Asian Architecture, co–author with Tan Hock Beng (1997); Asian New Urbanism (1998). Besides Contemporary Vernacular, the other four are a compilation of his lectures and articles on a broad range of subjects. Presently, Lim is President of AA Asia, a board member of LaSalle–SIA College of Arts (Singapore) and an editorial board member of Solidarity–current affairs, ideas and the Arts (Manila). He is also an Adjunct Professor of the Royal Melbourne Institute of Technology (RMIT).

of North and South Vietnam, there exists a remarkable stability in the political boundaries of the new nation-states in the region. Therefore, not surprising that most Southeast Asian states are still in the process of working out how to handle their multi-ethnic, cultural and religious diversity.

1997 marked an important political watershed for Southeast Asia as the Association of Southeast Asian Nation (ASEAN) celebrated its 30th anniversary. ASEAN also decided to enlarge its membership to include Laos and Myanmar. With the eventual realization of ASEAN 10-notwithstanding the temporary delay to formally admitting Cambodia until after her election-the Association will embrace the whole of Southeast Asia as geographers define it. ASEAN will attempt to facilitate closer economic, political and cultural relationship for the mutual benefits of all member states. Its policies and collective actions have increasing impact with outside powers as well as on each other.

The ten ASEAN countries are Brunei, Cambodia, Indonesia, Laos, Malaysia, Myanmar, Philippines, Singapore, Thailand and Vietnam. These countries differ greatly in many aspects, including: land area, population, per capita income and the stages of economic development. [3] However, these countries also have much in common. Their shared experiences include centuries of cross-cultural influences from different Asian regions, imposed western domination (with the exception of Thailand), a modernity of the other-those outside the orbit of western civilization-and a similar climatic imperative. These differences and commonalties are reflected in the architecture and urbanism of each country and their relationship with each other.

In the West, modernity is seen as the process of historical transformation of Europe and later of the United States. Modernity is based on the Greco-Roman traditions and its subsequent development from the middle ages and Renaissance to the industrial revolution and beyond.

Historically, the West generated the basic ideas and the necessary energy for the initial development of modernity, and more recently in relation to the rapidly changing values and lifestyles. It is therefore understandable that many Westerners still have a strong sense of its possession. For many, irrespective of whether their affinities are classical or modern, Asian architecture appears excessively decorative and even ostentatious. Their unfamiliar design principles and aesthetic rules have conveniently resulted in their exclusion from main stream architectural discourse. Gulsum Baydar Nalbantoglu, a Turkish scholar writes: "I need to turn to the Vitruvian heritage .... in the unequal architectural encounter between the colonizer and the colonized, the lineage of western architectural theory governs the limit for all possible architectural identifications."[4] Fletcher with impeccable clarity considered in his writing that non-western architecture should be classified as non-historical styles. The prefix 'non' signifies lack. According to Fletcher: "styles that lack history are marked with ornamental excess".

An assumed historical truth, interpreted primarily from Euro-American viewpoint for a long time insisted on treating Southeast Asia merely as a meeting point of cultural influences derived from neighboring parts of Asia, particular as a southward extension of China and as an eastward extension of India and beyond. The significance and nature of those encounters with indigenous cultures were never seriously examined.

Over the last three or four decades, new ways of interpreting Southeast Asian cultures have evolved. According to Clarence Aasen: "Most important, and increasingly explored and accepted, is the possibility that there have been significant indigenous underpinnings for their cultural developments: that they were not entirely, or even primarily, derivative, and that the foreign factors should be viewed less as 'influences' and more as 'exchanges'." [5] In other words, the so called 'soft' cultures, i.e. the indigenous cultures of Southeast Asia, cannot be easily dismissed to be naturally subservient to the stronger and more aggressive cultures they have encountered over the centuries. In fact, their cultures have often proven their flexibility and ability to survive adversities and oppressions over long period of time.

The Architect Sumet Jumsai, speculated with considerable scholarship in his book Naga–Cultural Origins in Siam and the West Pacific–that Southeast Asia was the original location of the water based civilization, memories of which prevail even today in the psyche of her people. The built record of this civilization is rather impermanent. Its population is relatively mobile and always lives alongside water. Let me quote: "Broadly speaking there are only two types of civilization on earth: one whose instinct is mainly based on tensile material and the other on compressive material. The former is the result of the aquatic skill and the survival instinct .... when it was necessary to travel with the minimum of impediments." [6]

Today, there is an urgent need to look at Southeast Asia on its own terms, to provide intellectual space for a re–interpretation from an Asian perspective and to recognize the inherent strength, complexity and special characteristics of Southeast Asian cultures. We need to overcome the perceived dominance of the metropolis. We must be at ease with the contemporary and be able to share its modernity, including information technology and the global network society.

The architecture of Southeast Asia in the 20th century cannot be easily presented in a systematic manner. To list and describe selected buildings based on time of completion cannot possibly represent or reflect the complex mosaic of these societies. The architectural experiences of these countries differ widely because of their varied pace of social, economic and political developments. Other crucial factors are the nature of the anti–colonial struggle, cold war ideological involvement, the quality of governance and the commitment and capability of the political leadership.

Research and comprehensive publications on Southeast Asian architectural history are scarce. Analytical discourse particularly on the regional basis has only just begun. In this essay, I will attempt to define its architectural history into four processes with over–lapping time periods for different countries. They are: 1) the late colonial era; 2) heroism and identity; 3) metropolitan dominance and contemporary vernacularand; 4) shock, pause and way ahead.

1. The Late Colonial Era

The single unifying factor of the region is the common experience of different countries during the late colonial era from 1900 to 8 Dec 1941, i.e. the beginning of the Pacific War. The economic impact of World War I and the great depression was transmitted to the region with various degrees of severity. However, the colonial powers continued to rule with minor modifications according to their accustomed styles. Commenting on Singapore, the two expatriate authors of *A History of Singapore Architecture wrote*: "The inter–war years were deceptively calm, marked by a steady separation of the colonial officials and European expatriates from the Asians in the community, and an increased snobbishness, complacency and blindness to what was going on around them. In most ways this was really the twilight of the Empire, ultimately shattered by WWII." [7] Western intellectual and racial arrogance continued to manifest itself in social relationship as well as in cultural perception of the colonized.

During this period, most important public, institutional and commercial buildings had been designed by western architects exhibiting the last vestiges of neo–classicism. In colonial cities, western aesthetic dominance of important civic spaces provided forceful psychological symbolism to express the unchallengable power. According to Winand Klassen, the Philippines was an exception to this in as much as Americans carried out a policy of benevolent assimilation, particularly in education and health and the provision of a much needed infrastructure.[8] Young Filipino architectural students after completing their studies in the U.S. returned home to practice. The best known was Juan Arellano. He designed the Manila Post Office (1926) in neo–classic style and Art Deco Metropolitan Theater (1931).

However, the most famous concentration of private development in Asia is not in this region. They are the foreign business centers known as the Bund in Shanghai and the Art Deco Marine Drive in Bombay. At their best, these buildings deserve their rightful places in our architectural heritage notwithstanding their foreign origin. New Central Market in Phnom Penh, Cambodia by Jean Desbois and Louis Chauchon is one such magnificent building. According to Brian Brace Taylor, this building "is one of the great modern edifices of the early 20th century in Asia, yet one whose remarkable qualities–even its very existence–seem to have gone unnoticed since it was erected in 1937." [9] Other notable examples are the hybrid Aula I.T.B., Indonesia (1920) by Maclaine Pont, the exciting art deco Villa Isola, Indonesia (1931) by Wolff Shoemaker and the Railway Station, Singapore (1933) by Swan & Maclaren. Comprehensive research and documentation on a pan–ASIAN basis are urgently needed to list and record the important works by western architects during this period.

The royal patronage of Thailand and in some instances the protectorate states of Peninsular Malaysia indulged in independent aesthetic preferences for their palaces and religious institutions. They were also able to foster a hybrid architecture of their own choices. Two Thai examples include a well–known hybrid neo–renaissance building, Phra Thinang Chakri Maha Prasat in the Grand Palace (1882), and Vimanmek Palace (1901).

Ubudiah Mosque (1917), Malaysia, is an excellent example of a work derived from the Moghul architecture of North India, which was introduced by British colonial administrators owing to their long familiarity with indigenous pre–colonial culture of British India. On the other hand, the Kenangan Palace (1931), now, the Perak State Royal Museum, Kuala Kangsar, Malaysia was designed to suit the ruler's personal lifestyle. To this end, the palace displays a strong mixture of indigenous Malay vernacular design and construction mixed with a roof adapted from non–traditional source.

In Europe, the intellectual discourse on modern architecture continued with great vigor during the inter–war years. Major activities were the Athen Charter 1931 and the various meetings of Congrés Internationaux d'Architecture Moderne (CIAM). Important educational institutions were developed during this period, such as the Bauhaus in Germany and later the AA School of Architecture in London. Le Corbusier, Mies van der Rohe and Gropius, among others, exercised an enormous influence through their writings and buildings. Experimental projects were built and many new ideas were presented and were critically examined. However, the impact of modern architecture in Southeast Asia was at best marginal and only some less prestigious buildings were built in the modern idiom. Interesting examples include Pablo Antonio's Far Eastern University dating from the late 30s, Philippines, Singapore Improvement Trust Flats, at Tiong Bahru Singapore (1936–41); and Kallang Airport Singapore (1937). Its impact continued after the Second World War. It is particularly noticeable in such buildings as the Federal House, Malaysia (1954); Asia Insurance Building, Singapore (1954); and Lee Yan Lian Building, Malaysia (1959).

Up to 1941, the bulk of urban structures in central areas of major cities in the region consisted of carefully regulated two to four story terrace shophouses built in various vernacular design and hybrid styles. These buildings had four to six meters wide frontages and varied depth. They catered for various types of usage on the ground level, and with usually residential accommodation above. In later years, the more affluent moved to the suburbs, and the residential density increased rapidly so as to accommodate the working–class and new migrants. In many instances, these buildings became very seriously over–crowded and fell into terrible physical condition. In the meantime, new squatter settlements were created and surrounding villages were absorbed by them to cater to the rapid urban expansion. Attempts were sometimes made by well–meaning colonial officials to improve urban facilities and to provide public housing for the urban poor. However, these could at best only be viewed as welfare tokenism and had no significant impact on the deteriorating urban environment and the critical housing situation.

2. Heroism and Identity: the Post War Years

Japan occupied all Southeast Asia except Thailand up to its unconditional surrender on 15 August 1945. The war did great damage to the economies and generated years of hardship and suffering for the population. From this experience, local people learnt that colonial powers were not invincible, and that the Japanese behaved just like any other colonizer. After the war, the European powers were still reluctant to surrender their colonies. The Dutch stayed till the end of 1949, and the French continued to occupy Vietnam until her defeat in battle. Malaysia and Singapore had their own emergency to deal with. This gave rise to the Domino Theory and the subsequent tensions of the Cold War in Southeast Asia. The intellectual environment of the region was increasingly compromised by the Macarthyish nightmare, particularly after the escalating U.S. involvement in the Vietnam war. Even the third force of non-aligned nations, led by Nehru, Nassar and Sukarno was not beyond suspicion.

During the guided democracy period of President Sukarno (1957-1965), modern architecture was introduced with great conviction to Indonesia as a symbol of power and modernity. The ideology inherent in the modern movement as a rejection of the old order suited the strong tide of nationalism. Numerous large buildings and important national monuments together with major highways were constructed. The programme continued with more sophistication and commercialism after Sukarno's fall in 1965. These projects had unprecedented political significance and were sometimes described as visionary and heroic.[10] Selected important projects were Hotel Indonesia (1962), Selora Bung Karno Sports Centre (1962) and Tugu Monas National Monument (1978). These works were not unlike those built in the time of Marshall Phibul, who instituted grandiose modern urban designs for Bangkok, the most poignant example being the Middle Rachadamnern Boulevard Row House (1946) during the guided democracy period.

After WWII, modern architecture was accepted by the authorities and many leading educational institutions in western Europe and United States. A popular version of modern architecture was celebrated through the realization of the Festival of Britain in Harvard under Gropius, Illinois Institute of Technology under Mies and other educational institutions in Western Europe became the nerve-centers for serious architectural discourse. Le Corbusier was idolized in UK and in much of Western Europe.Important and exciting projects were built everywhere. New ideas were explored. It was indeed an exciting time for architects.

Young Asians including many Japanese studied at these enlightened institutions during the fifties and beyond. In so doing, they were exposed to an incredible dose of intellectual and creative discourse on architecture and urbanism. They could also enjoy first-hand experience of the distinguished master works of the period. Southeast Asian students attended the first tropical architectural course introduced at the AA in the mid-fifties by Maxwell Fry and Jane Drew. In the meantime, Le Corbusier was designing Chandigarh with the same team. He made an extensive use of the Parasol –an overhanging roof protecting the spaces beneath from sun and rain together with the brise-soleil as the vertical sun breakers. Chandigarh, the Maison Jaoul and Chapel at Romchamp were major departures from the more regulated designs and theories of his Purist period.[11]

Many young graduates returned with modern architectural ideas and aesthetic approaches that extolled a set of values that seemingly had universal validity. They embodied the imprint of Le Corbusier and other modern masters as well as having a general understanding of the dynamic and exciting architectural debate at the time. This intellectual stimulation, coupled with the excitement of the newly won political independence, brought young Asian architects to seek an international legitimization for their architecture. Much effort was made in many buildings to serve the climatic imperative as well as cultural interpretation and identity. Their heroic efforts produced very interesting results. Selected examples include Singapore Conference Hall, Singapore (1965); Negri Sembilan State Mosque, Malaysia (1967); Geology Building, Malaysia (1968); Telephone Board Exchange, Singapore (1969), British Council, Thailand (1970); People's Park Complex, Singapore (1973) and Golden Mile Complex, Singapore (1973),and Science Museum, Thailand (1977).

Tan Kok-Meng wrote on The Singapore Conference Hall / Trade Union House of 1965: "its seemingly neutral 'tropical modern' image somewhat suitably reflected the modernization of Singapore's economic and social processes .... The nagging dilemma of identity still remained a vital concern–in creative and ethical conscience of the authors .... The prevention of closure of representation, both symbolic and instrumental .... already points to possibilities of framing the 'problem of identity.'" [12]

In this exciting architectural environment, an informal pan–Asian collaborative group called Asian Planning and Architectural Consultants (APAC) was formed in 1969. Its members are Fumihiko Maki and Koichi Nagashima from Japan, Tao Ho from Hong Kong, Charles Correa from India, William Lim from Singapore and Sumet Jumsai from Thailand. They met regularly to exchange ideas and experiences as well as to examine and develop the directions of architecture and urbanism in the Asian region. [13]

Philippines has the longest history in Southeast Asia of architectural education. The first architectural school was established there at Mapus Institute of Technology in Thailand soon followed in 1930 in establishing a School of Architecture at the National School of Arts and Crafts. It was hardly surprising that the cultural environment in the Philippines should prove to be fertile ground for the gifted Leandro V. Locsin. From his first project the Chapel of the Holy Sacrifice (1955), he became instantly famous. According to Winand Klassen, the most convincing reason for the sudden rise and sustained achievements of Locsin was his constant striving, unconsciously and consciously, for an architecture which is truly Filipino. Unfortunately, his strong American orientation minimized opportunities for any serious intellectual architectural discourse with his Asian counterpart. He dominated the architectural scene in the Philippines for decades until his untimely death in 1994.[14] Important projects by Locsin included Theater of Performing Arts, Cultural Center, (1969), Philippines International Convention Center (1976) and the National Arts Center of the Philippines (1976).

During this period, many major buildings ranging from educational institutions, club houses to hotels and commercial premises were constructed incorporating strong ethnic and cultural images. These modern buildings with over–riding local cultural specificity were easy responses to tradition–oriented clients. However, when this design approach was applied to tall buildings, even their symbolic pretensions becomes ludicrous i.e., C.K.Tang, Singapore (1982). In this context, we need to acknowledge

Hijjas Kasturi's struggle to provide a recognizable, ethnic-based cultural symbolism. We see this architectural language in his many tall buildings, such as Luth Building, Malaysia (1986) and Menara Maybank, Malaysia (1987). While the aesthetic and architectural quality of these projects may be contested, their significance as a process in search of a national and a cultural identity must be recognized.

Needless to say, there is much general searching for identity in the region. Cross-cultural influences have to be identified and acknowledged. The rich mosaic of Southeast Asian cultural and architectural heritage is still increasingly being discovered and re-appreciated. In 1985, a leading Indonesian intellectual Soedjatmoko argued that "the architectural identity of a nation, or of a culture, in order to be authentic, and not pastiche, will have to be rooted in and will have to be a response to the real problems of the society."[15] He also warned that identity is not a fixed, permanently shaped commodity, but a constantly changing socio-cultural essence.

3. Metropolitan Dominance and Contemporary Vernacular

With its strong government dedicated towards economic growth, Singapore would opt from the early seventies to become a global city like Hong Kong, thereby to positively attract MNC's investments. In the process, the island state had to quickly re-position and re-structure itself in order to maximize its benefits. The English language was accorded over-riding importance, nuclear and small families were encouraged and large-scale urban re-development were implemented. The incredibly rapid economic growth of Singapore was followed by Malaysia, Thailand and Indonesia and subsequently by China and other Southeast Asian countries. We can clearly witness rapid economic and social transformation of these countries particularly in the major urban centers. Increasing self-confidence has allowed Asians to overcome their multiple complexes arising from their shared colonial past and economic backwardness. However, the recent economic openness in these countries has often resulted in the aggressive introduction of contemporary arts, fashions and lifestyles, along with Hollywood-style entertainment, junk food and commercialized corporate architecture.

Wall Street and Fifth Avenue become inspiring images for our urban development and architectural ambition. It is not surprising that the authorities actively introduce and encourage International Style architecture particularly when designed by large corporate practices overseas. These metropolitan architects often bring their ideas and taste with them, constructing an architecture which ignores the environmental context, is disinterested in climatic conditions and has no cultural references.

Furthermore, many local practices are prepared to play subsidiary design roles, to learn the professional and technical know-how, and subsequently to produce similar design products. Once they have even learnt the art of packaging the latest architectural stylistic fashions from their metropolitan masters, these practices are able to export their professional services to other emerging economies in the region and beyond. The underlying intellectual and creative energy of the origin or any kind of architectural theory is seldom needed, understood or appreciated. It is therefore not surprising that thousands of high–rise buildings and millions of other speculative units are being constructed in Southeast Asia with total disregard for basic design principles. Many projects have been constructed incorporating the symbolic use of traditional imaginary, such as the pseudo–classical fronts and the 'historical hats' placed on top of tall buildings. Replication is also widely accepted. However, such replication is carried out too frequently and indiscriminately, the historical importance of the original loses its meaning and significance. Past architectural styles are viewed as an archive to be raided in order to achieve historical legitimacy. Thus, replication comes to replace innovation as a creative process.

Under such circumstances, promising architectural experiments by serious local architects could not be readily accommodated and had to be suppresed. Marginalised voices and remnant efforts continued. However, we need to recognize: Robot Building, Thailand (1988); Central Square, Malaysia (1988); Tampines North Community Club, Singapore (1986);[16] the Kampong Bugis Development Project, Singapore (1989); [17] the Nation Building, Thailand (1991); Abelia Apartment, Singapore (1994); Nation Tower, Thailand (1995);[18] and the Marine Parade Community Club, Singapore (1999).[19] These projects are barely visible against the backdrop of relentless large–scale construction in an ugly commercialism and stylistic imitation.

The one exception is the international recognition accorded to Ken Yeang. Yeang has invariably in–corporated a bioclimatic factor in his design equation,[20] such as we find in his Menara Mesiniaga (1992). This form of climatic rationalization has enabled him to give his high–rise a different character from that of Norman Foster and followers. Furthermore, he has introduced design complexity in the external enclosures of his recent projects such as the Shanghai Armory Tower (1997) and the Nagoya Tower (2005).[21] Unlike Charles Correa, Geoffrey Bawa and others, Yeang is perhaps the first Asian architect outside Japan to have been accepted by the metropolitan architectural elite on their own turf.

In the meantime, the importance of our heritage as a cultural anchor and counterweight to the global culture is coming to be increasingly recognised. Heritage gives meaning to the past, explains the present and provides internal strength and confidence for the future. Conservation and adaptive re–use of traditional areas are beginning to be taken seriously.[22] There are increasing exchanges and sharing of experiences among heritage organizations in Southeast Asian countries. Two of the most exciting and successful adaptive re–use proposals in the region are the Bu Ye Tian Conservation, Singapore (1982);[23] and Central Market, Malaysia (1986)[24]. Both were saved from the bull–dozers through timely interventions by concerned individuals to change the mind–set of the respective authorities.

To resolve the post–colonial intellectual blockage of self–discovery, it is essential to interpret and integrate the past pluralistically, as a living tradition that will enrich our lives. The notion of a contemporary vernacular in architecture can be defined as a self–conscious commitment to uncover a particular tradition of unique responses to a particular place and climate, and thereafter to re–interpret these formal and symbolic identities as creative new forms which are able to reflect contemporary reality including values, cultures and lifestyles. Cultural traditions can no longer be seen as external and contradictory to the process of modernity.

A growing public awareness of the rich vernacular heritage in Southeast Asian has accentuated the search for one's roots, and the need to recover the vital underpinnings that linked architecture with the past. It is in this context that many leading Asian architects are actively pursuing an engagement with tradition and with specific of localities with renewed vigor. These architects have developed their own interpretation in relative isolation. It is only in recent years that they have begun to have noticeable influence on one another.[25] Some manage to extract and re-invigorate the underlying features inherent in the vitality of the vernacular. In particular, I refer to the writings and built-works of Robi Sularto of Indonesia, Jimmy Lim of Malaysia and William Lim of Singapore as well as the delightful tourist resorts of Kerry Hill, Singapore. Among the finest works of this production one may cite: Walian House, Malaysia (1984); Reuter House, Singapore (1990); Eu House, Singapore (1993); The Datai, Malaysia (1993); Bali Serai, Indonesia (1994); Floirendo Family Villas, Philippines (1994).

Speed, greed and density have been the dominant underlying factors in the current rapid development of major urban centers in emerging economies of the region. The combination of these factors has created historically unprecedented conditions totally different from the western experience. Perhaps, most of these cities are still ableto maintain their attractiveness and dynamism, because of their chaotic order, pluralistic richness, and unintentional complexity.[26]

Rapid economic development has established clear images in many aspects of modernization. However, modernization cannot be automatically equated with modernity in non-western countries. Another process of modernity, evolving continuity and linkages of traditions to contemporary life must still be established through consciously discarding, re-interpreting or even re-inventing the history of the colonial andpost-colonial past.

4. Present Crisis and Way Ahead

The recent unexpected economic turbulence that started in Thailand around mid-1997 and which soon after affected Indonesia, Malaysia and South Korea, and thereafter spread to other countries in East and Southeast Asia, led to a situation in which currencies and stock markets have greatly depreciated throughout the region, with the result that many economies are in recession or worse. Those countries who are most affected are in a state of shock. Indonesia is in the worse situation. Many disbelieve that decades of hardwork and economic progress could suddenly come to naught. Some political leaders even blame foreigners for having had a hidden agenda. With hindsight,it is easy to identify the fault lines, such as escalating corruption, uncontrolled cronyism and poor management. However, even Singapore and Hong Kong-long idolized internationally as ideal capitalist models-are also badly affected. It is only recently that more sober analysis begins to identify the key-the out-of-control, free-for-all, government supported property boom-in everyone of these countries. Greed, speed and speculation have been the order of the day. A disproportionate amount of financial and human resources has been involved. The incredible escalation of land and property prices have hurt business, have distorted investment priorities and have frustrated aspiring young middle income earners aside from increasing the cost of living for everyone.

In the meantime, the controversy on Asian values continues. The economic success of the past decades in the Asian region and the friction, which has arisen over trade protection,democracy and human rights, have turned the Asian values debate into a highly–charged political exercise. Strong advocates of Asian values are mostly senior politicians and diplomatic intellectuals from Southeast Asia.[27] Serious reservations are made by others, including the many speakers of an International Conference in Tokyo on'Asian Values and democracy in Asia'[28] A timely article in the Economist recently subtitles, "Asian values did not explain the tigers' astonishing economic success and they do not explain their astonishing economic failures"[29] has hopefully put to rest at least for the time being a direct relationship between Asian values and the region'seconomic earthquake.

It is in this context that we must examine the possibility of a meaningful surge towards quality in architecture and urbanism in Southeast Asia. Now is the time to pause and reflect critically on what we have done and learn from our mistakes. We can take stock of our accumulated knowledge and experience. The crucial human resources and institutions are already present, but they should be positively supported in order to enlarge their capability.

Today, cross–cultural exchanges become increasingly meaningful and mutually beneficial. Creative arts and great ideas from anywhere in the world can be understood and appreciated across cultural frontiers. With the availability of the mass media, these arts and ideas can be transmitted quickly and convincingly. New values and lifestyles are evolving at an ever more rapid pace. These can be creative, artistic and enlightened,or offensive, decadent and trivial. This contemporary world culture generates exciting new possibilities, but sometimes with disturbing consequences.

All the arts in Southeast Asia are flourishing. Inter–action has greatly intensified both within the region and beyond. Exhibitions, workshops and seminars are held frequently everywhere. Art institutions are developing rapidly and their teaching standards are improving. In recent years, many younger scholars have shown their commitments towards more controversial and sometimes politically sensitive research. The subjects, which often have pluralistic interpretations, include colonial and post–colonial legacies, re–interpretation of history and heritage, Asia values and modernity, and the meaning of being contemporary etc.

The present multi–directional development in urbanism, architecture and the arts, reflects the spirit of creative freedom and rebelliousness. Increasingly, pluralism is becoming the acceptable norm. The criteria for excellence is being modified, developed and expanded continuously. There is now no single standard solution which can be applied effectively. We should have no hang–up about ISMs—be they Modern, late–Modern, late–modern or post–Modern.

Independent from the professional establishments, there are presently two organizations actively promoting architectural and design discourse. They are Design Forum (Malaysia) and AA Asia (Singapore). They focus on East–West discourse and pan–Asian issues respectively. Their recent publications include *Asia Design Forum #7*[30] and *Contemporary Vernacular: Conceptions and Perceptions*.[31] Theoretical investigations continue unabated. Current issues include: metropolis versus provinces, Asian urbanism in crisis, ecology and sustainability and, contemporary vernacular in the context of tradition and modernity.

Amidst the boom and doom of the economies, we can identify a younger generation of dedicated architects. They are teaching and practicing with great conviction and designing innovatively, as we may judge from the Lem House, Singapore (1997) and Dialogue House, Malaysia (1997).[32] Others are writing creatively in different professional journals and magazines, such as art4d (Thailand) edited by Duangrit Bunnag. Southeast Asia is steadily building a network of active professionals who can activate a meaningful architectural discourse and dialogue among ourselves and with others.

Architecture has to be viewed beyond its utilitarian functions. The committed architects need to contribute beyond being effective tools to fulfill development objectives and corporate ambition or worse to satisfy the greed of speculative developers. Architecture must be accepted as an art in order to effectively contribute to the quality of our environment for the enjoyment and benefit of all.

In the final analysis, it is critically important that design excellence and ideas of urban innovation must be recognized and adapted. Their development must inevitably depend on our talents, commitment and capability. We need to identify the limitations of those who with great confidence generate solutions painlessly based on well–established formula. In contrast, we should also identify those who agonize, question and challenge the accepted norms so as to arrive at innovative and creative alternatives. The distinctive roles between the doer and the artist, the pragmatist and the intellectual, or the main–streamer and the outsider must be understood by the informed public, and acknowledged and accredited by decision–makers.

Notes:

1. Iwan Sudradjat. A Study of Indonesian Architectural History. A thesis submitted in fulfillment of the requirement for the degree of Doctor of Philosophy, Department of Architecture, University of Sydney. 1991.

2. Brenda S.A.Yeoh, Contesting Space : Power Relations and the Urban Built Environment in Colonial Singapore. Kuala Lumpur, Oxford University Press,1996.

3. Regional Outlook: Southeast Asia 1997–98. Singapore, Institute of Southeast Asian Studies, 1997.

4. Gulsum Baydar Nalbantoglu. (Post)Colonial Architectural Encounters.Unpublished article, 1998.

5. Clarence Aasen. Architecture of Siam : A Cultural History Interpretation.Kuala Lumpur, Oxford University Press,1998.

6. Sumet Jumsai. NAGA Cultural Origins in Siam and the West Pacific. Bangkok,Chalermnit Press, 1988.

7. Jane Beamish & Jane Fergusaon. A History of Singapore Architecture. Singapore, Graham Brash, 1985.

8. Winand Klassen. Architecture in the Philippines. Cebu City, University of San Carlos, 1986.

9. Brian Brace Taylor. "Inventing a Colonial Landscape, The New Central Market in Phnom Penh" In : Form, Modernism, and History. Edited by Alexander von Hoffman.Cambridge (Massachusetts), Harvard University Graduate School of Design, 1996.

10. Iwan Sudradjat. A Study of Indonesian Architectural History. A Thesis submitted in fulfillment of the requirement for the degree of Doctor of Philosophy, Department of Architecture, University of Sydney. 1991.

11. William S.W.Lim. 'De–Styling of Architecture–from Corb to Gehry '. Paper prepared for book Architects on Architects to be published by Watson–Guptill, USA in 1999.

12. Tan Kok Meng, Critical Weave: Inter–Woven Identities in The Singapore Conference Hall/Trade Union House of 1965. Unpublished article. [1998]

13. Contemporary Asian Architecture: Works of APAC Members. In : Process Architecture No. 20. Tokyo, Process Architecture Publishing, 1980.

14. Winand Klassen. Architecture in the Philippines. Cebu City, University of San Carlos, 1986.

15. Soedjatmoko, "Opening Address" In UNU/APAC Meeting on "Architectural Identity in the Cultural Context" ", held at United Nations University Headquarters, Tokyo, 29th–30th July 1985. Edited by Catharine Nagasima

16. 1986–1999 William Lim Associates Exhibtion Catalogue. Melbourne, RMIT University, 1997.

17.Robert Powell. Line, Edge & Shade–The Search for a Design Language in Tropical Asia. Singapore, Page One Publishing, 1997.

18. Brian Brace Taylor and John Hoskin. Sumet Jumsai. Bangkok, The Key Publisher, 1996.

19. 1986–1999 William Lim Associates Exhibtion Catalogue. Melbourne, RMIT University, 1997.

20.Ken Yeang. The Skyscraper–Bioclimatically Considered. London, Academy Editions, 1996.

21. Yeoh Lee. Energetics: Clothes & Enclosures; ADO Exhibition. 22 May to 19 June 1998, KL . ADF Management Sdn Bhd, 1998.

22. Robert Powell. Living Legacy : Singapore's Architectural Heritage Renewed. Singapore, Singapore Heritage Society, 1994.

23. Singapore River, Bu Yu Tian : A Conservation Proposal for Boat Quay, Singapore, Bu Yu Tian Enterprises Pte Ltd, 1982.

24. William Lim Associates & Chen Voon Fee. "Central Market" In : MIMAR, Architecture in Development No 21 July/September 1986. Singapore, Concept Medi, 1986.

25. William S. W. Lim & Tan Hock Beng. Contemporary Vernacular–Evoking Traditions in Asian Architecture. Singapore, Select Books, 1998.

26. William S.W.Lim. Asian New Urbanism. Singapore, Select Books, 1998.

27. Mishore Mahbubani. Can Asians Think? Singapore, Times Books International, Tommy Koh. The Quest for World Order. Singapore, Federal Publications, 1998.

28. "Asian Values and Democracy in Asia". Proceedings of a Conference Held on 28 March 1997 at Hamamatsu, Shizuoka, Japan, as Part of the First Shizuoka Asia–Pacific Forum: The Future of the Asia–Pacific Region. Tokyo, The United Nations University, 1997.

29. "Asian Values Revisited : What would Confucius say now?",. In The Economist. July 25/31,1998. p. 23

30. Asian Design Forum #7. Edited by Leon van Schaik, 1996.

31. Contemporary Vernacular : Conceptions and Perceptions. Edited by Christopher Chew Chee Wai. Singapore, AA Asia, 1998.

32. Robert Powell. Urban Asian House : Living in Tropical Cities. Singapore, Select Books, 1998.

Introductory Essay–The Oceania: From Nowhere to Somewhere and Beyond

Jennifer Taylor

Editor: Jennifer Taylor

Jennifer Taylor is a highly regarded architectural critic and historian, especially noted for her writing on Australian and Japanese architecture. She undertook her architectural studies at the University of Washington, Seattle, graduating B. Arch. (1967) and M. Arch. (1969). From 1970 to 1998 she taught at the University of Sydney and currently is at the Queensland University of Technology, Brisbane. She is an enthusiastic teacher and in 1998 was awarded the RAIA Marion Mahony Griffin Inaugural Award for writing and teaching. While an Australian by birth she has spent much of her life in Europe, Asia and America, and has taught in architectural schools in many centers throughout the world. She was awarded the Japan Foundation Fellowship in 1975 and 1994–1995. She received the honorable mention in the UIA Jean Tschumi Prize for architectural Criticism, 1999.

Her previous writings include *An Australian Identity: Houses for Sydney 1953–63*; *Architecture a Performing Art* (with John Andrews); *Appropriate Architecture: Ken Woolley*; *Australian Architecture since 1960*; "Oceania: Australia, New Zealand, Papua New Guinea and the smaller islands of the South Pacific", Banister Fletcher, *History of Architecture*. Her current writings include *Tall Buildings in Australian Cities* and *Fumihiko Maki*.

Introduction

Over 30,000 islands of Oceania are scattered through the vast region of the South Pacific. They vary in size from the large land mass of Australia to minute atolls. Geologically they range from living coral reefs, to ancient flattened continental terrain, to precipitous volcanic outcrops. The majority of the islands lie in the tropical zone and with few notable exceptions, such as Australia, have high rainfalls. Natural disasters are common as many are located in cyclonic and earthquake belts. Through most of the region heat is the major climatic factor for consideration in building. The vernacular architecture of Oceania is lightweight and impermanent but, to a variable extent across this huge section of the globe, traditional building resources, primarily of timber and other vegetable matter, are now supplanted by masonry, concrete and steel. [1]

Aside from Australia and New Zealand, less than 7 million people live in the other 22 South Pacific countries, and just over 4 million of those live in Papua New Guinea. While this part of Oceania houses only 0.1% of the world population, it contains one third of the world's languages, hence there is wide cultural diversity. Across all Oceania the indigenous people are of distinct racial groups including Australian Aborigines, New Zealand Maoris, Micronesians, Melanesians and Polynesians. Historic settlement includes that of the indigenous peoples, as well as European settlement of 200 years duration, and the more recent influx from East Asia and India.

The large and small islands share a history of colonization by European nations and the present authoritative cultures on many of the islands evidence strong European influences. This history has greatly conditioned building practices with a decline in traditional customs and the dominance of European and (later) American methods and styles. Some countries, such as Australia, Papua New Guinea and Western Samoa, attained independence in the 20th century, whilst others, such as French Polynesia, retain colonial status. Typical of the region are large population growth rates and increasing urbanization (yet in the smaller islands three out of four people still live in rural areas). These characteristics are coupled with limited resources (with the exception of Australia and New Zealand and the larger islands of Melanesia) making many of the South Pacific countries economically fragile; hence there is a wide range of architectural development through the region.

For the most part, little change to ruffle the waters of the South Pacific accompanied the shift from the nineteenth century to the twentieth century. Australian and New Zealand forces fought in Europe and the Middle East, but World War I had few repercussions on the local architectural scene. Generally attitudes remained conservative with the building traditions and architectural styles inherited from Europe continuing to hold sway. Major incursions into the area occurred during World War II, as in Papua New Guinea and the Solomon Islands, with the establishment of airfields and military bases as evidenced by an imported, mainly American, prefabricated building heritage,such as the Quonset huts at Honiara. In the second half of the century the tourist industry has provided the primarily stimulus for explicative architecture in the smaller islands, and more recently other overseas investment interests have given rise to intruding inappropriate construction, as can be seen in Vanuatu. An increase in independence and the growth of nationalism throughout the less developed South Pacific has in recent years resulted in a reexamination of traditional buildings in search of identity and more environmentally responsive designs than those introduced from temperate northern zones. In these areas only in recent decades has there been conscious effort to produce a modern architecture appropriate for both culture and climate. The more developed nations, such as Australia and New Zealand, are moving towards a mature architecture appropriate for local conditions.

1
Ratana Branch Church,
Raetihi, North Island, New
Zealand. Year: unknown
Built by the Maori
community. Ph. Grant Bolley

1

Early Twentieth Century

In the first half of the century the villages of the indigenous people on the smaller islands existed reasonably independently of the European derived settlements of the colonial powers. The colonial architecture of the South Pacific was not particularly distinctive, rather, it resembled that of similar colonies throughout the world. Some interesting church architecture merging both cultures was built such as the nineteenth century coral churches of the English missionaries on the Cook Islands, for example the church at Avara; and the sculptural Ratana churches of this century, such as Raetihi Ratana Church, built by the Maoris of the North Island of New Zealand. [2]

Nationhood for Australia raised a degree of nationalistic spirit given expression primarily in decorative motifs such as gum leaves, and even koala bears, found in plasterwork and the like. The most inventive architecture of the region at the beginning of the century is to be found in Australia in the Federation Style of domestic design. [3] This was a generous high roofed, verandahed style, with decorative painted woodwork of barge–boards and railings. It had some allegiance to the romanticism of the Queen Anne style in England. New Zealand architecture too remained indebted to British precedent. The Parliament Building, Wellington, was commenced in 1912 to a Classical design by John Campbell and in domestic, commercial and public buildings a reduced classicism was common. However, the romantic school was also highly evident with fine picturesque residences clearly in line with the tradition of form and fine workmanship derived from the Arts and Crafts Movement and the buildings of Edwin Lutyens. Further, New Zealand architecture of the late nineteenth century had demonstrated considerable influence from West Coast America domestic design and this pattern continued into the twentieth century.[4]

In both countries the impact of American architecture was felt in domestic design in the 1920s with the dark and sheltering Bungalow Style for the new houses of the spreading suburbs. In Australia the Bungalow was joined by a Neo–Colonial revival led by W. Hardy Wilson, who both celebrated Australia's Georgian buildings of the late eighteenth and early nineteenth century, and sought to temper these with the lessons he discovered in Chinese architecture, thus providing one of the first architectural endeavors in Australia to learn from the example of Asian neighbors.[5] Rivaling the interest in Neo–colonialism, was the work of Leslie Wilkinson, the first Professor of Architecture in Australia (Sydney University) who taught that appropriate precedent for building in Australia's climate was to be found in Mediterranean

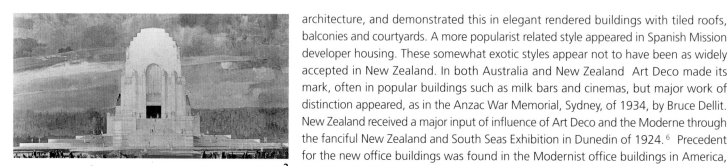

2

2
**Anzac War Memorial, 1934,
Sydney, Australia arch.
C. Bruce Dellit, Drawing
courtesy Victor Dellit**

3
**City Mutual Life Assurance
Building, 1936, Sydney,
Australia, arch. Emil
Sodersten. Source: Sir
Banister Fletcher: A History
of Architecture, 19th Edition,
John Musgrove (ed.),
Butterworths, London, 1987,
p. 1504A**

4
**Capitol Theatre ceiling, 1924,
Melbourne, Australia,
arch. Walter Burley Griffin
and Marion Mahony.
Ph. Wolfgang Sievers**

3

4

architecture, and demonstrated this in elegant rendered buildings with tiled roofs, balconies and courtyards. A more popularist related style appeared in Spanish Mission developer housing. These somewhat exotic styles appear not to have been as widely accepted in New Zealand. In both Australia and New Zealand Art Deco made its mark, often in popular buildings such as milk bars and cinemas, but major work of distinction appeared, as in the Anzac War Memorial, Sydney, of 1934, by Bruce Dellit. New Zealand received a major input of influence of Art Deco and the Moderne through the fanciful New Zealand and South Seas Exhibition in Dunedin of 1924. [6] Precedent for the new office buildings was found in the Modernist office buildings in America, and these stood side by side with the continuing Neo–classical examples still finding favor in the transitional climate of the period. The 1936 City Mutual Life Assurance Building, Sydney, by Emil Sodersten, with its powerful stepped–back massing and grand corner–commanding entry regaled by handsome metallic relief patterning, is among the finest Australian examples of these; while Gray Young with the Australian architects Hennessey and Hennessey designed the powerfully formed Prudential Building in Wellington, 1934. Also, the State Insurance Building, Wellington, 1938–1942,by Gummer and Ford and Partners, is a handsome building with a stepped facade and roof profile, confidently forming a corner site in Wellington's business area. [7] It marked the maturity of the 1930s styles and, with its plain facade and metal–framed fenestration of the Chicago School family, it was a harbinger towards the emerging modernism.

The influence of the Prairie School arrived with Walter Burley Griffin who moved with his wife Marion Mahony to Australia from Chicago after winning the 1912 competition for the plan for the new national capital at Canberra. [8] But in Australia the Griffins were regarded as eccentric and little credence was accorded their ideas. They later moved to India and left in Australia the foundation of the Canberra Plan, and innovative residential developments, as well as civic, educational and commercial buildings including the Capitol Theatre, Melbourne, 1924. As in America, the cinema,as represented by Griffin's Capitol, the Civic Theatre, Auckland, by Bohringer, Taylor and Johnson, 1929, and the State Theatre, Sydney, 1929, by Henry E. White, rejoiced in an eclectic escapist extravaganza adding new landmarks to the cities and towns.

European Functionalist Architecture of the 1920s and 1930s was not well understood or readily accepted despite the popularity of such journals as *Architectural Review*, and increasing travel by young architects to England to further their experience. In the local journals modern architecture was reviewed more in terms of form than the theories that laid behind it. The taut elevated frame buildings were rejected in favor of buildings that sat heavily on the ground. In part, this was due to the interest in the work of Willem Dudok, as evidenced in Australian buildings such as the Macpherson Robertson's Girls High School, Melbourne, 1934, by Seabrook and Fildes, and in New Zealand by the buildings of W. H. Gummer. Inspired by European social housing and mass–production, the Government Housing Construction Department was established by the New Zealand Labor Party in 1940 and the Berhampore State Flats, Wellington, 1940, by Francis Gordon Wilson, who was Chief Architect for the Housing Construction

Division, provided an example of grouped housing modeled on such European thinking. [9] Construction, while clearly derived from European models retained a sense of weight in its massing and brick details. Berhampore State Flats were followed in 1943 by the sleekly modern Dixon Street Flats, horizontally defined by the fenestration and open access balconies. The Dixon Street Flats provided New Zealand's first example of a high-rise apartment building. By the 1950s a confident, elevated lightweight architecture had appeared as exemplified by the Wanganui War Memorial Hall,1960, by Newman, Smith and Greenhough. The horizontal streamlined buildings of Mendelsohn also found favor in Australia and Aalto's Paimio Sanitarium provided the model in the 1930s and 1940s for a series of elegant hospitals banded by balconies on each level, as in the work of Stephenson and Turner. A major contribution to the development of modern architecture and theory came through the founding, in 1946 in Wellington, of the Architectural Centre, which, through publications, competitions and projects, promoted modern architecture. Similarly, Group Architects, a collaborative formed in Auckland in 1949, aimed to produce functionalist housing adapted for local conditions. The Depression followed by World War II, however, slowed major building activity in both Australia and New Zealand until the 1950s.

5
Massey House, 1948–1957 Wellington, New Zealand, arch. Ernest Plischke (Plischke and Firth). Ph. Gordon H. Burt. Courtesy Gordon Burt Collection, Alexander Turnbull Library, Wellington, New Zealand

6
MLC Building, 1957 Perth, Australia arch. Bates, Smith and McCutcheon Ph. Ronald H. Armstrong Pty Ltd. By Courtesy of the Architects

Later Twentieth Century

Further knowledge of modern architecture was carried to Australasia by migrating architects from Europe and shown in such buildings as Frederick Romberg's streamlined Stanhill Flats, Melbourne, designed in 1943 but not built until 1950, and Ernst Plishke's (Plischke and Firth) curtain-walled Massey House, Wellington, for which the design commenced in 1948 but the building was not completed until 1957. [10] Romberg, who was of German descent, had developed a successful practice in Switzerland. He arrived in Australia in 1938. Plischke, an Austrian, who had worked for Peter Behrens and was known for his disciplined designs in modern architecture, reached New Zealand in 1939. In the mid-forties Harry Seidler visited his family in Sydney and decided to settle there. While not educated in Europe, Seidler was Austrian by birth and studied under Gropius at Harvard. [11] His Rose Seidler House, 1949, and subsequent houses in Sydney introduced unadulterated examples of the International Style into the conservative local milieu. Although Seidler's houses were admired for their startling difference, the modern houses of the leading Australian-born architects, such as Sydney Ancher in Sydney and Roy Grounds and Robin Boyd in Melbourne, retained a certain identifiable local flavor. Also evident in the work of all three was an interest in traditional Japanese design.

In the 1950s and 1960s Australia experienced a financial boom and, with the drive to international status and its representation in prestige modern office building, the low-scale modest cityscapes of Sydney and Melbourne were transformed by curtain-walled high-rise towers following the American model. The work from firms such as Bates, Smart and McCutcheon, using lightweight construction, was highly advanced technically for its time. Of particular note was a series of curtain-walled buildings by Bates, Smart and McCutcheon for MLC that appeared in the major cities in the second half of the 1950s. Fully glazed buildings soon proved to be unsuitable for the Australian

6

7
John Andrews' House, 1980,
Eugowra, New South Wales,
Australia,
arch. John Andrews Inter-
national, Ph. David Moore
By Courtesy of the Architects

7

sun and the consequent rapid fluctuations in temperature, so that the 1960s saw a move away from lightweight steel and glass to concrete construction. The use of sun-shielding devices, notably as precast concrete panels, dramatically altered the appearance of the city towers. Seidler's Australia Square in Sydney, 1967, drew acclaim for its rational engineering (consultant Pier Luigi Nervi) and for the amalgamation of multiple city sites that allowed for the provision of a generous public plaza.

The prosperity of the country was further reflected in the 1950s and 1960s in the building of cultural centers in the major cities. The competition for the Sydney Opera House was held in 1955 and the winning building by Jorn Utzon established new standards and expectations for architecture in Australia through its landmark imagery, its design quality, its excellent relationship to the city and the harbor, and its challenge to the building industry. [12] The Olympic Games in Melbourne added a further boost to building in that city, leaving the legacy of the dramatic structurally expressive Olympic Swimming Pool, 1956, by John and Phyllis Murphy, Borland and McIntyre.

While the importation of models from the northern hemisphere for housing and city building was hailed in many quarters, the loss of a regional rational and aesthetic was decried in others. In the 1950s architects such as Bruce Rickard and Peter Muller introduced to Sydney an earthy, organic architecture inspired by Frank Lloyd Wright and traditional Japanese buildings, which were seen as more appropriate models for the Australian life style than were those following the European rationalist precedent. This romantic movement was accompanied by a fresh appreciation of the aesthetic qualities of the Australian landscape, and building became closely attuned to the site. By the 1960s Brutalism was introduced by Australian architects primarily working with the London County Council. English Brutalism and the appeal of the buildings of Aalto, had added further dimensions to this architecture responding to the place. As in Australia, architects returning from England to New Zealand in the 1950s introduced new concepts, among these was the understanding of Brutalism derived by architects, such as Miles Warren, while working for the London County Council. Warren and Peter Bevan, both practicing in Christchurch, modified the Neo-Brutalism of Europe with regional considerations.

By the 1960s a quite distinctive style of a brick, earthy, architecture attuned to rugged sloping sites, had became apparent in the Sydney region, notably in domestic design. [13] The work of the Sydney School remained a major influence throughout Australia for the next twenty years. The C. B. Alexander Agricultural College, Tocal, 1966, by Philip Cox and Ian McKay provides an early example of the application of the language of the Sydney School to an institutional structure. Cox's concern for a complimentary union of building and landscape was carried into his first major steel structure, the National Athletics Stadium, Canberra, 1974, where earth berms blend with a minimal mast structure of considerable grace. [14] Representative of Australia's lightweight wide-span buildings of distinction are the buildings for the 2000 Olympic Games in Sydney and Cox's celebratory sporting and exhibition buildings, which continue to combine a clear structural logic with the romanticism of form. The Andrews' Farmhouse at Eugowra, 1980, by John Andrews, with its imagery rooted in the past and the land, reflects the widespread concern in Australia for an authentic regional architecture that continued through to the 1980s. [15]

In the 1970s a further interest in responding to the Australian landscape can be seen in the architecture of the Port Philip area south of Melbourne from architects such as Daryl Jackson and Kevin Borland. [16] This was a muted, yet complex, timber architecture with pitched roofs and layered screening walls, inspired by work such as Sea Ranch on the West Coast of America. As the Sydney School architecture matched the rough textures and burnt colors of the Sydney region, the Melbourne work blended with the soft landscape of tea-trees and sand-dunes.

Queensland also witnessed a revival of concern for an appropriate architecture for its tropical, sub-tropical climate. James Birrell's inventive buildings for the University of Queensland shared some affiliation with the Sydney School architecture, while architects such as Robin Gibson and John Dalton designed buildings utilizing passive cooling elements, such as wide verandahs, roof vents, breezeways and courtyards. Gibson's Queensland Art Gallery is a particularly sensitive solution with generous and expansive galleries and lobbies enlivened by the use of pools and fountains. The buildings of Russell Hall, such as the Wilston House, Brisbane, of 1985,and the minimalist houses of Gabriel Poole, as represented by his own house at Doonan, 1997, and the preceding 'tent' houses he designed for the Sunshine Coast, were highly inventive in their response to the locale. Queensland architects, such as Birrell and Hall with Rex Addison, working in Papua New Guinea contributed to the development of a sound and expressive architecture for local conditions and ways of life. [17] Of particular note is Addison's Raun Raun Theatre, Goroka, 1982, a thatched timber-poled structure that creates a contemporary building rooted in local practices. The regionally inspired radical structures of Troppo Architects, Darwin, provide further examples of architecture strongly responsive to tropical conditions. Generally Australian architecture, notably in the north, is characterized by its response to land and climate, and this has been naturally extended into buildings concerned with ecological considerations.

New Zealand at this time was remarkable for the construction of the iconic Chapel of Futuna, Wellington, 1961, by the Maori architect John Scott, and for an upsurge of interest in the design of 'small homes', apparently inspired by the Case Studies Houses of Los Angeles. [18] In the 1970s and 1980s Wellington again became the center of architectural endeavor with an energetic group of young architects, led by Ian Athfield and Roger Walker, producing strikingly fractured buildings, with innovative planning and vigorous massing. Walker's Britten House of 1971 exemplifies the vitality and imaginative handling of form found in this architecture.

Through the 1960s and 1970s Australian architectural theory was primarily concerned with the balance of international and regional expectations and influences and their representation in architectural expression. As the Australian landscape is the most distinctive characteristic of the country, the attention of those seeking a regional expression mostly had been directed to rural, generally domestic, buildings, at the

8

8
Queensland Art Gallery, 1982, Brisbane, Australia, *arch*. **Robin Gibson. Courtesy the Architect**

9
Gabriel Poole House, 1996, Doonan, Queensland, Australia, *arch*. **Gabriel Poole. Ph. and Courtesy Jennifer Taylor**

9

10

11

10
Britten House, 1974.
Wellington, New Zealand,
arch. Roger Walker.
Ph. Gillian Chaplin, By
Courtesy of the Architect

11
Church of Resurrection,
1976, Keysborough, Victoria,
Australia.
Ph. John Golling.
Source: Jennifer Taylor,
Australia Architecture since
1960, 2nd Ed., RAIA, 1990,
p. 208

12
American Express Tower,
1976, Sydney, Australia,
arch. John Andrews
International. Ph. David
Moore. By Courtesy of the
Architect

12

expense of concern for appropriate designs for the cities. Under the influence of Robert Venturi's theories on the ordinary and in reaction against the 'bush myth' architecture, Melbourne architects turned to the suburbs as the true representation of Australian life. Of particular note was the work of Peter Corrigan who in attitude and aesthetic championed the concerns and preferences of the suburban dweller with houses, churches, schools, designed for the context of the norm of everyday existence. [19] Typical is the Church of the Resurrection, Keysborough, 1976.

The cities also received fresh attention under the direction of the Federal Labor Party in the 1970s. Government expenditure on the restoration and re-vitalization of the inner-city suburbs, such as Glebe and Woolloomooloo in Sydney, has ensured centrally located housing available to lower income groups. Also, the convenience of the inner suburbs of the cities became increasingly apparent to more affluent groups and previously run-down suburbs, primarily those with terrace housing, were revitalized, for example Carlton in Melbourne and Paddington in Sydney. [20] The same process occurred with the inner-city workers cottages a little later in New Zealand, with Ponsonby, Auckland, providing an example. General interest in conservation blossomed first in Australia in the 1970s and in New Zealand shortly after, but it was too late to prevent the destruction of much of the historic fabric of the inner cities.

In the immediate postwar years demolition and rebuilding characterized the central business and shopping districts of the major cities of Australia. The car and the tall building with its 'plaza' transformed the city pattern. The pedestrian was forgotten. A change of sensibility accompanied the 1970s, much of this coming from grassroots level. Since that time more enlightened policies have resulted in cities of increasing amenity and delight. Further, increasing sophistication and awareness, together with the input of the post-war migration policy that has transformed Australia from a parochial Anglo-Saxon culture to a global multi-racial society, have revolutionized the tempo of urban life style, and consequently the character of the urban environment. Yet for the most part the individual buildings have borne the stamp of international sameness with notable exceptions, such as John Andrews' American Express Tower in Sydney, 1976, which celebrated the sun in the dynamic patterns of its sun shielding, and its location on the busiest intersection in Sydney by its setbacks and other gestures of public goodwill, such as seating for waiting bus passengers. Denton Corker Marshall's elegantly paired Governor Phillip and Governor Macquarie Towers, 1994–1995, provided a further landmark for Sydney with restrained sophistication of the handling of form and materials, and the drama of the geometric grided skyline. [21] In design is Renzo Piano's wrapped and folded Macquarie Street tower destined to join the profile of Sydney's skyline. [22]

Australia's capital, Canberra, presents a microcosm of Australian architecture in the second half of the century as most of the leading architects have built there. Griffin's design has continued to provide the blueprint for the framework for development, with its geometries reinforced by the planning of the Parliament House of Australia by Mitchell Giurgola Thorp, 1988. The Parliament House, located on the apex of Capital

Hill at the pivot point of Griffin's radial planning, was conceived as a democratic image submerged into the hill and swept over by grass ramps that extend the lines of the diagonal avenues of Griffin's plan, and allow them to symbolically span across the nation.

Over the past two decades the central urban areas of Australia's cities have undergone considerable metamorphoses, notably as they have turned to address their previously neglected watersides. Abandoned land has been reclaimed for new public and private use, enhancing appearance and amenity. Brisbane's South Bank has been under redevelopment since the 1970s and Seidler's Riverside Centre, 1986, provided the example of possibilities offered in the central city by the winding Brisbane River. In subsequent years the city has been transformed by riverside development and walkways along both banks. Similar development has enlivened the banks of the River Yarra in Melbourne. On South Bank the vitality of the mixed development of offices, housing, restaurants and the Casino, is balanced to the west by the dramatic geometry of the cool and refined Exhibition Centre by Denton Corker Marshall, 1996.[23]

13

Of New Zealand's cities it has been Wellington that has moved to enhance its waterfront and to offer engaging public space in the city. Earthquake legislation resulted in the demolition of 250 buildings in central Wellington in the 1980s, resulting in a dramatic new building output. As part of the regeneration of the waterfront, Te Papa Tongarewa, the Museum of New Zealand, 1998, by JASMAX was located at the western end of the urban land on the bay. In size and form it is a dominating building, containing a sensitively designed series of progressive spaces culminating at the Maori 'marae' on the upper level overlooking the bay. The Wellington Civic Square development adjoining Ian Athfield's engaging Wellington Library, 1992, and the library itself with its nikau palm–tree colonnades, have provided new landmarks and generated activity in the central city. His following Palmerston North Public Library, 1996, is even more densely enmeshed in its setting, and has invigorated a previously run–down part of the town through the stimulus of visual interest and user activity.

14

The cultures of both the Australian Aboriginal people and the New Zealand Maoriis were given well over–due recognition in the 1980s. In New Zealand Maori building traditions, and ornamental arts conspicuously impact on the design and decoration of recent buildings, as in the National Museum of New Zealand, and the Maori architect Rewi Thompson's 1995 Puukenga, the Centre of Maori Studies, on the UNITEC Campus, Auckland. Aboriginal culture, while increasingly receiving respect and admiration, is not so visible in architecture. Museums and galleries of Aboriginal work, such as Greg Burgess's Brambuk Living Cultural Centre, Halls Gap, 1990, both in line and materials attempt to embody Aboriginal spirituality and craft. The light–weight pavilion buildings of Glenn Murcutt owe something to Aboriginal attitudes to building in Australia. This becomes specific in his 1994 Marika–Alderton House for an Aboriginal client living in Yirrkala Community in the Northern Territory. Both directly, and through the work of architects such as Burgess and Murcutt, an awareness of traditional Aboriginal living patterns and building practices is exerting an influence on Australian architecture.

13
Museum of New Zealand Te Papa Tengarewa (model), 1998, Wellington, New Zealand, arch. Jasmax Architects. Ph. Grant Shoehan. By Courtesy of the Architects

14
Puukenga School of Maori Studies, UNITEC Institute of Technology, 1995, Auckland, New Zealand, arch. Rewi Thompson. Ph. Dushko Bogunovich. By Courtesy of Dushko Bogunovich

While global culture generally is moving away from concern with the particulars of regional individuality, the newly independent nations of the South Pacific are exploring symbolic form and insignia as an expression of identity. The new Parliament buildings of Fiji, Papua New Guinea, Vanuatu and Western Samoa, take as their starting point traditional building forms, such as the 'haus tambaran' and the 'haus baran' in Papua New Guinea, and the 'bure kalou' in Fiji. Renzo Piano's Cultural Centre Jean Marie Tjibaou for Noumea, due for completion in 1998, is a politically balanced Mitterrand commissioned complex bridging between Kanak civilization and the continuing French presence. [24] It offers a technically advanced solution to the integration of global/local values, forms, and building techniques. Following tradition, the three 'villages' of the complex are linked by a long walkway. Low buildings are located on the lagoon side of this passage, while tall conical forms, ventilated through their double–layered faces, turn their backs to the reef side. These are of glulam timber construction clad externally by iroka wood from Africa and manufactured by pre–fabrication in France. So generally, recent decades have seen an increasing recognition of the qualities of the architecture and art of the indigenous people of Oceania, and a sensitivity is emerging that blends the universal and the local, though most investors and architects remain of expatriate origin.

Architecture in the twentieth century as found in the widely scattered lands of Oceania covers a spectrum from the most modest vernacular hut to the Sydney Opera House. The larger nations of Australia, New Zealand and Papua New Guinea house most of the population, and hence have produced most building. Australia and New Zealand with their predominantly European descended population offer a particular case in a region elsewhere inhabited principally by indigenous peoples. However, through all of the diversity of architecture resulting from different cultures, resources and stages of economic development, a shared strain of colonial and post–colonial thinking and practice can be detected in the island countries of Oceania.

Notes:

1. Information on architecture in the Pacific Islands is not easily obtainable. The South Pacific Commission is a reasonable source for general comment and statistics, for example, the various essays in *Pacific Islands Social and Human Development*, South Pacific Commission, Noumea, 1995.

2. Diedrie Brown, UNITEC, Auckland, has undertaken a major study on Maori architecture. The Ratana churches are discussed in her unpublished paper "Morehu Architecture"

3. See Trevor Howells and Michael Nicholson, *Towards the Dawn: Federation Heritage in Australia, 1890–1915*, Hale and Iremonger, Sydney, 1989.

4. This is discussed in an interesting essay by William Toomath, "New World Origins", *Architecture New Zealand*, March/April, 1997. pp.21–24.

5. W. Hardy Wilson wrote several books on early Australian architecture including *Old Colonial Architecture in New South Wales and Tasmania*, Union House, Sydney, 1924.

6. Greg Bowron discusses this exhibition in "A Brilliant Spectacle, *Zeal and Crusade*"; *Modern Architecture in Wellington*, (Editor John Wilson) Te Waihora Press, Wellington, 1996, pp.39

7. Bruce Petry covers the building in "A Break with Tradition", *Zeal and Crusade; Modern Architecture in Wellington*, pp 47–52.

8. Griffin's work is discussed in Donald Leslie Johnson, *The Architecture of Walter Burley Griffin*, Macmillan, South Melbourne,1977. Roger Pegram has provided an account of the planning and

development of Canberra in *The Bush Capital*, Hale and Iremonger, Sydney, 1983.

9. For a discussion of public housing of the 1930s and 1940s in Wellington see Julia Gatley, "For Modern Living", *Zeal and Crusade; Modern Architecture in Wellington*, pp.53–60.

10. Linda Tyler has written the story of Massey House in "Modernity Arrives", *Zeal and Crusade; Modern Architecture in Wellington*, pp.103–109.

11. Several books are available on Seidler's architecture. For the early work see *Houses, Buildings and Projects, 1955–1963*, Horwitz, Sydney, 1963.

12. The Sydney Opera House has been subject to numerous publications. A recent text is Philip Drew, *Sydney Opera House: Jorn Utzon*, Phaidon Press, London, 1995.

13. See Jennifer Taylor, *An Australian Identity: Houses for Sydney 1953–1963*. Department of Architecture, University of Sydney, Sydney,1984 (First Edition 1972).

14. For the architecture of Philip Cox see *Philip Cox, Cox Architects: Selected and Current Works*, 2nd. edition, Images Publishing and Craftsman House, Mulgrave, Victoria, 1997.

15. John Andrews' career up to the early 1980s is discussed in Jennifer Taylor and John Andrews, *John Andrews: Architecture a Performing Art*, Oxford University Press, Melbourne,1982.

16. For information on Jackson see *Daryl Jackson: Selected and Current Works*, Images Publishing, Mulgrave, Victoria, 1966

17. *Australian Architects: Rex Addison, Lindsay Clare & Russell Hall*, RAIA Education Division,Manuka, ACT, 1990.

18. For the Chapel of Futuna see Russell Walden, *Voices of Silence: New Zealand's Chapel of Futuna*, Victoria University Press, Melbourne, New York,1993.

19. See Conrad Hamann, *Cities of Hope: Australian Architecture and Design by Edmond and Corrigan 1962–1992*, Oxford University Press, Melbourne, New York, 1993.

20. Sydney's story is told in G. P. Webber, *The Design of Sydney: Three decades of Change in the City Centre*, The Law Book Company, Sydney, 1988.

21. The earlier work of the firm is covered in *Australian Architects: Denton Corker Marshall*, RAIA Education Division, Manuka, ACT, 1987.

22. See Lawrence Nield, "Macquarie Street, Sydney: Matter and Form: Renzo Piano's New Sydney Tower"*Content* 3 1997.pp.50–61.

23. See Denton Corker Marshall, "Exhibition Centre, Melbourne", *UME* 2 1996. pp.18 –27.

24. For a coverage of the project to date see an interview with Piano, "Renzo Piano Building Workshop", *Architecture and Urbanism*, December 1996, pp. 92–103.

Editor's Acknowledgments

I am grateful to the nominators for their continuous support including the selection of projects for the cover page, back page and spine of the book as well as providing additional titles for the bibliography. I am also greatly indebted to Professor Kenneth Frampton who painstakingly edited this essay with understanding and professionalism.

Special thanks must be given to student Sonja Berthold who was my research assistant and who also co-ordinated materials submitted by the nominators. Subsequent follow-up by other students include Mark Low, Lim Ching Tung and Lee Kah-Wee. Acknowledgment should also be given to Sally Mah and Mabel Koh who provided valuable and painstaking secretarial support.

Last, but not least, personal thanks must be given to my wife, Lena who has always commented critically on the substance of my papers and corrected my English. She also operates a very specialized bookshop, which provides me with an incredible resource.

William S. W. Lim

I wish to thank Susan Clarke, Senior Research Assistant, University of Sydney, for her outstanding contribution to the production of this section. Her intelligent, dedicated and good humored pursuit of research and organization over a period of two years has been greatly appreciated. I also want to acknowledge the enormous effort of Zhang Qinnan, Volume Co-Editor , for his critical role in the production of this book. In particular I would like to thank him for his efforts and persistence in obtaining illustrations of the buildings which was a very time-consuming task.

I am much indebted to the nominators for their initial involvement in the selection of buildings for inclusion and for their later writings and advice for the production of the individual buildings covered and the provision of illustration material from their own collections. In this regard I would like to thank Neville Quarry, Andrew Metcalf, Philip Goad, Julia Gatley, Russell Walden and Rahim Milani. In addition I would like to thank Deborah Deering for her essay and Ken Costigan for his advice on the projects in New Guinea.

So many people helped in the collection and provision of the illustrative materials. Credits are given in the relevant pages, still special mentions should be given to:

Reverend Monseignor J. M. Harrington of the Catholic Presbytery, Christchurch, New Zealand for permission to use the plan and photographs of the Cathedral of the Blessed Sacrament; The Honorable Speaker of the Parliament of Fiji for approval to use the ground floor plan and photographs of the Parliament House; The National Parliament of Papua New Guinea for approval to use the plans, elevations and photographs of the Parliament House; Lady Bettine Grounds for permission to use the plans and photographs of the Grounds House.

We have had warm responses from the architects, architectural firms, photographers, studios, libraries, archives, museums, journals and publishers, among them are

Architects: Ian Athfield, James Birrell, Ron Burgess, Neil Clerehan, Paul Frame, Don Gazzard, Robin Gibson, Romaldo Giurgola, Glen Murcutt, Russell Hall, Harry Seidler, Gerald Melling, Peter Miller, Allan Morse, Bruce Rickard, Gordon Smith, Roger Walker, David Wilkinson, Ken Woolley.

Architectural firms: Ancher/Mortlock/Woolley (Gloria Meyer); Architects Pacific (Anumala Chand); John Andrews International (Maryanne Hampton); Bates Smart and McCutcheon; Gregory Burgess Pty Ltd (Peter Ho); Cox Richardson Taylor (Charlotte Cox); Jasmax Ltd (Ivan Mercep); Denton Corker Marshall (Anna Long); Russell Hall Architects (Danielle Adermann); Daryl Jackson Pty Ltd (Thihou Gill); Katsalidis Pty Ltd (Catherine Hyde); MGT Architects (Leslie Mckay); Renzo Piano Building Workshop (Giovanna Giusto); Vitia Architects (Filipe Tauva); Warren and Mahoney Architects (Thom Craig).

Photographers and studios (who directly provide their works): Wolfgang Sievers, Marc Strizic (through Anne Shields, Viscopy), Eric Sierens (Max Dupain and Associates) and architect James Birrell.

Archives, Libraries and Museums: Alexander Turnbull Library, National Library of New Zealand; Art Institute of Chicago (Hsiuling Huang); Estate of Robin Morrison, Auckland War Memorial Museum (Gordon Maitland): Image Library (Jody Ward); Mitchell Library (Kevin Leamon); National Archives of New Zealand (Adam Stapleton); La Trobe Picture Collection, State Library of Victoria (Dianne Reilly and Michael P. Galimany).

Journals and Publishers: Alistor Taylor Publisher (Alistor Taylor), Architecture Australia (Jo Metcalfe), Independent Group (Brenda Willmuth Sharp) and the Ove Arup Journal (David J. Brown).

The Architectural Society of China wants me to convey their deep appreciation to those who not only supplied the materials requested but contributed to its Library their very valuable works: Zeny Edwards, Daryl Jackson, Donald Leslie Johnson, Wolfgang Sievers, Mark Strizic and David Wilkinson.

The support came from so many sources that I ask forgiveness in case of some inadvertent neglect.

Jennifer Taylor

SELECTED BUILDINGS ▶

Vol. **10** SOUTHEAST ASIA

1900–1919

Vimanmek Palace

Location: Bangkok
Architect: Prince Narisaranuwatiwong
Year of Completion: 1901

1

1
The eastern approach.
Steps ascending to the
Photo−albums Room

2
The spiral staircase that
leads from the fourth to the
ground floor

2

Vimanmek was rebuilt as the main royal residence at Suan Dusit Palace. The idea of the building was conceived when King Rama V visited the seaboard provinces and saw the uncompleted Mundhat Ratanaroj Mansion. The golden teakwook building was demolished and was taken to be rebuilt here and the construction took only seven months to complete.

The beautiful structure was built in the shape of the Roman letter L with its two wings–one running westward, the other northward–joining at an angle of 90°. Each wing is 60 meters in length while the width in general is 15 meters, though certain parts are as wide as 35 meters. The height measured 20 meters from the fourth–floor ceiling or 25 meters to the top of the superstructure.

Vimanmek is framed by four canals so the lowest story of the building is only made of stucco, the rest of the structure is made entirely of golden teakwood which is now extremely rare. The building consists of three stories with the exception of the octagonal end of the west wing whose additional fourth floor was used by the King's private quitters. Beyond the end of the west wing was a large green house as the nursery of the garden palace. (Duangrit Bunnag/Sumet Jumsai)

4

3
Second floor plan (1. The East Room; 2. The Blue and White Room; 3. The Bronze Room; 4. Big Game Trophy Room; 5. The Octagonal Room; 6. The Pink Apartment; 7. The Piano Room; 8. The Photo–Albums Room; 9. The Porcelain Table Room)

4
The Octagonal Hall on the second floor was the King's private Living Room, now used for displays of porcelain

5
The Anteroom in front of the King's Bed Chamber on the fourth floor in the West Wing

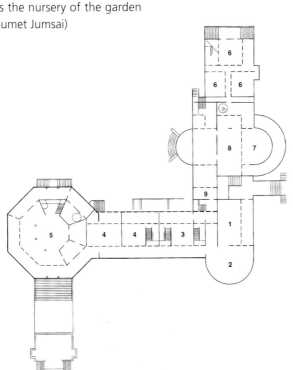

3

5

6
**The spacious Throne Hall in
semi–circular shape on the
third floor Loggia**

7
Fretted staircase spirals up from second to third floor in the North Wing

8
The semi–circular room above the western entrance seen from the gallery through the fretwork craftsmanship of the window

9
The Long Gallery on the fourth floor that surrounds the Octagonal Room

Drawings provided by
Duangrit Bunnag
All photographs courtesy of
Skyline Studio.

7

8

9

Istana Sri Menanti

Location: Sri Menanti, Negeri Sembilan
Architect: None
Builders: Tukang Kahar & Tukang Taib*
Years of Design and Construction: 1902–1908

1

1
Exterior view from north

2
Location plan

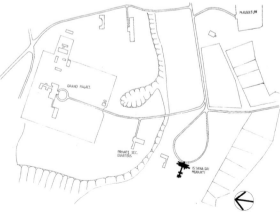

2

Malaysia, home to one of the world's oldest tropical rain forests, has a long tradition of building in timber from humble houses to royal palaces. The Malay palace, Istana, residence of the sultan, was the symbol of Malay culture and tradition and was of paramount importance to the lives of his people. The last, large timber palace was built for the 7th Ruler of Negri Sembilan, one of the four Federated Malay States, under the British Resident system. The palace was in use as the official residence of the Ruler until 1931, when a new and modern palace was built close by. Since then, the 'old' palace has been put to many uses; it is the present State's Royal Museum and remains in good repair.

Using timber from the nearby forests, the four main pillars of the central tower measure 65 feet rising the whole height from the ground. Typically, the ground floor is left open and no nail is used in the construction. The plan form and the whole design is however not typical of traditional Malay house type of the area.

The first floor's public rooms held State functions; the long verandah along the whole length of the front was lined by courtiers with the ruler's throne on a dais at the left end and local chiefs at the right. The second floor was occupied by the royal family; the third by His Highness. The fourth floor, which was in the central tower, housed the Royal Treasury and Archives, reached only by a steep stairs from the royal apartment.

The outside of the wooden posts and beams are profusely decorated with floral motifs, examples of the rich craftsmanship of the Malay carver. (Chen Voon Fee)

* Tukang—Malay for skilled craftsman

3

3
Exterior view of entrance

4
First floor plan

5
Roof plan

6
Section

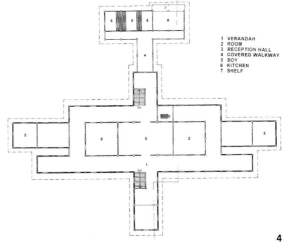

1 VERANDAH
2 ROOM
3 RECEPTION HALL
4 COVERED WALKWAY
5 BOY
6 KITCHEN
7 SHELF

4

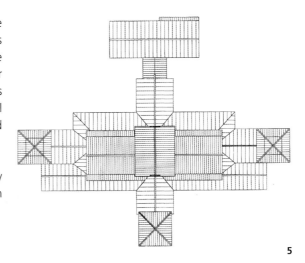

5

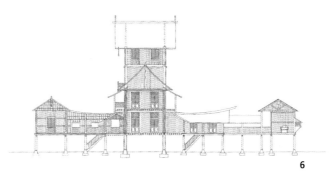

6

7
Interior view of Long
Gallery/Verandah and Royal
Dais

8

8
Carved decoration of evolving leaves on wooden posts and fascia

9
Exterior view of Central Tower

10
Detail of carving on posts of foliated design

Drawings provided by Chen Voon Fee, photographs courtesy of Photo Unit, National Museum of Malaysia

9

10

11

Pyre For Rama V

Location: Bangkok
Architect: Phraya Rajasongkram (Korn Hongsakul)
Year of Completion: 1911

1

1
The complex of buildings for
the cremation of the royal
bodies

2
Elaborate decoration at the
base of the building

2

Along with Buddhism, Cremation came to further India as well as Siam, where it has become customary. When King Chulalongkorn (Rama V) died in October 1910, his cremation took place by the end of march 1911. The place for Royal cremation is located at the northern part of palace complex.

The establishing of a place of cremation in proportion to the greatness and fame of his predecessor is the first care of a Siamese King on ascending the throne. The governors of the four northern provinces, where the best teak wood is found, are requested to provide, one each, the four main columns of the Phrameru. These pillars must be of the best variety of wood, absolutely straight, and 60 to 75 meters long. This applies equally to the governors of the other provinces, who have to provide big quantities of poles and wood for construction work, to be sent to the capital. Next to the main building where the cremation is going to take place, galleries are also built, including corridors and covered space for the mourners and the whole court. Further a great number of other buildings for several other purposes are also built, so that the whole are resembles a small town. The buildings completely covered with gold ornaments and glittering mirror mosaic, they are a striking copy of the gorgeous Siamese temples. Numerous umbrellas of honor with 7,9 and 11 tiers surround the whole crematory. The main building which has a square floor, is closed in by a wall. In the four corners of the wall are big, high towers. (Duangrit Bunnag/Sumet Jumsai)

3
Elaborate Thai painting
4
Mourning procession with urn
5
Inside the temporary building for the King
6
The temporary building for the new royal family to sit during the cremation ceremony

All photographs courtesy of National Archives of Thailand

4

5

3

6

Ubudiah Mosque

Location: Kuala Kangsar, Perak
Architect: Arthur Bennison Hubback, P.W.D.
Years of Design & Construction: 1913–1917

1

1
General view of exterior
(courtesy of Photo Unit,
National Museum of
Malaysia)

2
Site plan

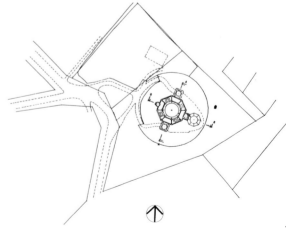

2

Located in Bukit (Hill) Chandan opposite the Royal Mausoleum, this beautiful mosque was started in 1913 by Sultan Idris, the 28th Sultan of Perak to fulfill a vow. It was opened in 1917 by his successor, Sultan Abdul Jalil. The design by A. B. Hubback, Government Architect in the Public Works Department of the Federal capital, Kuala Lumpur was an outstanding example of the imported style of North Indian Moghul Architecture. This was first introduced in the Sultan Abdul Samad building in Kuala Lumpur (1894–97), a deliberate choice of the State Engineer, C. E. Spooner.

Symmetrically designed, its plan form is an octagon with the main axis oriented as required in Islam, in the direction of Mecca as indicated by the traditional niche. The mosque is surrounded by a circular fence with a segment broken off the main circle to direct the faithful to enter the mosque by the side porticos as the approach is facing the back of the niche. The prayer hall is surrounded by an ambulatory verandah and roofed over by an onion–shaped dome which is surrounded by four tall, slender minarets capped by chatry. Five smaller domes roof over the mihrab niche, the ablution and the two porticos; in between are sixteen smaller minarets in descending pairs. The impression is of the central dome emerging from a grove of minarets and domes. The whole is gracefully proportioned and balanced. Ubudiah is justifiably regarded as the jewel in the crown of the country's moghul architectural heritage. (Chen Voon Fee)

3
View of 'chatry' of minaret (courtesy of Akitek Suria)

4
Floor plan

5
Section AA

Drawings provided by Chen Voon Fee

3

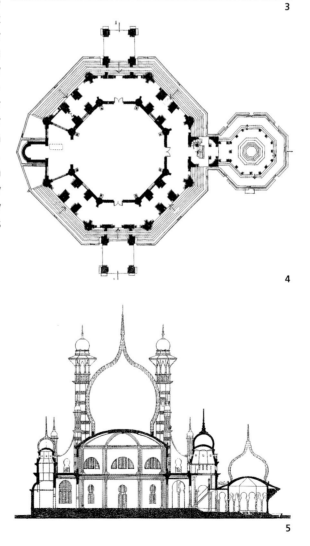

4

5

1920–1939

Aula ITB
(Institut Teknologi Bandung)

Location: Bandung
Architect: Henri Maclaine Pont
Year of Completion: 1920

1

1
Exterior front view of the
Aula

2
Axonometric view

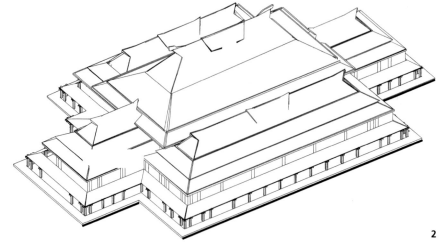

2

The Aula ITB was designed in 1919 by Henri Maclaine Pont (1885–1971), a noted Dutch architect born in Meester Cornelis (Jatinegara), Indonesia. As it was common to Dutch families born in Indonesia in those days, he went to Holland to study in 1894, and in 1902 he enrolled in Technische Hoogeschool Delft to study architecture. Actually, he was the first alumnus of architecture who was of Dutch–Indonesian descent.

The city of Bandung lies well below the site in the south, while the mythic and legendary mount of Tangkubanperahu (literary: upside down vessell/prau) is exactly due north, recalling the North–South main axis of the keraton. By putting the main entrance in the south, Pont opened up, upon entering the campus, a vista of a flattend mountain top of Tangkubanperahu in the up north, which was, and still is, the visually northern benchmark. On each side of the axis-road are the twin aula buildings, the West and East Aula, a perfect symmetry, connected with covered walkways which are at same time part of an open verandah encircling the aula, thus creating a peristyle. These covered walkways, connecting all other buildings, would be the pedestrain circulation system around the campus in anticipation of long rainy season of the year.

The aula itself is actually a cluster of buildings, each has its own roof. They were built attached to each other in such a way so that the roof overhang ends onto a concrete gutter. The largest building, with the size of 16m x 32m, being in the center has also the highest ceiling, consequently also the highest and the most sophisticated roof structure, has a very unconventional truss which stands on an elongated arch of laminated wood of more than 10m high. It seems that a durable glue has yet to be invented at the time, so Pont used the available glue with iron clamps and bolts instead which he painted black, in sharp contrast to the bright brown color of the wood, so that it looks like bamboo stems from below. The lower goes the arch, the thicker it becomes; the thickest are of more than thirty layers of board/panels. It was a structural tour-de-force indeed!

The building materials are decidedly of high-quality teak wood, while the roofs are of hard and durable wooden tiles, i.e. shingles, locally called sirap (Eusideroxylon

3
Ground plan
4
North elevation
5
Exterior view with landscape

5

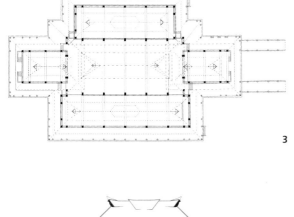

3

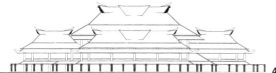

4

6
Interior showing the structure

7
Interior sketch (by the Architect, 1919)

8
Column Foot

6

7

8

zwageri). Noting that it was built in the late 1910's, in the scarcity of the aftermath of WWI, and done by local workers and utilizing local materials, with all those minimal conditions notwithstanding, the joineries were just superbly done and most certainly they must have demanded the highest degree of craftsmanship. It was interesting to see how the concrete gutter meet the wooden structure! And it still stands for 80 years up to now (it seems that a lot of bitumen and sheets of lead were used around the sharp and creaky corners to withstand any wooden structure shrinkage). The column footings, where the lateral force of the arch should be neutralized, were also resolved handsomely. It reminded one of the footings of candis, which by that time Pont must have familiarized with , albeit the gigantic steel clamps, bolts and nuts were uninhibitedly exposed.

Architecturally speaking, it is hard to deny the Wrightian atmosphere in the walkways along the peristyles, to see the design solutions in warding off showering rain. Pont not only used a nicely cut of roof angles, but he used also wooden struts one above the other criss-crosiing one another in an orthogonal way, jabbed in the upper part of each column/style to hold spreading vines of flowery plants. Surprisingly, the eaves, the struts, were also able to control the human scale along the lines of apple-sized-stones-studded columns. Indeed, it was really an elegant architectural solution in the tropics.

Maclaine Pont, by this very design, which was officially open in 1920, has been hailed as a pioneer in modernizing colonial architecture, for being able to develop new forms out of local, traditional or vernacular architecture. His ideas have inspired architectural students for many generations. But still, the aula ITB (Institut Teknologi Bandung) was, and still is, one-of-a-kind architectural piece that have never been surpassed or likened. It is just beyond compare, so the saying goes. (Yuswadi Saliya).

9
Interior sketch
(by the Architect, 1919)
10
Detail of Construction

Illustrations provided by Yuswadi Saliya

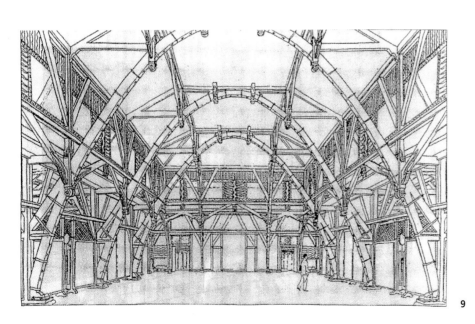

9

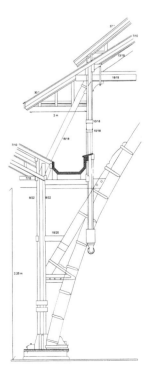

10

Majestic Theatre

Location: Singapore
Architect: Unknown
Year of Completion: 1927

1
Exterior view (Courtesy:
National Archives of
Singapore, Collection of
ZTan Kok Kheng)

Across the road from the heart of Singapore's Chinatown, the Majestic Theatre was built by the rich philanthropist Eu Tong Sen in 1927 as the Tien Yien Moh Toi Theatre for Cantonese operas. Later it was converted into a cinema for Chinese films and renamed Queen's Theatre; the name was later changed again to Majestic Theatre. The Chinese motifs on the facades was one of the earliest attempts in Singapore to imbue a sense of cultural origin in a building type that is essentially western in character. The motifs themselves were 'modernized' mosaic versions of traditional Chinese patterns. The cavernous interior reveal the rhythm of the concrete structure and as in Chinese tradition, decorated in a Chinese art–deco style. The proscenium arch is presently concealed behind tacky renovations done in the sixties and one hopes with bated breath that this queen of Chinatown will one day be restored to her original beauty. (Richard K. F. Ho)

2

2
Exterior view (provided by
Richard K. F. Ho)

Istana Kenangan

Location: Kuala Kangsar, Perak
Architect: None
Builders: Haji Sopian & sons Zainal, Abidin and Ismail
Years of Design & Construction: 1929–1931

1

1
Exterior view from
north–east

2
Site plan

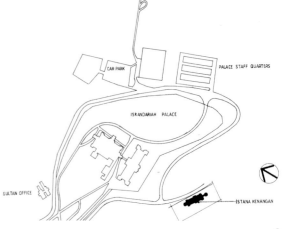

2

This unique palace was built as a temporary residence of the late Sultan Iskandar Shah of Perak State in Malaysia, who used it as his official residence until 1933 when the present Iskandariah Palace was completed. It was later occupied by the Perak Royal family. Today it houses the Perak Royal Museum.

Typical of Malay Dwellings, it is raised off the ground and constructed in timber without nails. A typical though unusual form, 41.75m long, unlike any of the main Malay house types, consists of linked polygonal shapes giving a series of shaped rooms, roofed over by hipped, half–gabled and jack–roofs covered in belian shingles, a hardwood grown only in Sarawak State. The distinctive feature is the in–fill wall panels made entirely of woven bamboo strips or kelarai. The woven pattern is further highlighted by the State colors of black, yellow and white giving the facade an overall lattice grid of diamond shapes. The ridges, fanlights, roof and floor fascias show another form of the artistic Malay craftsmanship in the finely carved, filigreed friezes. (Chen Voon Fee)

5

3
First floor plan

4
Section

5
Kenangan Palace as Perak Royal Museum

6
Exterior view of southwest side

7
Detail of woven bamboo wall and carved friezes

Drawings provided by Chen Voon Fee
Photographs courtesy of Photo Unit, National Museum of Malaysia

6

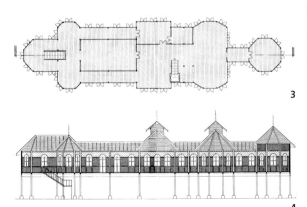

3

4

7

25

Metropolitan Theater

Location: Manila
Architect: Juan M. Arellano
Year of Completion: 1931

1
Front facade of the
Metropolitan Theater

The Metropolitan Theater was designed by Juan Arellano, a Filipino architect. He was educated in the United States at the Drexel Institute where he graduated with a Bachelor of Architecture in 1911. Upon his return, he joined his brother Arcadio and later joined the Bureau of Public Works. He was also a painter whose works followed the ideas of the expressionists and impressionists. As an architect, he was also responsible for the design of other civic buildings in Manila, particularly the Post Office Building and the Philippine Legislative Building, both neoclassical based on the Federal style of the United States. These structures were part of the Master Plan developed by Daniel Burnham for Manila.

The Metropolitan Theater first came into conception in 1924 when the then Senator Alegre submitted to the Philippine Legislature a proposal for the creation of a theater for Manila. As such, there was created a Metropolitan Theater Committee and Juan Arellano was selected as the architect for the project. He was then sent by the Committee to the United States to study and consult with Thomas W. Lamb (1871–1942). Lamb was then one of the best theater designers in USA and was famous for the designs of the Court Theater, the Rivoli Theater and the Loew's Theater in New York. It was under his tutelage and guidance that Juan Arellano designed the Metropolitan Theater.

It was during this period that the influence of the Exposition des Arts Decoratifs et Industriels held in Paris in 1925 was felt throughout Europe and the United States. Art Deco's characteristic playfulness and geometry in ornamentation was a major influence in Arellano's work for the Metropolitan Theater. Yet the plan of the Theater is still influenced by the Ecole des Beaux Arts. Symmetrical in plan and elevation, the theater exhibits the formality and order that allows it to stand out as a object building in the urban fabric of Manila. The main volume of the theater is a series of tiered masses that culminates in an arched roof. The perimeter of the roofs is further punctuated by vertical buttresses each capped with finials. These finials are similar to the minarets found in mosques as seen in the southern part of the Philippines which is perdominantly Muslim. The center of the volume is a rectangular stained glass window that depicts different tropical plants found in the Philippines. This is set against a representation of the rays of the sun adding a strong tropical flavor to the otherwise western architectural style. The other exterior motifs include hand made tiles that mimic traditional Malay tapestries and garments and have the appearance of being draped over the structure. The main volume of the structure houses the theater and the lobby. It is flanked on two sides with arcaded shops, restaurants and other establishments. The arcade has been successful in tropical climates and effectively shelters the pedestrians from the elements and as such is responsive to the urban texture in then Manila.

Arellano continues the use of indigenous motifs with regard to the interior of the theater. The decorative systems were Filipino in origin but playfully transformed into the Art Deco style. Included were mangos and bananas, tropical garlands of Philippine fruits and flowers. Within the main lobby are two murals done by the national artist Fernando Amorsolo, appropriately entitled "The Dance" and "The Spirit of Music". Other decorative elements include glass lamps in the shape of bamboo, capiz lamps and other works depicting birds of paradise. This strong adherence to the language of the Art Deco style was transformed in its vocabulary to include local plants, animals and fruits. Collectively, they create an architecture that has the ability to exude a strong cultural tradition that is the embodiment of Philippine culture.

Other rooms in the structure include a ballroom, a studio theater aside from the main gallery. Throughout these spaces, the use of the language and vocabulary of the Art Deco style was maintained creating a consistent and coherent image. The main gallery seats approximately 1339 persons and was then considered small for the population of Manila. Despite its size, however, the theater became a Manila landmark for decades to follow. (Francisco "bobby" Mañosa)

2
The arcade at the side of
the Theater
3
The main entrance

2

3

4
The artistically crafted stained glass

5
Detail influenced by Art Deco

Photographs provided by Daniel Lichauco

4

5

Clifford Pier

Location: Singapore
Architect: Public Works Department
Year of Completion: 1931

1
General exterior view
(Courtesy: National Archives
of Singapore, Collection of
Lim Choo Sie0)

1

Clifford Pier was named after Sir Hugh Charles Clifford, Governor of the Straits Settlements (1927–29). It was officially opened by Governor Sir Cecil Clementi (1930–34) on 3 June 1933. Previously the Pier was known as Johnston's Pier which was dismantled in July 1933. Johnston's Pier was erected in 1854 and named after one of the first businessmen and a founder of the Chamber of Commerce, Alexander Laurie Johnston, a friend of Sir Stamford Raffles. Clifford Pier was built by the Singapore contractor Who Hup. Steel piles were hammered into the seabed to create the foundation of the Pier by the local company which had then acquired the expertise to complete the task.

The Pier has a magnificent hall supported by elegant concrete arched trusses which till this day imbues one with a great sense of arrival–such was the romance of travel in those days. The Pier stood in front of a row of impressive buildings along the waterfront–the old Ocean Building, Alkaff Arcade, Maritime Building, Hong Kong and Shanghai Bank Building and the Fullerton building–all of which, except for the last, have been demolished in the name of 'progress'. In its heyday, the Pier was fondly referred to by the locals as the Red Light Pier, both as a reference to a red lamp in the old Johnston's Pier and also the ladies–of–the–night plying the Pier with offers of carnal pleasures. The Pier is still heavily used till this day. (Richard K. F. Ho)

2

2
Arched trusses (provided by Richard K. F. Ho)

3
Concrete arched hall (provided by Richard K. F. Ho)

4
Entrance view (provided by Richard K. F. Ho)

3

4

Sultan Sulaiman Mosque

Location: Klang, Selangor
Architect: L. Kesteven
Year of Completion: 1932

1

1
Old general view of the
mosque from the mihrab
side (Courtesy: Photo Unit;
National Museum of
Malaysia)

2
Site plan

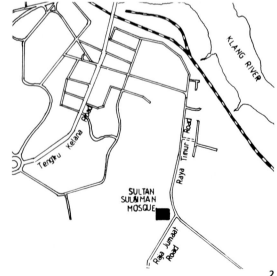

2

Like the Ubudiah Mosque, this is a royal mosque built for a Malay Ruler, sultan Alauddin Sulaiman Shah, sited close by the Shah Alam Palace in the royal capital of Klang. Like its predecessor, its plan form is an octagon with the main axis determined by the qiblat, direction of Mecca, indicated by the traditional niche directly facing the entrance. Along this axis between the *porte cochere* and the mosque proper rises the tall, domed minaret topped by a crescent finial replacing the old weather vane. The prayer hall is similarly surrounded by an ambulatory and has a western–type dome instead of the onion–shaped dome of Ubudiah. The central dome is supported by a ring of buttresses which transfer the dome onto the inner octagonal walls with clerestory lighting in between. The dome has a crown–like cupola surrounded by a ring of lighting finials with metal decoration. Four smaller domes roof over the porticoes of the cross axes. Still smaller domes cap the towers on the surrounding outer walls. Inside, the main dome floats over the Prayer Hall which has a kaleidoscopic, multi–colored glass ceiling. Stylistically this mosque derives its idiom from turn of the Century Secessionist Movement, the chief architectural exponent of which was the Viennese Otto Wagner whose work was probably known to the architect. (Chen Voon Fee)

3
Interior view of dome's ceiling (Courtesy: David Hashim)

4
Ground floor plan

5
Section

Drawings provided by Chen Voon Fee

3

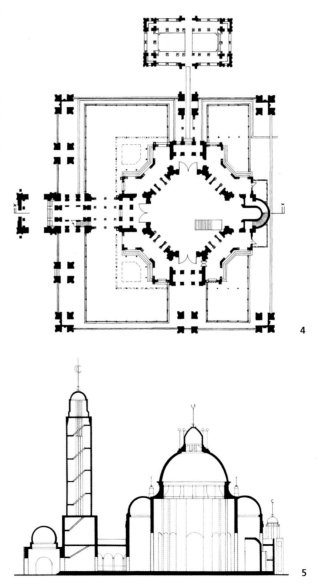

4

5

Singapore Railway Station & Hotel

Location: Singapore
Architect: Swan & Maclaren
Year of Completion: 1932

1

1
Front view

The Railway Station was officially opened by Governor Sir Cecil Clementi Smith in 1932. The dignified building in neo-classical style has been claimed to have its inspiration from Eliel Saarinen's Helsinki Station.

Completed in 1932 after three years of construction, its 72 feet (24 meter) reinforced concrete vault with exposed arches must have elicited gasps of wonder in those days. Between the arches are interesting panels of ceramic tiles depicting local scenes such as shipping, tin mining, paddy planting and other Malayan activities of that era. The exterior front facade has four heroic figures representing Commerce, Agriculture, Industry and Shipping. The 2 platforms covered by umbrella-form einforced concrete roofs were capable of accommodating the longest trains of that period. It is unfortunate that this magnificent structure has been marred by insensitive additions and poor maintenance over the years. (Richard K. F. Ho)

2
Reinforced concrete arches.

Photographs provided by
Richard K. F. Ho

2

Municipal Offices Building (Now The Rangoon City Development Corporation or YCDC)

Location: Rangoon
Architects: A.G. Bray and U Maung Tin
Year of Completion: 1933

1

1
Front view of exterior

Photographs provided by
Brian Brace Taylor

British colonial architecture of the late 19th and early 20th century, particularly in Asia, can be usefully characterized either as uninspired transplanting of architectural styles fashionable at that point in time in the British Isles, or as conscientious efforts to create amalgams of local and Western vocabularies–the latter was usually politically motivated and imposed upon the Western designer. Burma, which was a province ruled by the British Raj, first from Calcutta and then New Delhi until it obtained a separate status in 1937, was no exception to the two scenarios just cited: the capital, Rangoon, possessed numerous governmental buildings with an Edwardian cast, while the new university in the northern city of Mandalay has a purely neo–Greek main portico. However, it is the new Municipal Offices in Rangoon, a single building designed and executed in two phases by the British architect A. G. Bray which presents a critical turning–point in monumental institutional architecture of British colonial, as well as post–colonial, Burma. It reflects the conscious decision on the part of the Rangoon Municipal Council to require that features of Burmese architecture be incorporated into the second portion of the edifice–after it had already been designed.

Located at the junction of Dalhousie Street and Sule Pagoda Street, to the northeast prestigious Sule Pagoda, the offices occupy the site of the previous town hall (between 33rd and 34th Streets) suitably enlarged to accommodate the monumental new structure of reinforced concrete. The first section, containing both office space and the Council chambers, was designed by Bray for the rear portion of the site, constructed and officially inaugurated in November 1927. Conceived around a central interior court and surrounded with galleries, which was entirely appropriate given the hot, humid climate, this wing has a rather sober, two–story, neo–classical facade facing the narrow street behind. Tenders for the second section had been received in January 1928 when the proposal to modify Bray's project in order to render it more 'Burmese' was made and hence, approval of the construction was postponed. A Burmese, U Maung Tin, a trained architect employed by the municipal administration of the time as an assistant engineer, was given the responsibility of "completing the design and preparing all working drawings"

(Municipal Report 1929–1930).

Although plans of the building are at present unavailable, written description mentions that the program for the second phase involved formal reception spaces and the Town Hall Banquet Room. Not unlike French architect Tony Garnier's town hall in the Paris suburb Boulogne–Billancourt, Bray's secular building must have been intended to rival in importance its neighbor, the greatly venerated Sule Pagoda. The new office building, by its height and volume, may have prompted the discussions as to the appropriateness of its stylistic expression being either Burmese or Western. It seems that U's efforts were directed primarily to the decorative schemes of the reception spaces, and of course, to the principal facade on Dalhousie Street. Judging from the exterior alone as it exists today, U Maung Tin has attempted, with the mixed success such endeavors have known in other cultures (e.g., in medieval Russia), to introduce forms borrowed from traditional wooden architecture into–in this caseóconcrete. Even though Burma has a rich tradition of monumental Buddhist building in masonry in Pagan, the towers and ornamental latticework on the second building of the municipal offices derive ostensibly from wooded architecture of northern Burmese Buddhist monasteries and temples.

The significance of this project within the framework of modern Burmese architectural development, which has been extremely conservative, is that it set a precedent by opening the door to discussion about the future character and expressiveness of an architectural vocabulary indigenous to Burma. Its completion in 1933, some six years after the first section by Bray alone was inaugurated, coincided with the rise of Burmese nationalist activity. This edifice was the first by a member of the pre–1940 generation of architects, which included U Tha Tun (ARIBA) who was educated in Britain and U Maung Maung (ARIBA) who studied in India, that participated in the transition to an architecture in the period after independence. Other buildings followed, such as the new Railway Terminal, in this neo–Burmese idiom but none were of comparable prestige as a result of the site, scale and function.
(Brian Brace Taylor)

Villa Isola

Location: Bandung
Architect: Wolf Shoemaker
Year of Completion: 1933

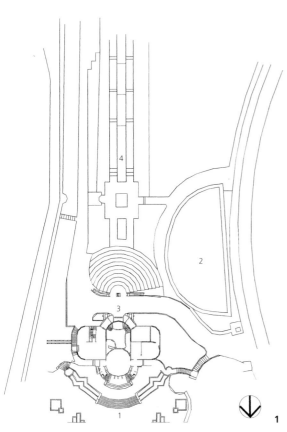

1

2

1
Site and ground floor plan
(1. Main entrance; 2. Pool;
3. Garden; 4. Backyard)

2
Exterior view with landscape

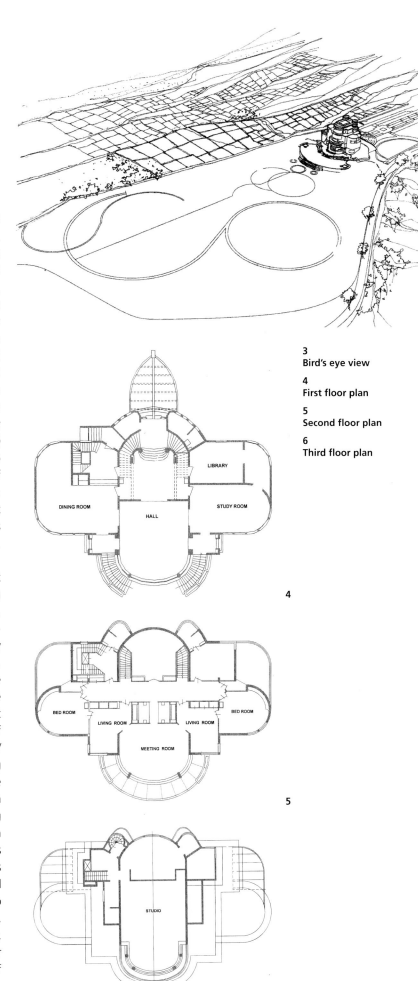

The villa was designed by C. P. Wolff Shoemaker and completed in 1933 for a rich Dutch merchant, D. W. Berrety. Shoemaker was a prominent Dutch architect with a lot of projects in several cities in Java. He had done a lot of studies on Javanese traditional architecture, just like his contemporary Maclaine Pont. While Pont was trying to develop the indigenous, Shoemaker seemed to be coming in from outside with a ready made proposal albeit with a keen understanding of the local culture. Shoemaker viewed the Javanese traditional architecture from the Hindu perspective. Thus the Villa Isola was supposedly an abstracted form of an Indian temple (candi), that is to say that Villa Isola, just like any other buildings in Java, consists of foot (foundation/floor) body (walls/column) and head (ceiling/attic/roof). To articulate and emphasize those building parts, a sum of horizontal moldings of some sort should be applied. On the other hand he was also familiar with modernist thinking of de Stijl and Art Deco. Then the problem was how to combine the two. Villa Isola was a case in point.

The layout is along a classic north–south axis of about 600m long site, with 4–5% inclination, the north being the higher, pointing straight to Mount Tangkubanperahu. The site is to the west side of the winding Bandung–Lembang Road (Lembang is a small town 16km away from Bandung, at the foot of Mount Tangkubanperahu). Shoemaker took the entry point some 200m from the north, cutting the axis from the east directly into the entrance porch and a vestibule. It turned out to be that the vestibule is slightly higher than the second floor of the villa. Going down a step one enters a large family/meeting room (salon), dining room, library, working room/secretarial works place. Going down one more floor, we reach the ground floor for a service area (kitchen, storage, servants rooms, etc.) and a playing room which is annexed to a vast open verandah, with plenty of symmetrical curvilinear stepped terraces following the existing contour and the stepped rice fields in its environs. Going up from the vestibule to the third floor, approach the bedroom, which are extended into a space with a very large sliding door to the balcony, covered with special glass to ward off rain water, structured by steel cantilever. The fourth floor is for studio, loggia, mini bar and guest–rooms, with a roof terrace on the top.

3

3
Bird's eye view

4
First floor plan

5
Second floor plan

6
Third floor plan

LIBRARY

DINING ROOM

HALL

STUDY ROOM

4

BED ROOM

LIVING ROOM

LIVING ROOM

BED ROOM

MEETING ROOM

5

STUDIO

6

7

7
Side exterior view

8
Exterior view at time of
completion

9
South elevation

10
North elevation

8

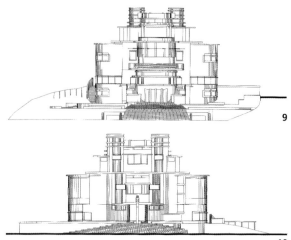

9

10

The main formal feature of the villa is that the walls are curved all around, just like a composite of several cylinder of different sizes, ordered in such a way so as to comply to the existing primary north–south axis. As to the horizontal linings, Shoemaker applied extensive moldings, to emphasize slices of openings with a thoughtful fenestration design. From the third floor upward, the floor area became smaller, with the roof terrace as the peak. The end result is a commanding symmetrical mass of solid and void, handsome and proud, but still conforms to its undulating environs.

The size of the four–floor villa with the studio plus a roof terrace itself is about 1400m². The rest is an open space within a lot of about 5ha, parks (pool, sculpted fountain) in its northern and outdoor landscape (pool, sculptures, curvy staircases, long winding footpaths to stroll) in its southern. Looking northward, one could see the legendary skyline of Mount Tangkupanperahu. Looking southward from any floor, Bandung terrain lies bare in front of one's nose, about 8 km away and some 100m below!. (Yuswali Saliya)

11

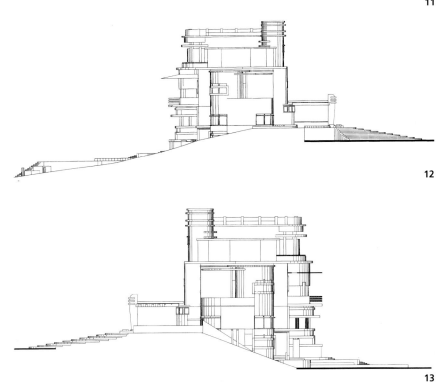

12

11
Interior staircase

12
East elevation

13
West elevation

Drawings and photographs
provided by Yuswadi Saliya

13

Grand Lycee Yersin

Location: Dalat
Architect: J. Lagisquet
Years of Design/Completion: 1934/1935

1
View of the north facade
and tower of the Grand
Lycee Yersin. Note the open
corridors serving the
classrooms on the middle
levels

1

Of the few remarkable structures actually erected in Vietnam as a whole during the French colonial administration of the years 1920-1950, the new extension to the Grand Lycee Yersin stands out prominently. It is historically significant as practically the only building which was constructed on the site originally designated for it in Ernest Hebrard's Master Plan; and it is geographically prominent, situated on the crest of a hill where its architectural qualities are visible at great distance. Designed by the French Beaux-Arts-trained architect J. Lagisquet, who had lived and worked for many years already in Indochina, the Grand Lycee Yersin extension is neither an attempt to re-interpret a local, traditional style nor to create a hybrid vocabulary of Eastern and Western. The school is of a frankly modernist design - so much so that it probably could have been inserted into a contemporary, 1930s context in France without shock to aesthetic tastes-yet, the actual siting is so deftly handled by the architect, the plan of the edifice so carefully thought through, the detailing as well as the execution of such high quality, that it is an outstanding achievement.

The Grand Lycee Yersin represents a 'breath' of modernity and cosmopolitanism in the best sense, in spite of some regionalist elements that were included, such as the stair tower and belfry, and the double-pitched roof. Structurally, it is of fired, red brick bearing wall construction, and reinforced concrete for floors, roof beams, lintels, balconies and columns. Typical of much European design of the 1930s, the openings have concrete framing which projects slightly from the smooth outer surfaces of the facade, creating bands that accentuate the horizontality. Here they have been painted and contrasted with the warm color of the brickwork. The exposed brick has been executed with considerable care.

The siting of this large edifice has been masterfully handled, both in relation to the topography and to the existing buildings on the premises. The first buildings of the Grand Lycee Yersin, completed in the mid-1920s, are located on a level plateau along the summit of one of Dalat's many hills; they are simple, three-story, plastered brick structures with double-pitch, wooden roofs and shutters, and generally speaking, lacking in aesthetic interest. On the other hand, Lagisquet designed a building which curves in a long, gentle sweep from northeast to southwest along one edge of the plateau, and which is linked at each end to other buildings by galleries of low, concrete domes on concrete columns. This linking device frames, in a sense, the new school building, which is larger and taller (four stories) and seemingly more monumental; at the same time, it achieves a coherent grouping around a central playground. Its overall volume is nonetheless within the scale of the older buildings, unifying hitherto disparate parts.

In plan, the school is clearly sensitive to the climate. The region receives approximately 150 days of rain a year, and temperatures vary from 32 to 2°C, with an average of 18°C. Hence, the classrooms have all been located along the southern side of the building for the best natural light and heat in the cold season. However, there is good cross ventilation, since the corridor giving access to the classrooms on levels two and three runs along the north side and is open towards the playground. On the ground floor, with arched openings and high ceilings, there are spaces for group activities; this floor as well as the attic floor have a central circulation system.

A tower, which rises nearly twice as high as the main body at the western end, houses the main stairs to the upper levels. It is visually the most striking vertical feature, its high, sloping roof culminating in a belfry. However much it may recall a European, perhaps alpine, vernacular tradition, one finds the tower curiously ambiguous in style, non-specific in its allusions and certainly not a pastiche.

Since Vietnams independence from France, it has become a teachers' college. (Brian Brace Taylor)

2
Partial view of the stairs tower and concrete vaulting of the galleries connecting the new building to the older ones

3
General view of the Grand Lycee Yersin from the south

4
Detail of the stair tower and classroom wing of the Grand Lycee Yersin from the south. The ground floor has sun–screens of cement to filter the sunlight

Photographs by
Brian Brace Taylor

3

4

The Central Market

Location: Phnom Penh
Architects: Jean Desbois with Louis Chauchon
Years of Design/ Construction: 1934/35;1935/37

1

1
Exterior view at night

2
Interior view of dome

Photographs provided by Brian
Brace Taylor

2

A truly exceptional building in the emergence of modern Southeast Asia architecture in this century, the Central Market in Phnom Penh is the centerpiece of the city's first Master Plan, which sought to unify and to extend the existing neighborhoods. The Market was radically different in form, scale and construction materials from its predecessors locally and even regionally. Moreover, it represents a tentative effort at introducing a modernist architecture into a colonial setting at one of the farthest limits of the French Empire.

The conception differs from the typical shed-like structures of metal, wood and sometimes glass which were designed for covered markets throughout the world during the last 150 years: it consists of an octagonal central space, 45m in diameter and covered by a dome 26m high, with 4 wings projecting from the core. The structure, built entirely of reinforced concrete poured in-situ, nevertheless responds perfectly to the two major functional requirements of the brief: adequate natural ventilation and protection from the tropical sun. The projecting wings are largely open on the sides, with screen-like vents in the tiered roofs, while the central space has similar openings for indirect light and evacuation of warm air.

Jean Desbois, a French architect residing in Indochina at the time, was originally commissioned by the municipal council to produce four different preliminary designs for a market, with the stipulation that each represent the most advanced ideas for covered markets to be found in Europe in the 1920s and early 30s. Inspired specifically by publications on the new central market in Leipzig (1928) which had several cupolas each with a 76m clear span, Desbois proposed a more modest building that is nonetheless unique in its composition of spaces, monumental in scale and grandeur both inside and from

without, and yet bears no stylistic traces of a particular tradition in the East or West.

The preliminary project was selected from among Desbois' four submissions and served as a basis for a limited competition between French public works companies who bid on future construction, and in addition the services of an architect for preparation of working drawings. In this way, a second architect, Louis Chauchon, living in Saigon, contributed to the final version of the Central Market, modifying the shape and structure of the dome slightly, as well as the elevations of the radiating wings.

Apart from its outstanding qualities as a building, the Central Market gained in importance because its location at the very core of a master plan to extend the main business district of the Cambodian capital and to tie together the somewhat disparate quarters of the city into a more coherent and unified plan. Situated on infill of a previously swampy area, the market was surrounded by blocks of planned shop-houses of mixed commercial and residential use. The generally flat topography of the city as a whole. Broken only by the artificial hillock of the phnom itself, thus received a new, 26m high 'hillock'. The potential symbolism which this 'artificial mountain', rivaling only the existing phnom on the landscape, may have offered some of the religious communities cannot be neglected. It became both an organizing element for planned, future urban expansion within a network of streets and building typologies, as well as the focus of social and religious activities. For a single building with a clearly modernist aspect, and without any overt symbolism, in plan or in decorative motifs, to achieve such a role is indeed a remarkable accomplishment.
(Brian Brace Taylor)

Anglo-Oriental Building

Location: Kuala Lumpur
Architect: A. O. Coltman, Booty, Edwards & Partners
Years of Design and Construction: 1936, 1937-1940

1
Exterior view of entrance

2
Site plan

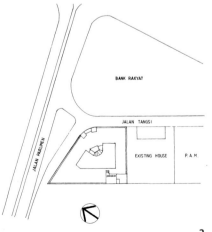

Located at a corner quadrilateral site, the Art Deco, 3-story building makes a strong sweep round the corner on Parliament Road. Its twin towers, grooved and topped by typical flagpoles flank the corner entrance shaded by a projecting canopy; the strong verticality sets off the horizontality of the sides. The latter's tripartite facade design is repeated on the two visible, unequal street frontages. The ground floor colonnade supports a grooved frieze suggesting a classical entablature. Piano nobile windows are individually canopied while the top floor windows are continuously shaded by a deep overhang, giving the effect of an attic floor.

Internally, the entrance hall leads to the main staircase contained in a stair drum in the central open court, now roofed over, following the introduction of air conditioning in the 1960s. The stairs bifurcate and turn round to reach the first floor rooms, all reached from corridors surrounding the court; the same arrangement is repeated for the second floor. The strong Art Deco features on the facades are carried through internally to the details of doors and timber paneling of the corporate offices. This is a fine pre-World War II building leading to the rise of Modernism in the next decade.
(Chen Voon Fee)

4

3
Interior view of steps

4
Interior view of the atrium

5
First floor plan

6
Section

Drawings and photographs provided by Chen Voon Fee

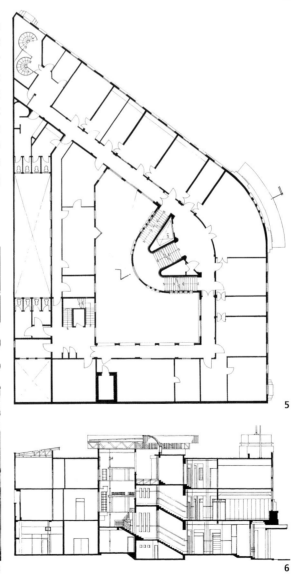

5

6

3

1940–1959

Tiong Bahru Flats

Location: Singapore
Architect: Singapore Improvement Trust (SIT)
Year of Completion: 1941

1

Photographs provided by
Richard K. F. Ho

In 1927, the British colonial government set up the Singapore Improvement Trust (SIT) to look into the problems of overcrowding and acute housing shortage in Singapore. The Tiong Bahru flats was the first public housing project undertaken by the SIT built on land which were originally the site of a Chinese cemetery. 'Tiong Bahru' is an amalgam of two words: 'tiong', a Chinese Hokkien work for cemetery and 'bahru', a Malay word for new. Although New Cemetery is certainly an inauspicious name for a public housing estate built to house the living, it nevertheless reminded subsequent generations of the area's origin. Between 1936 and 1941, the SIT built 784 flats housed in two and three story blocks, 54 tenements and 33 shops in Tiong Bahru. The Tiong Bahru flats were advertised for sale when completed but the sale was a failure (SIT Report, 1953) probably due to its inauspicious name. Hence, they were rented out to tenants and by 1941, over 6,000 people including Europeans lived in the new estate.

The estate was largely planned based on the principles used for British New Towns where the emphasis was on small neighborhoods and the provision of open spaces in close proximity to the flats for recreation and to promote more sanitary conditions. The British architects, however, took local life-styles into consideration in the design of the flat layouts as evidenced by the modified traditional shop-house plan with air-wells and back lanes. Urbanistically, the estate layout has great integrity with memorable spaces for the community to interact, and well-scaled buildings in the Art-Deco style. Corners are well-defined by the architecture and with shops and cafes catering to the local community. Considering that this estate was completed in 1941, it is miles ahead of many other public housing estates completed decades later in Singapore. The Tiong Bahru Estate is living proof that public housing does not need to be repetitive, boring and alienating. (Richard K. F. Ho)

2

3

Rachadamnern Boulevard
Row House

Location: Bangkok
Architect: Chitrasen Abhaiwongse
Year of Completion: 1946

1

1
The special row house at the
corner of the main junction

2
Plan (provided by
Duangrit Bunnag)

3
The simple design facade of
the middle row house

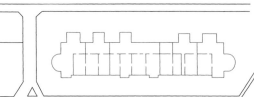

2

3

Since 1868, the national policy to develop the country has acquired western civilization. The community has extended beyond the Royal Palace to streets together with the creation of row-houses and shop-houses in order to lodge foreigners as well as to serve for the Thai and foreign businesses. Some of these buildings have been transformed later into governmental offices due to the working convenience.

Before the Thai revolution in 1932, there were some students who finished their architectural study from aboard under the Thai government scholarship or their own support and become the civil servant in the design office in replacement of the foreign architects the number of which have been reduced only for the necessity. As a result, all the buildings along Rachadamnern Avenue was designed by the Thai architect graduated from France.

The building designs were applications of western architecture and basically emphasized accommodating local weather conditions and the efficient use of space. Buildings were designed in a simple manner, and were not decorated in detail. A characteristic feature was the use of architectural design to counter the effect of the tropical sun-horizontally above exterior windows helped shade the buildingís interior. The vertical and horizontal reinforced concrete slab were used to serve as decorative function and shaded the exterior walls. Sculptural effect forms were used in the corner of the road. With the exception of the buildings in the middle of the row there is no step reduction of mass. The opening was emphasized to natural light according to the real function. The horizontal and vertical reinforced concrete fins were simply designed with these openings to protect the sunlight and the rain. Texture paint was mainly utilized with ivory color for the fins and dark brown for window frames. (Duangrit Bunnag/Sumet Jumsai)

4

4
Geometrical shape row house with reinforced concrete slab overhangs

5
Intervention of solid planes and voids, light and shadow as created by geometrical shapes

6
Rows of shop houses on the first boulevard of Bangkok

Photographs courtesy
Skyline Studio

5

6

55

Federal House

Location: Kuala Lumpur
Architect: B. M. Iversen
Years of Design and Construction: 1951, 1952–1954

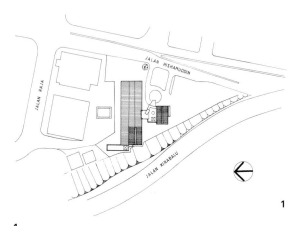

1
Site plan

2
Exterior view from Jalan
Hishamuddin (Courtesy:
Photo Library, Ministry of
Information)

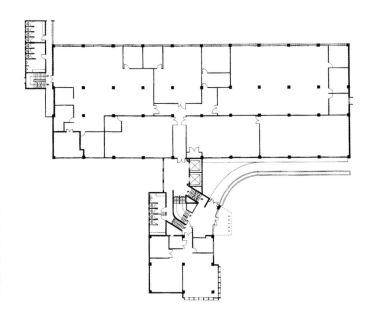

The Federal House, completed just three years before the country's independence, was the winning entry in a Government invitational architectural competition. Built to house various government offices, it consists of two (an 8 & a 9–story) blocks linked by a tower block housing the main staircase, lifts lobby and an entrance hall measuring 84 feet from ground to top.

The reinforced concrete structure was designed with cost–saving secondary beams and slabs of uniform span and size. The roof is a light R. C. curved slab insulated from heat with hollow pre–cast blocks. Rainwater is drain via downpipes on the face of each column from the roof gutters along the edge of the curved slab, supported by paired edge beams.

The typical office floor of 16,000 square feet was an open plan with flexible, demountable office partitions later provided. Flexible telephone and electrical services installation were other early innovations for office buildings. Originally 30 cars and 200 bicycles were planned for in the semi–basement apart from forecourt parking.

The facade design was one of the first to use steel framing filled with wall panels of green Vitrolite; French windows are in the center of each bay and a continuous top light of louver glass runs along the entire floor admitting adequate natural light to the middle of the office floor. Solid brickwork was finished with hammered plaster and ornamental key–lines; small squares of gold leaf glass mosaic decorate the front gable wall. Arrows of round portholes punctuate the edge of the solid gable wall and layers of curved fins shade continuous glass windows walls above the entrance canopy. Old Malayan civil servants remember their office as the 'Dutch Barn' because of its unusual roof design. (Chen Voon Fee)

3

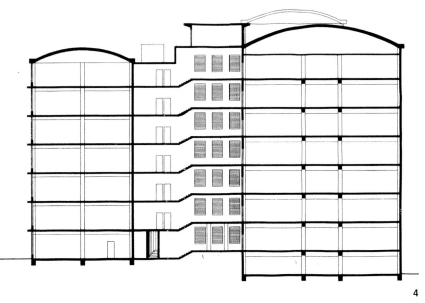

4

5

3
First floor plan

4
Section

5
Interior view of entrance hall and stair case (Courtesy: Chen Voon Fee)

Drawings provided by Chen Voon Fee

Asia Insurance Building

Location: Singapore
Architect: Ng Keng Siang
Year of Completion: 1954

1

Exterior view

1

The Asia Insurance Building was the tallest building in Singapore at the time. Ng was one of the Singaporeans who returned from architectural education in Britain and brought back with him the influence of the Modern Movement and Art Deco styles. It was one of Ng's first buildings in Singapore. This art–deco building commands its position well in the corner of Raffles Quay and Finlayson Green. The building with its beige marble finish has aged remarkably well. Its horizontal bands of sun–shading the stepped crown of a roof give it a distinctive presence which till today is still significant in spite of much taller and bigger neighbors. (Richard K. F. Ho)

2
Close–up of exterior

Photographs provided by
Richard K. F. Ho

2

Lee Yan Lian Building

Location: Kuala Lumpur
Architect: E. S. Cooke
Years of Design and Construction: 1949–1959

1

1
Old view from Jalan Hang
Lekiu (courtesy of the New
Straits Times)

2
Old aerial photo of Jalan Tun
Perak/Jalan Hang Lekiu
junction (courtesy of Photo
Library, Ministry
of Information)

2

Named after its owner, the 17-story office building occupying the entire corner site formed by Jalan Tun Perak's junction with Jalan Hang Lekiu and Jalan Raja Chulan was the tallest of the first generation of high-rises in the country from the 1950s till early 60s. Planning started in 1949 as an 8-story building but throughout the planning and building stages the design was affected by many changes of the owner's requirements.

The raised ground floor with a mezzanine gallery houses a bank with the entrance at the splayed corner of Jalan Tun Perak and Jalan Hang Lekiu. Another entrance leads to a lift lobby directly off Jalan Tun Perak with the main stairs going round three sides of the two-lift shaft. Office floors are in various configuration with the owner's penthouse on the 15th floor. The toilets and other service rooms are on the plain Jalan Raja Chulan side. A sub-basement houses storage and plant room. There was no provision for a carpark.

The broken-up massing and the facades design–no two alike–put this building in a class of its own without a peer. Two dissimilar street frontages interlock at the corner held together by a tower; Jalan Hang Lekiu's has a 2-story podium fenestrated with two rows of boxed windows and a set-back tower block; Jalan Tun Perak's has a more conventional curtain wall cladding until the twelfth floor above which the 6 upper floors break up into unequal juxtaposition of three varying boxes with strip windows in deep box frames.

The original interplay of geometric blocks and facade treatment with different materials express the three functions of public, office and private space. Not until the revival of deconstructivist architecture in Europe of the 1980s was anything like this seen. In Malaysia Lee Yan Lian Building remains unequaled. (Chen Voon Fee)

3

3
Jalan Hang Lekiu exterior view (By Chen Voon Fee)

4
Jalan Tun Perak exterior view (By Chen Voon Fee)

5
Jalan Raja Chulan exterior view (By Chen Voon Fee)

4   5

1960–1979

Parliament Building

Location: Kuala Lumpur
Architect: W. Ivor Shipley, J.K.R.
Years of Design and Construction: 1957–1960; 1960–1963

1

1
General exterior view
(Courtesy of Photography
Library, Ministry of
Information)

2
Site plan
(Courtesy: Chen Voon Fee)

3
First floor plan

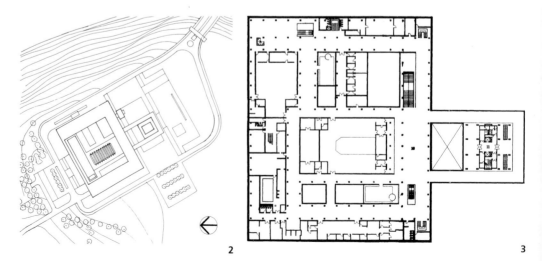

2

3

Like many of the first post–Independence (1957) buildings, the Parliament Building was the brain–child of Tunku Abdul Rahman, the country's first Prime Minister. As befitting a newly independent and democratic nation the architectural idiom chosen was the modern International Style. Located on top of a low hill in the Lake Garden area visible to all, the Building is set among manicured lawns, reflecting pools and formal planting. A ceremonial parade ground, Parliament Square, overlooked by the office tower is where State guests and important dignitaries are formally welcomed.

The design concept was based on the podium and tower block, a well–known early exponent being New York's Lever House. Planned symmetrically along a N.W.–S.E. axis, the 18–story podium at first floor level. Rising from the large podium is on the main axis is a striking, triangular folded plate structure, joined corcertina–like with 11 pinnacles, symbolizing the country's initial eleven States. Beneath this sits the House of Representatives (Dewan Rakyat) the people's elected government. The smaller chamber of the Senate (Dewan Negara) is nearby. The distinctive architectural treatment given to the facades is a total skin of pre–cast concrete sun–shading grilles, creating an elegant tracery of pattern and scale. (Chen Voon Fee)

4
Interior view of House of Representatives
(courtesy of Photography Library, Ministry of Information)

5
Exterior view of Tower
(courtesy Chen Voon Fee)

6
Section

Drawings provided by Chen Voon Fee

5

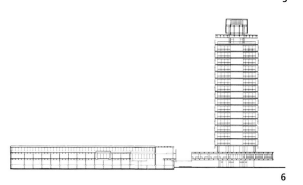

6

Singapore Conference Hall And Trade Union House

Location: Singapore
Architect: Malayan Architects Co–Partnership
Year of Completion: 1965

1

1
External Detail

2
Exterior view

2

The design of this building was the subject of an open architectural competition announced on 14th June 1961 and won by Malayan Architects Co–Partnership, a triumvirate of British–educated architects; Lim Chong Keat, Chen Voon Fee and William. S. W. Lim. The architectural competition was significant as it was the first major open architectural competition to be conducted in accordance with RIBA conditions in Singapore after the Second World War.

The imposing building houses the Conference Hall and offices of the National Trade Union Congress. Topped with a dominant cantilevered upturned butterfly roof supported by square columns and five monolithic cores of staircases and lifts, it is symmetrically ordered along the inverted ridge of this roof along the north–south axis. There are three parts to this building: to the northern end, an auditorium with naturally ventilated foyers extending into cantilevered terraces projecting beyond glazed wall–screens demarcating the inside and outside; to the southern end are the offices of the National Trades Union Congress which incorporates a resource library at the 3rd and 4th stories.

In between these two parts is a large central space that reaches the underside of the main roof with day–light let in through a jacked middle portion. Functionally, this space is used for temporary exhibitions at the ground level. The direction of entry is perpendicular to the axis of symmetry thusforming a central concourse from the western and eastern faces of the Conference Hall. From this concourse, two symmetrically placed staircases reach to the upper concourse on the second story which in turn brings one to the foyers of the auditorium on the third story. On the walls of these foyers are stylized motifs in brightly colored glass mosaics inspired by indigenous patterns and colors of the traditional Malay mengkuang mat (woven from the leaves of the pandanus plant, pandanus aurantiacus). At the Trades Union Congress office section, where walls are exposed directly to the outside, there are vertical louvers of dark tropical hardwood (merbau) forming another layer behind the row of columns Here, strategies constitutive of the new architecture abound: clarity of structure with the associative separation of enclosing elements from the structure; a clear, fluid composition of interpenetrating elements and planes that enclose and demarcate spaces; the freeing of the ground story – in this case, only partially creating a public concourse; and the blurring of boundaries between inside and outside through the use of extensive glazed panels.

4
Section

5
Ground floor

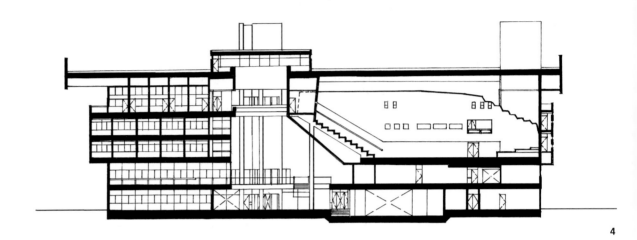

4

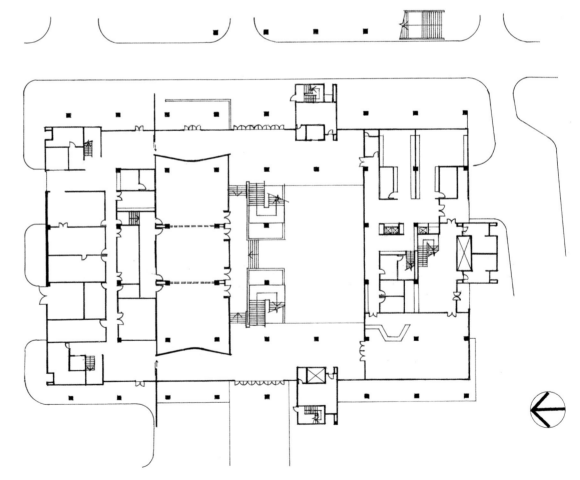

5

The quintessential distinguishing mark of the new architecture, the roof garden was also present in the competition drawings of the architects on the 'butterfly' roof, but was later omitted by the client with advice from the jury which considered it 'overdone', and may not be seen much by visitors. Most visually dominating, the deeply cantilevered upturned roof is a strange and questionable reaction to the specificity of the local climate of torrential rains and hot weather. Chen Voon Fee has suggested that this is a reinterpretation of the deep overhanging eaves of the prototypical traditional Malay house. While the Malay roof pitches steeply downwards to dispel rainwater rapidly, the upturned 'butterfly' roof does not seem a rational response to the problem. What it does however is to enable most of the glazed facades under it to be in constant shade. The effect is that the depths of the interior is clearly seen through the shaded glazed panels with little interference from reflections. Its interior is effectively revealed this way. In fact, the view extends all the way through the building to the other side where the carparks are. It seems all structure; 'walls' thus disappear, or appears insignificant. It is this character of the building that recalls the traditional buildings of South East Asia where the roof is generally very expressive while the walls are typically non-load bearing infills. Aesthetically, the varying portions of the facades that come under shade at changing times of the day seem to add another dimension to the elevational composition. The aesthetic is thus one of layering, of degrees of transparencies and reflectivity. This poetically brings out the qualities of tropical shade, with its rich tones, shielded from the harsh tropical light. The Corbusian use, typified at Chandigarh, of chiaroscuro, of modulation of shadow versus light and mass versus voids, especially the aesthetic function in the use of the brise-soleil, is most sensitively transformed here into a modulation of layers of transparencies and tactility that almost acquires a textile quality. Also left out from the original scheme is a large reflecting pool in the forecourt that stretches the entire length of the building.

Presently dwarfed by surrounding high-rise buildings, the Conference Hall manages to maintain a presence that its neighbors many times its size could not command. Its timeless qualities have withstood the test of time. (Richard K. F. Ho)

6
Entrance view

6

La Cité Sihanouk

Location: Phnom Penh
Architects: Vladimir Bodiansky, Gerald Hanning with Vann Molyan
Years of Design/Construction: 1963–1964/1964–1965

1

1
Floor plans of typical
apartments.

2
Aerial view of La Cité
Sihanouk soon after its
completion in the late 1960s.
The row of apartments in
the upper right are those
with patios, while those in
the lower left foreground
are the less expensive units.

Photograhs provided by
Brian Brace Taylor

2

La Cité Sihanouk in Phnom Penh, built in 1964 as part of a larger urban complex that extended the capital southwards along the edges of the Bassac and Mekong rivers, was comprised of some 300 housing units in two parallel, multi-story rows separated by a park. A civic center, which included a municipal theater and an exhibition hall were located between one of the apartment buildings and the river. Seen in its entirety, the urban planning as well as the apartment types represent a rare, if not the sole, example of the CIAM rationalist approach to urban design originating in the European modernist movement, and actually achieved in what was formerly French Indochina. In fact, the apartment-types were conceived by former close associates of the French architect Le Corbusier, namely, Gerald Hanning (1919–1978) and Vladimir Bodiansky (1898–1966), who came to Cambodia after independence as consultants to the United Nations. Hanning lived in Phnom Penh from 1959 until 1963, while Bodiansky resided there only periodically.

The approximately 160 apartments in the building overlooking the Bassac River were intended for Cambodians of an upper income – bracket, such as civil servants; the second building, further from the river, had slightly fewer units, was lower than its neighbor, but possessed less spacious apartments and , hence, was aimed at potentially less well-to-do inhabitants. However, the apartments run across the entire structure in both buildings, so that all of the units have facades to the east and west. This offers excellent natural ventilation for all. The patios of the higher income units (as well as the terraces of the more economical complex), participate admirably in this adaptation to the tropical climate of Cambodia.

Yet the patio of residential units here reflect–as did the beehive dwellings in Casablanca by ATBAT–Africa–a sensitivity to local culture and customs. As with the indigenous Muslim populations of North Africa, many rural, and even urban, Cambodians prefer to prepare meals outside the house, on porches or terraces: in the new apartments, the kitchen is placed immediately adjacent to, if not actually in the patio. Moreover, typically one enters the apartments not from a corridor nor from a vestibule but directly into the patio, which is usually a double-height space onto which the living room opens from one side. It acts as a kind of verandah. The most private rooms, such as bedrooms, were placed farthest from the entry. Finally, in a manner altogether typical of traditional rural houses on pilotis in Cambodia, the ground level of the complex does not have dwellings, but could accommodate small shops or other activities.

The structures which permitted the relatively open ground floor, and the inclusion of the high-ceiling patios is a post-and-beam skeletal structure of reinforced concrete; the infill is brick with rendering. Floors were concrete slab. Window and door frames and shutters were of wood.

Unlike most of the housing built in Cambodia between independence from France and the tragic events in the country as a direct result of the Vietnam war and its aftermath, La Cité Sihanouk was not a private speculative endeavor. The Public Sector Pensions Administration invested the money necessary for constructing this housing, selling off a portion with 13-year mortgages and leasing directly the remaining units.

Although it was designed by foreign consultants to the Cambodian government but built after their departure, it nevertheless benefited from their previous vast experience in housing design for hot, tropical or arid climates and for non-European cultures. The potential influence of these dwellings as a model for future economical mass-housing in southeast Asia was, in large measure, nullified by more than 30 years of war and destruction in Cambodia itself. This project passed unnoticed in the outside world. It is only recently that its "rediscovery" had shed some new light on the modernist architectural heritage in the country, including the built work of the major local figure of that period, Vann Molyan, with whom Hanning, Bodiansky and others collaborated to produce the Bass River development project. (Brian Brace Taylor)

State Mosque, Negeri Sembilan

Location: Seremban
Architect: Malayan Architects Co–Partnership
Years of Design and Construction: 1963, 1966–1967

1

1
Exterior view
(Courtesy of David Hashim)

2
Location plan

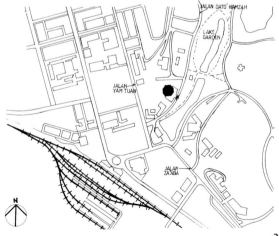

2

The State Mosque of Negeri Sembilan was the winning entry of a national architecture competition held in 1963. It is sited in the landscaped setting of the Lake Gardens in the heart of Seremban, the State capital. Based on the number 9 (Malaysembilan) in the State's name, the raised prayer hall is a nine-sided polygon, roofed over by nine conoid sections meeting in the center with their outer edges shaped upwards in shallow curves. The motif is repeated by nine slender, U-shaped pylons set in between the bays, forming the outer ring of supports for the flared roofs. Nine smaller cones in the center of each bay support the upper gallery for women, separated as required in Islam. The mosque office administration, ablutions and all ancillary rooms are on the lower level with turfed banks shaped up to the window openings. 'Burying' – the secondary accommodation highlights the prayer hall which further extends outwards as roof terraces over the lower rooms. The soaring, arched openings of each bay are infilled with tall central timber panels pierced into diagonal patterns with continuous side glazing enclosing the prayer hall. Except for the cone-shaped mihrab and a simple mimbar there is no other feature in the prayer hall. With the whole structure finished in white, the single space is designed to enhance the ambiance for the faithful in the oneness of the religion. (Chen Voon Fee)

3

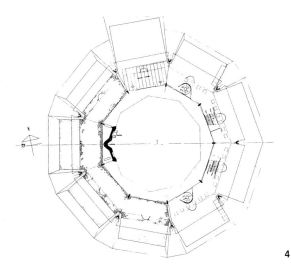

4

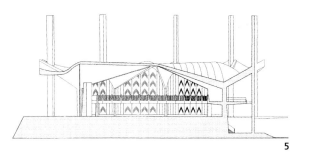

5

3
Interior view of Prayer hall, mihrab & mimbar, pierced panel & glazing

4
Upper floor plan

5
Section

Drawings provided by Chen Voon Fee

Geology Building, University of Malaya

Location: Kuala Lumpur
Architect: Malayan Architects Co-Partnership
Years of Design and Construction: 1964–1966, 1966–1968

1

1
Exterior view from south

2
Site plan

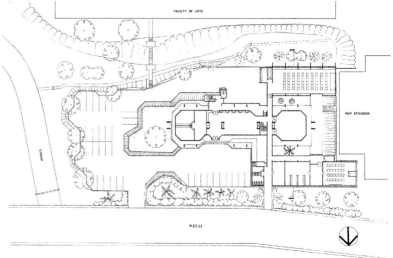

2

The Geology Department's building outside the main Science Faculty complex is designed as three parallel, linked blocks on a N–S axis; a walkway joins the single-story north block and the 2–story south block with two informal courts between them and the main 3–story block at the west end. The main forecourt serves as a transition space between road and entrance.

The massing of the central block shows a clear tripartite hierarchy of spaces. Three large, column–free laboratories are on the top floor forming the 'roof'; structurally slung below is the first floor of smaller research rooms and staff offices; the ground floor has administration, lecture hall and a museum. The reinforced concrete structure is boldly expressed in off-form work and finish. Three pairs of full height pylons support a deep beam from which is suspended the middle floor. Another six pairs from the E–W spine of the main block, which also houses service ducts.

Careful consideration is given to shading by setting back the three floors of the main block; vertical fins and metal louvers are also used on the lower blocks. Natural lighting was provided by roof lighting details. New planting adds shade and buffer to the surrounding campus. Professors remember this as 'the best designed building in the campus'. (Chen Voon Fee)

3

3
Exterior view of entrance forecourt

4
Exterior view of west

5
Elevation

6
Section

Drawings and photographs provided by Chen Voon Fee

4

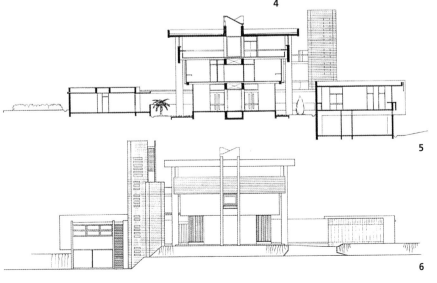

5

6

Theater of Performing Arts –Cultural Center of the Philippines

Location: Manila
Architect: Leandro V. Locsin and Associates
Year of Completion: 1969

1

1
Front view
2
Plan

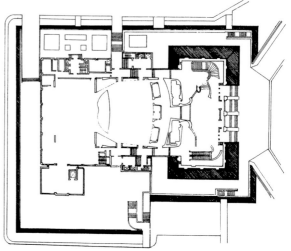

2

The Theater of Performing Arts was completed in 1969 as a venue aspiring to embody the cultural heritage of the Filipino. It is a performing arts center that would manifest the dreams of a nation working together with one culture. As such the Theater had, in its conception, the civic responsibility of being a symbol of the cultural development and expression of the Filipino race. With this task in mind, the architect was also given the responsibility of creating a structure that would not only meet the functional requirements of the theater but cross the realm of the practical and become monument within the urban landscape. It was with this goal that the architect Leandro V. Locsin set about the design of the theater.

Leandro V. Locsin was educated at the College of Architecture of the University of Santo Tomas, Manila. What is significant about his education is that he spent the first two years in college pursuing a degree in Music with intentions of becoming a concert pianist. He abandoned these aspirations and attend the College of Architecture eventually completing his Bachelor of Architecture and proceeded to practice. He is one, if not the most prominent Philippine architect of his generation. He influenced the architecture in the Philippines for decades and his works are often seen as exemplary by students and professionals alike. Other examples of his work include the Istana Nural Inan in Brunei and the Philippine International Convention Center in Manila.

The Theater of Performing Arts is but one of his major accomplishments that explore the expression of Philippine Architecture within the context of the modernist movement. In the design of the theater, Locsin was able to create a duality in the image of the structure, that of a heavy mass floating above the ground plain. These contradictory concepts and ideas led to the creation of a building that was both monumental in scale and mass while being light and graceful in form. The theater is basically a travertine clad rectangular box floating above a podium. This image is reinforced by a reflecting pool at the base of the podium that acts as a foreground to the overall composition.

The theater includes a main auditorium, a smaller theater,

3

3
Lobby

4
Entrance

rehearsal halls and administration offices. It is divided into two distinct masses, the first is the proscenium space housed in a non–descript rectangular box and the second is the foyer and lobby and main theater housed in a large cantilevered rectangular box. The foyer is set above a podium that rises from the ground and is accentuated by a graceful ramp that allows access to the lobby. The exterior mass is supported by graceful curved columns that seem to bend with its weight of the form reinforcing the feeling of lightness in the main structure.

Color, materials, texture and contrast play important roles in reinforcing the idea of the floating slab which has been attributed to the large mass and volume of the nipa hut (grass hut) which is supported by thin and spindly bamboo poles. This image of an unsupported large forms floating above the ground is characteristic of Locsin's work and will be seen in the other buildings that he designed. It was a move towards the creation of an architecture that had strong allusions to regionalism and towards a strong Philippine identity.

With regard to the interior of the theater, Locsin takes on a more literal direction in expressing Filipino culture with its structures. Although deeply rooted within the Modernist idiom, the extensive use of local materials clearly express a direction towards regionalism in design. The capiz chandeliers that hang gracefully above the lobby are a local adaptation of the western tradition. The translucent capiz shell add a distinctive glow making the lobby friendly and warm while maintaining its sense of grandeur. The exterior wall of a mix of shell, coral and concrete if brought into key elements in the interior including the sweeping balustrade for both main stair and escalator. On the walls, the bright colors of the tapestries and murals executed by different Filipino artists are successful in the expression of the uniqueness of the

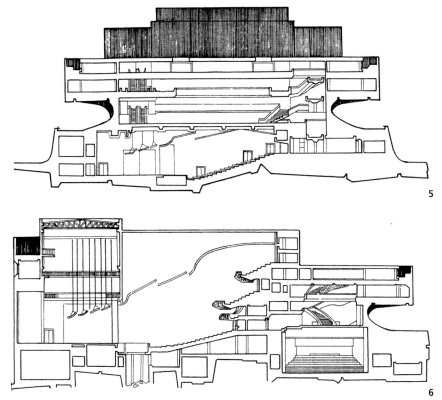

5

culture. Another expression of a Philippine tradition is in the main theater with its mural by Filipino artist H. R. Ocampo, cone in different hues of red and orange. As interesting contrast to this mural is the design of the interior walls which include laminated wood pillars, bronzed wire mesh all assembled in a pattern that is reminiscent of a bamboo wall with the bamboo nodes expressed in an orderly rhythm of alternating horizontal lines. The main theater includes box seating that are cantilevered over the interior space. Again the contrast with the concrete boxes and the softer richer fabric allow the different materials to work together to create a memorable space. (Francisco "Bobby" Mañosa)

5
Longitudinal section

6
Transverse section

Photographs provided by
Daniel Lichauco
Drawings courtesy:
Winard Klassen

Panabhandhu School, Classroom and Dormitory Building

Location: Bangkok
Architect: Ongard Architects
Year of Construction: 1969–1970

1

1
Site and roof plan

2
West facade

2

The background of this spherical multi-purpose building started from the need to increase the number of classroom which were insufficient for utilization. The new building in the limited front space is then required. The area is so small and nearly become a triangular shape with the road on the southern side. The initial design concept was a two-story rectangular building facing the street. However, the outcome model seemed too tight for the given area and when the new building is seen from that road, the old adjacent one was hardly been recognized. The new circular shape model was then created without the front or the back view, every side seemed to be front view. Seeing from the model, the circular shape seemed to be the most suitable for this building due to its simplicity.

There are various stacked elements of the new school. Vertically each layer occupies part of a broken circle. Most of the internal arrangement need a four-side form because of the class-room type. It was therefore designed according to the required function with a circular fin suspended from the rectangular column grid, acting as a sunshade device. That exposed concrete sunshade create the various views of shadow on the exterior wall. This building is served for tutoring, dormitory as well as an administration purpose allowing the top floor to be as a conference room. The building is exposed concrete finish with brick-wall and no paint. (Duangrit Bunnag/Sumet Jumsai)

4

3
Section

4
Various elements of the building seen from the ramp

5
Various architectural elements, stairs, column, sunshade device and auditorium mass

Photographs courtesy Piboon Patwichaichoat, Drawings provided by Duangrit Bunnag

3

5

81

British Council Building

Location: Bangkok
Architect: Sumet Jumsai & Associates
Year of Design and Construction: 1969–1970

1

1
The building in new color
(courtesy of Skyline Studio)

2
Second floor plan

3
Ground floor plan

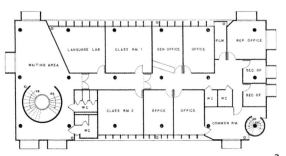

2

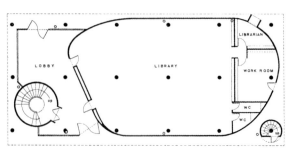

3

Progressive Architecture (USA) October 1970, "The British have eschewed any supposed stuffiness in one notable architectural instance: the British Council Building in Bangkok." The architect has expressed the various elements in the three – level structure so clearly that the building looks as if it were constructed from a toy assembling kit. The central mass of the building is finished in gray mosaic on the second and roof levels; it is wrapped around two massive red stair towers which appear to be carrying the first and third floors. Color inside are primary, with a grid of red and blue columns placed with nonchalant reference to other elements, such as door, windows, partitions.

In 1996, the British Council moved into new premises and the old building is now converted into a music shop. The original floor plans and color scheme have been modified considerably, although the facades, a little altered, remains. In all, despite the alterations, the spirit of fun and game of the old building survives.
(Duangrit Bunnag/Sumet Jumsai)

4
Elevations West

5
The building in the original color (Courtesy: SJA Co. Ltd.)

6
The new color of the stair– well tower at the corner (courtesy of Skyline Studio)

7
Elevations East

Drawings provided by Duangrit Bunnag

5

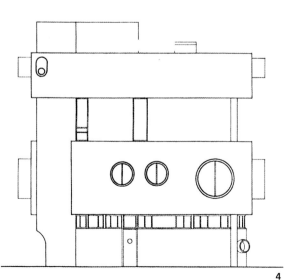

6

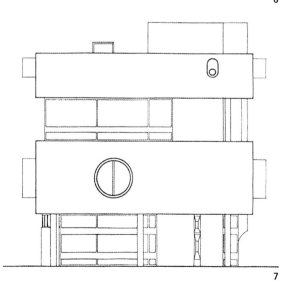

4

7

83

People's Park Complex

Location: Singapore
Architect: Design Partnership
Year of Completion: 1973

1

1
Exterior view

The People's Park complex was one of the 14 urban sites offered for sale in 1967 to private developers by the Urban Redevelopment Authority (URA) in its lst. Sale of Sites Programme. Designed by William S.W. Lim, Goh Siew–Chuan and Tay Kheng Soon of Design Partnership, this 31–story complex was the first of its kind in South–East Asia for its multi–use concept and the slab–block on a podium 'urban solution'.

It set the pattern for many subsequent commercial developments in the region. The slab block houses studio apartments which must be ahead of its time in that era. The shopping center which occupies the first three floors, is still one of the busiest in Singapore and its city room– a large covered atrium, captures much of the festive character of China town just across the road. Presently undergoing renovation, we can only hope that the original architecture will be respected and not changed beyond recognition as is the case of many old buildings in Singapore. (Richard K. F. Ho)

2
Interior view

Photographs provided by
Richard K. F. Ho

2

Golden Mile Complex

Location: Singapore
Architect: Design Partnership
Year of Completion: 1973

1

Photographs provided by
Richard K. F. Ho

This building (formerly known as Who Hup Complex) was one of the 14 sites offered for sale in 1967 in the 1st. Sale of Sites Programme of the Urban Redevelopment Authority. The architects, William S. W. Lim, Goh Siew–Chuan and Tay Kheng Soon of Design Partnership conceived this building not as an isolated monument but as one of many along Beach Road with interconnected atriums and a continuous pedestrian spine. Unfortunately this heroic vision was not taken up by subsequent developments. The sloped form fronting what was once the sea and now a park gives the internal atrium a dynamism never achieved before in early seventies Singapore. The building leaves much to be desired and combined with a mix of very low budget shops, have marred the building and the atrium irretrievably. It still stands defiantly as one of Singapore's significant modern buildings which responded to the fast expanding city with a vision ahead of its time.
(Richard K. F. Ho)

2

3

National Arts Center of the Philippines

Location: Mt. Makiling, Los Baños, Laguna
Architect: Leandro V. Locsin
Year of Completion: 1976

1

1
Aerial view
2
Section

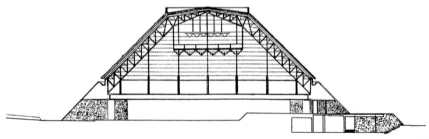

2

The primary objective of the National Arts Center of the Philippines was to foster the development of young and talented artists as to perpetuate the culture and heritage of the Philippines. The Center sits on top Mt. Makiling and the complex includes a theater, cottages, a club house/social hall and a dining hall. Dominant over the whole complex is the theater/reciting hall that was designed to have flexible seating and can accommodate up to 5000 persons with both interior and exterior seating. The Center sits on a Promontory that has a commanding view of the surrounding mountains particularly Mt. Makiling and the Laguna de Bay, which is the largest fresh water lake in the Philippines. The structure was designed by Leandro V. Locsin.

National Arts Center sits on top of a plateau on Mt. Makiling and has a commanding view of the Laguna de Bay. Its form is reminiscent of the Ifugao House, an indigenous Philippine house usually found in the mountain provinces. Its dominant structure is a large pyramidal roof that appears to hover above the ground as it sits on corner triangular stilts. There is an ingenious play between surfaces and textures in the roof structure. The stilts and a thick horizontal band of the roof accentuates a horizontal that gives the structure a heavy and massive feel. This is counteracted by an intermediate band of clay tile and capped with a solid fascia of the same material as the primary concrete band. This allows the structure to be read as a layering of different parts, diminishes the overall mass of the roof but accentuates the floating effect of the whole structure as it hovers above the ground plane.

There is a consistent use of geometry created by the pitched roof forming a pyramid with a flat top. This pitch is carried out in the plant boxed, sloped grass walls and other site amenities throughout the complex. The consistent use of the synthetic stone material on objects that hit the ground reinforce the image of the structure springing from the earth and hovering above the ground. The theater is open to three sides, This allows for the seating to expand and extend to the exterior of the structure. Strong sight lines have been maintained to allow the stage to be visible from all points.

The interior of the theater was designed against the backdrop of the view of the lake. In order to create an acoustically competent structure, the architects included a glass wall backdrop. This allowed the sound from the performances to be reflected to the audience as well as framing the commanding view of the lake and mountains. There was also an additional series of movable screens to cover the glass during performances as not to let the view distract the audience, so as to concentrate on the performance giving the interior space an inherent flexibility that is characteristic of traditional Filipino spaces. The main theater is finished with a local hardwood called Philippine Mahogany adding warmth and an intimate setting to the structure.

With regard to the plan, the theater consists of a semi-circular stage with the seating radiating from it. There is a proscenium, a larger stage backdrop and other support spaces in the rear at a half basement level. The total volume of the interior is executed in wood and resembles the exterior mass in shape. This allows for an effective space for the stage area.

Included in the complex are 104 cottages that have been grouped into five different clusters. These cottages were designed in the more traditional architecture of the Philippines and blend well with the natural setting. They house the dormitories and housing for staff, students and administration, private practice rooms and other recreational type facilities. Aside from these cottages, the complex also includes a dining hall/social hall that doubles up as cafeteria and a clubhouse. These structures are also equipped with small performance spaces designed for informal use.

The architecture of the support structures are reminiscent of the more traditional dwellings of the Philippines. The cottages are raised above the ground through the use of stilts and columns. Throughout the buildings, there is the consistent use of the anahaw as the decorative element that unifies the different structures.
(Francisco "Bobby" Mañosa)

Science Museum

Location: Bangkok
Architect: Sumet Jumsai & Associates
Year of Construction: 1976–1977

1

1
View of the northwest side.
The outside wall cantile-
vered out with recessed
outside wall in vertical
direction

2
Axonometric view

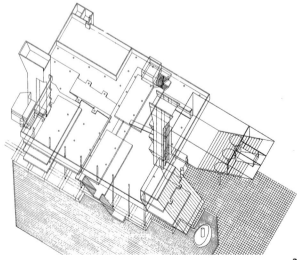

2

Besides normal museum facilities, the building also functions as a science teaching center for school children from all over the country who visit it on a rotating basis. The museum is conceived as a technological 'gadget' standing next to a 'Jcience Park' which is used for open air exhibits. The idea of the park stems from the need for corner parks and open spaces in Bangkok.

Entrance to the museum is from the science park under a giant 15–meter cantilevered concrete canopy. The public enters into a four–story main exhibit hall with receding mezzanines so that a general view of all display areas can be enjoyed at once. Space trusses above provide supports from which large objects can be suspended. A central staircase connects the hall to the auditorium and classrooms located above the main entrance, followed by a library, an audiovisual room, and a teachers' room. The latter are grouped into a single volume that projects from the central exhibition space over an area at a corner of the reflecting pool (where refreshments are served). A foot–bridge spans from the staircase across the main exhibit hall to the upper mezzanine, leading to a special exhibit room at the back.

Discarding the conventional museum (which, like the theater, consists of a front with things to be seen and an unseen part at the back where things are stored) the architects have decided to design a 'see–throughí building. Thus the mezzanine galleries are pierced through with viewing balconies which project over the back part of the building: storage, workshops, science laboratories, design and silk–screen studios, and offices. To allow visitors to see fully the museum at work, the walls of the laboratories, studios and offices facing the viewing balconies are glazed from top to bottom. (Duangrit Bunnag/Sumet Jumsai)

3

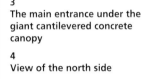

3
The main entrance under the giant cantilevered concrete canopy

4
View of the north side

5
South elevation

6
West elevastion

7
North elevation

8
Longitudinal section

Photographs courtesy: SJA Co. Ltd., Drawings provided by Duangrit Bunnag

4

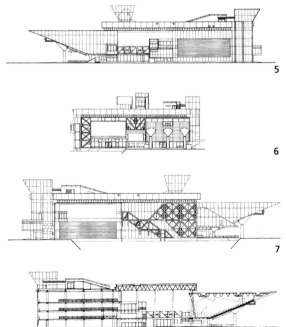

5

6

7

8

1980–1999

Bank of America Building

Location: Bangkok
Architect: Robert G. Boughey & Associates
Year of Construction: 1983

1

1
View from the main road

2
Ground floor plan

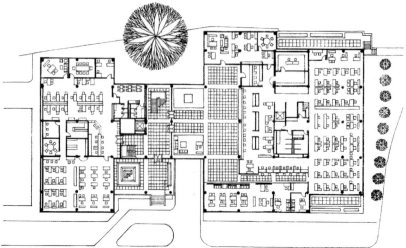

2

The building site was formerly a park and it was therefore important to keep as much of the existing greenery as possible. At the rear of the site was an existing waterway access and one large rain tree that needed to be saved because of its size and significance to the site. The building outline at the rear was dictated by the location of the tree. In addition the frontage trees along the main road were retained.

The owner also wanted a building that would properly represent them in Thailand. The site was on a street that was primarily a low rise residential area with much greenery. The building was kept low because of these conditions and the desire of the Bank of America to make a subtle but unique statement on their presence in Thailand. The major design objective was to create a building that was specifically tailored to the planning requirements of the Bank of America. Since this was essentially a single tenant building it was possible to accommodate these requirements. Since both the building concept and the interior were conceived at the same time it was possible to fully integrate the building volumes with the planning requirements.

The building form is scaled by plan indentations. This effectively reduced the plan mass of the building. The building steps back with large overhangs, which develops a profile similar to other traditional building forms. Horizontal bands of travertine are trimmed with horizontal louvers, which shield the glass areas of the building. The exterior walls are of laminated glass which act as a sound buffer on the busy street. It was the intention that the most appropriate materials and the latest technology be utilized in the building while not interfering with the residential scale of the project. The building interior was designed to be as open as possible so that the employees and other occupants could take advantage of the park like atmosphere of the site. The interior is either carpeted or surfaced with the same travertine as used on the exterior. The lighting and building automation systems are fully computerized.
(Duangrit Bunnag/Sumet Jumsai)

3

3
View from the rear of site

4
Customer Lounge overlooking rear garden

5
Sections

6
Elevations

7
Sections

Drawings provided by
Duangrit Bunnag

4

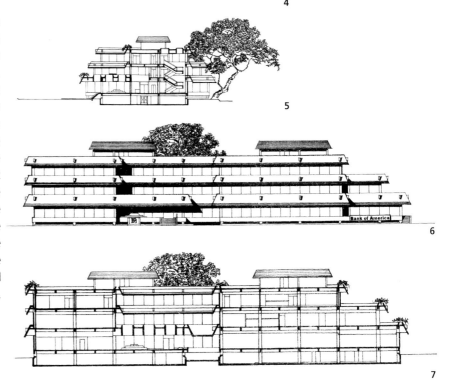

5

6

7

Walian House

Location: Kuala Lumpur
Architect: Jimmy Lim Cheok Siang
Years of Design and Construction: 1982; 1983–1984

1

1
Looking up from living
space to master
bedroom

2
Aerial view from northeast

2

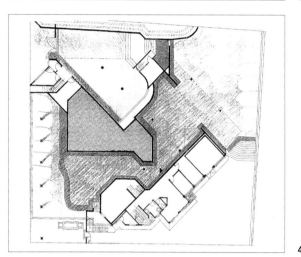

3
Upper ground floor plan
4
Lower ground floor plan
5
First floor plan
6
Section

A private residence, Walian House's L–shaped plan is designed in accordance with Feng Shui (Chinese: wind, water) principles of siting, hence its N.W.–S.E. axes. Located in a woody site in the exclusive, hilly, residential area northwest of the city, it consists of a three–story house with a guest unit separated by a large, roofed atrium. The pedestrian approach to this is deliberate and processional and hidden from view–privacy and security are paramount. (J. Lim) To induce maximum natural air flow the layered roof is raised 50 feet high over the atrium. Running water, an essential element in promoting good Feng–Shui cascades from the swimming pool over an angled wall to a lower pool. The atrium stays airy, cool and looks out into a serene view. The materials used are of the traditional vernacular buildings namely salvaged timber from old buildings, fair–faced clay bricks and floor tiles. The house has successfully incorporated traditional planning principles and use of building materials combined with the architect's admiration of Wrightian geometrics resulting in a clearly identifiable modern Malaysian vernacular.
(Chen Voon Fee)

3

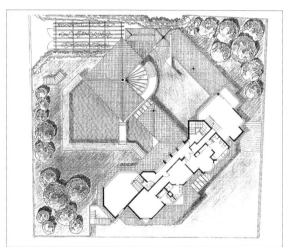

4

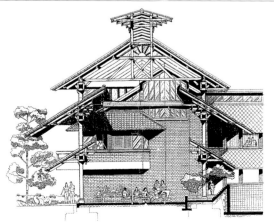

5

6

7

7
Silhouette of tiered roof

8
View from living space
towards kitchen

8

9
External views from
northwest of tiered roof

10
Northeast elevation from car
porch

11
Internal roof detail

9

10

11

Soekarno–Hatta
International Airport

Location: Cengkareng, Jakarta
Architect: Soejano & Rachman
Year of Completion: 1985

1

1
Exterior view of departure

2
Situation plan

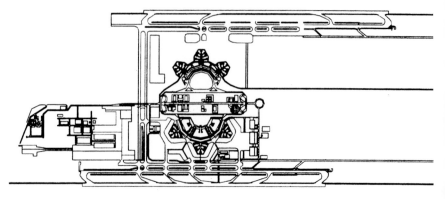

2

Cengkareng area was chosen after considering the distance from Jakarta (about 20 km to the west), the prevailing winds (90% from the west), and also after the requirements of IFR (Instrument Flight Rules) were fully met, and thus no airspace conflict world arise. The airport covers an area of 1800 ha (4500 acre) with two parallel runways of 36 m wide and 3050 m long each, separated 2400 m from each other, so that both runways can be used simultaneously, with passenger facilities situated in between. All those facilities were designed to handle about 9 million passengers yearly (completed in 1985), 2.5 million are foreigners. The whole floor space of the three terminals is about 125,000m². By the following stage, with the terminals of the second runway completed in 1992, the whole floor space came to cove 250,000 m².

Each runway has three terminals, attached to a fan-shaped departure hall, each with 7 boarding lounges arranged in an equilateral triangular shape to shorten the walkways leading to the boarding aero-bridges. Each terminal has a parking lot for 800 cars so that each runway has a lot for 2400 cars; for both runways the parking lots could contain 4800 cars.

Spaces between lounges are thoroughly landscaped, with carefully selected tropical evergreen trees and flowering shrubs, here and there adorned with rocks and artificial hills providing the atmosphere of a roughly tropicalized Japanese garden. It is quite a sight indeed, so much so that it was awarded the Aga Khan Award for Architecture 1995 for innovative landscape design.

Although emphasis was laid right from the very begining on keeping the building on a human scale, it was nevertheless to serve as a gateway to the country and express Indonesian art and culture as well as a tropical atmosphere. Thus, the 4–centrally–columned boarding lounges, each with a capacity to hold 400 persons, were designed with a special sense of place, of Indonesia. In effect, the roofs were constructed in traditional *joglo* style with its unique stepped profile , catching the eye instantly from the air and from afar. From these boarding lounges, passengers can directly embark the aircraft comfortably by way of aero–bridges. In the original design, these embarking upper floor walkways were provided with horizontal adjustable blinds, and thus directly exposed to the prevailing weather. There were times during the rainy season when the rain poured through the leaky blinds, driven by strong winds from the vast open airfield. Now, it is all glass–walled to ward off the wind, rain , aircraft noise and also the tropical nocturnal pests. (Yuswadi Saliya)

3
Terminal section

4
Departure gate section

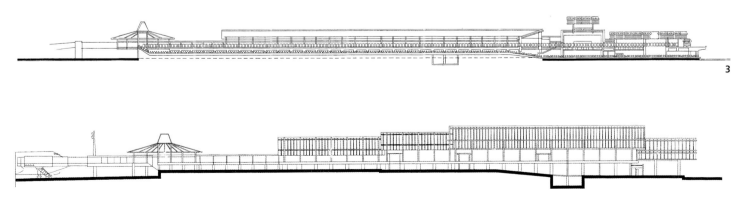

3

4

5

6

6
Exterior view of Arrival

7
Grand staircase and sculpture

8
Interior

Drawings and photographs
provided by Yuswadi Saliya

7

8

The Robot Building

Location: Bangkok
Architect: Sumet Jumsai & Associates
Year of Construction: 1986

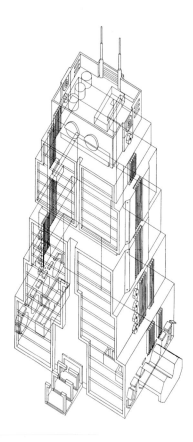

1

2

1
Full axonometric view
Inscription by Sumet Jumsai

2
Inside the banking hall
(Courtesy of Profile)

3
Overview from north–east
side (Courtesy: SJA Co. Ltd.)

3

The directors of the Bank of Asia belonged to the new generation of bankers and they were possibly the youngest amongst Thai bank executives. What they wanted was a design which would reflect a new generation, their own, and usher in a new era involving their new computerized banking service. What they have is in accordance with their wishes. But they have also unwittingly become part of a turning point in architecture. What has emerged is a building in the shape of a robot which is now given a host of attributes; user-friendly, 21st century, Post High-Tech, etc.

Although the design contains within it an element of humor, it is also a serious theoretical commitment, as well as being practical in its compliance to stringent municipal codes and structural and spatial requirements. In effect the staggered robot shape represents an optimum solution to the set-back regulations which entail an 18 degree incline from all four sides.

The architecture might be classified as Post High-Tech in the sense that it is the Post Modern treatment of the 'machine' as embodied by the robot and does not exhibit its mechanical parts. Instead it is a finished product wrapped in a stylized body. The eyes, arms, knuckles, chest and legs of the robot are abstract (but not inhuman), while the nuts and bolts and caterpillar wheels, instead of being a faithful reproduction of the 'machine', are mere abstractions of the mechanical parts.

Special lighting effects were originally designed for the eyes to 'wink' at night, with aircraft landing lights operated by automatic dimmers and high-power strobe lights. The glowing and dimming, as well as the free play of the high power strobe lights, were meant to give a repeating rhythm to the tune of an electronic composition called "The Robot Symphony".
(Duangrit Bunnag/Sumet Jumsai)

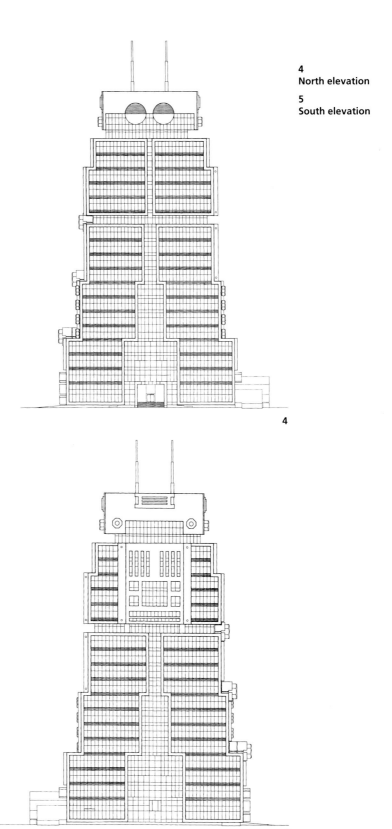

4
North elevation

5
South elevation

4

5

6
Sculptures at the entrance
inside the banking hall
(Courtesy: Profile)

6

7
Detail of caterpillar wheel
on west side (Courtesy:
Profile)

8
Back view (south–west)
(Courtesy: Profile)

9
Front (north) elevation at
night (Courtesy: Profile)

7

8

9

Menara Maybank Tower

Location: Kuala Lumpur
Architect: Hijjas Kasturi Associates Sdn
Years of Design and Construction: 1979; 1982–1987

1

1
Entrance tiered roof

2
Location plan

3
Exterior view

2

3

The winning entry of an international Architecture Competition, the Maybank Headquarterís design was based on two intersecting squares with the resulting center square divided by a cross providing passages to offices and banks of lifts with other core services. The two re-entrant angles, roofed over to house part of the high banking hall and the entrance foyer with stairs and escalators from the street form a strong diagonal line along the N.–S. axis.

The 54-story tower flares outwards for the lower 12 floors and its upper 9 floors slope up to a distinctive, sharp knife-edge roofline. From ground to top the design imparts an impressive sense of strength and power, important characteristics for the nation's premier bank.

The tiered roofs of the entrance derive from the country's traditional vernacular architecture reflecting hierarchical status. The mechanical floor's transfer girders with zig-zag patterns recalling ethnic weaves impart a sense of scale and contrast to the verticality of the millions.

Located on top a small hill in the city's bustling business center much of the spacious 8-acre site had been carefully landscaped, integrated with the traffic pattern and accessible to the public. Three basement floors of carparks accommodate over 1,700 cars. The Maybank Tower is a landmark building heralding the new generation of high-rises. (Chen Voon Fee)

4
Atrium and Banking Hall
5
Typical floor plan (13–34th floor)
6
Upper ground floor plan
7
Section

4

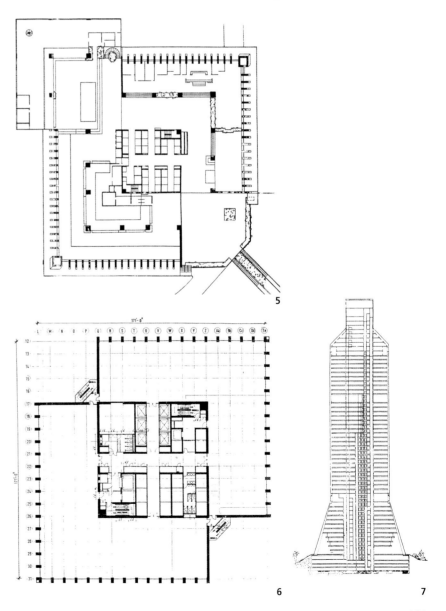

5

6

7

Central Market & Central Square

Location: Kuala Lumpur
Architect: William Lim Associates & Chen Voon Fee
Years of Design and Construction: 1985–1986; 1987–1988

1

1
Central Square view
2
Site plan

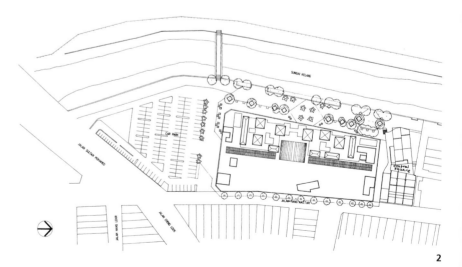

2

Two phases of a project in adapting old buildings for re-use in the heart of Kuala Lumpur's Chinatown reversed the trend of ìdemolish and rebuild during the city's building boom of the 1980s.

Kuala Lumpur's 50-year old wet market was earmarked for demolition when a private developer proposed a hitherto untried conserve-adapting design into a Covent Garden-type arts & crafts, food center. The city's largest ìsingle room was high enough to accommodate a mezzanine floor along half its length with six clusters of two-level shops linked across its central sky-lit mall by three bridges. Its containing box of strong Art Deco design was kept intact, cleaned and reprinted. The riverbank was pedestrianised and landscaped for outdoor dining and public performances on a small stage. It proved its commercial success from day 1.

The developer went on to adapt four turn-of-the-century shop-houses adjoining the Central Market on the North, inserting new fire-proof floors, re-roofing and upgrading all services. The back lane, roofed over into an atrium link the restored front shops with a rebuilt riverside lot housing the city's first 2 cineplexes. The shop-houses of early 20th Century western classical plaster moldings were repaired and painted afresh; while strong colors were used to dramatize the post modern forms of the new section. (Chen Voon Fee)

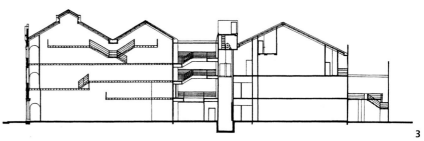

3

3
Scetion A–A

4
Central Square & Central Market along Jalan Hang Kasturi

5
Central Market, view of central mall shops

4

5

6

6
Adjoining lane between
Central Market and Central
Square

7
Central Square view

8
Plan

9
Section B–B

Drawings and photographs
provided by Chen Voon Fee

7

8

9

Reuter House

Location: Singapore
Architect: William Lim Associates
Year of Completion: 1990

1

1
Exterior

The generic form of this house can be traced to the colonial black and white bungalows of Singapore where the dominant and usually symmetrical front block has a smaller one–story rectangular service block as an appendage.

The square front block and the attached rear 'service' block are both present in this house but the architect has gone beyond replication by the addition of yet another rectangular appendage to the side which houses the private spaces (bedrooms) and skewing it at an angle to the front block, thereby creating a courtyard where a swimming pool is located. Yet another feature which is not typical of black and white bungalows is the forecourt one has to cross before entering a gateway set in the forecourt wall. This entrance sequence is typical of many traditional Chinese and south–east Asian houses. There are other architectural moves operating, for example the square living room being tilted at an angle within the square front block and the change in the use of materials on the same surface; all act together to remind one of the dynamic relationships set up with other blocks and objects in the composition. The architect has achieved a significant piece of architecture through the contemporary interpretation of a vernacular house form. It reminds of the past and yet is very much part of the present. (Richard K. F. Ho)

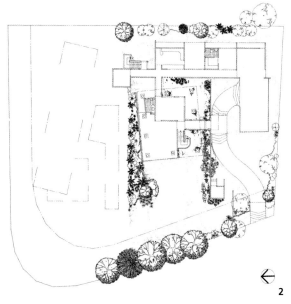

2
First story plan

3
Second story plan

Drawings and photographs provided by Richard K. F. Ho

2

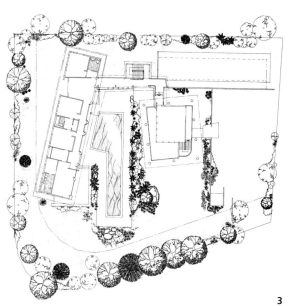

3

Menara Mesiniaga

Location: Subang Jaya, Selangor
Architect: T. R. Hamzah & Yeang Sdn
Years of Design and Construction: 1989–1991; 1990–1992

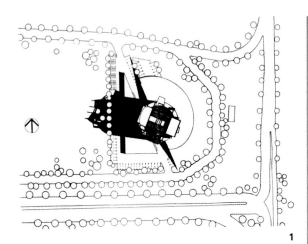

1

1
Location plan

2
View of skycourt

3
View showing the
planted ramp

2

3

The 14-storey circular tower of Mesiniaga Sdn Bhd (Business Machine Pte. Ltd.) incorporates the bioclimatic principles of designing tall buildings in the tropics propagated by the firm in the last decade. Passive low-energy features include planning lifts and toilet service core in the east segment, naturally ventilated and lit; so are the staircases. East and west windows are externally louvered, north and south sides are curtain-walled, clear glazed for maximum view and light. 'Vertical landscaping' occurs across the facades sweeping up from the turfed banks around half the tower's base and rising by staggered terraces 'sky courts' of the various floors. Recreational facilities–gym, swimming pool and cafè are on the top roof deck.

The R. C. frame and brick in–fill are sheathed in composite aluminum cladding; exposed Mesiniaga has the climate–responsive, high-tech, machine–look office tower. It won the Aga Khan Award for 1996. (Chen Voon Fee)

6
General view

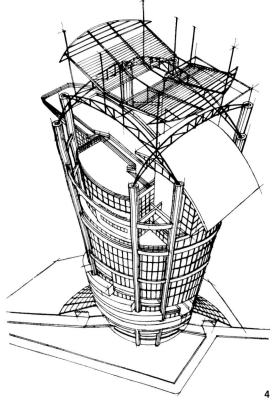

4

4
Study sketch
5
Terrace with pool
6
General view
7
Section

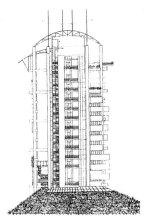

7

117

8
Entrance detail

9
Ground floor plan

10
Sunpath diagram

11
Detail of void

12
First floor plan

13
Mezzanine

14
12th upper floor

15
12th lower floor

Drawings and photographs
provided by Chen Voon Fee,
courtesy of the Architect

11

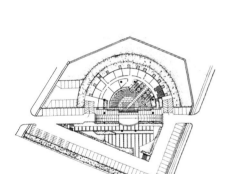

9

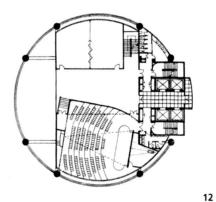

12

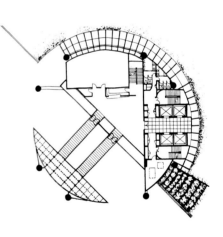

13

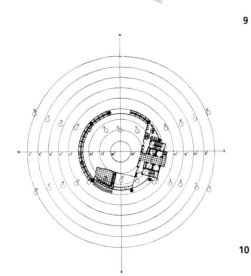

10

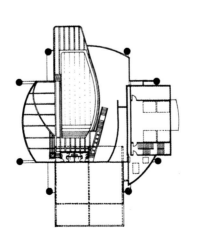

14

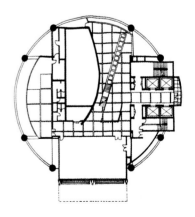

15

Eu House

Location: Singapore
Architect: Bedmar & Shi Designers Pte Ltd
Year of Completion: 1993

1

1
Exterior view from the yard

2
Site plan

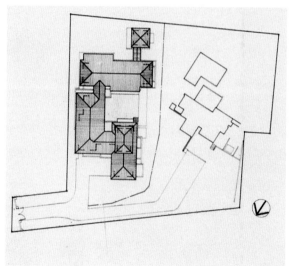

2

This house, conceived as four pavilions composed around a water courtyard, is located within the garden of the residence of the client's parents.

This is an architecture of grace and repose. Carefully choreographed and layered vistas reveal themselves as one crosses the entrance threshold and moves around the pavilions, not unlike the layering of Chinese traditional mansions. The play of light and shadow on surfaces finished in granite or sandstone with the well-proportioned and fine timber detailing, all contribute to the tactile quality and harmony of the ensemble.

Many influences have been cited about this house, Balinese, Thai, Chinese, but what is so successful about it is that it is all these and more, and architect Ernesto Bedmar has achieved it effortlessly and unselfconsciously. (Richard K. F. Ho)

3

3
Exterior view

4
Floor plan

5–6
Elevations

Drawings and photographs provided by Richard K. F. Ho

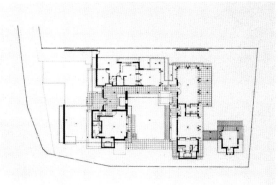

4

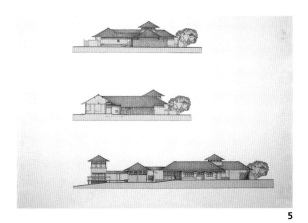

5

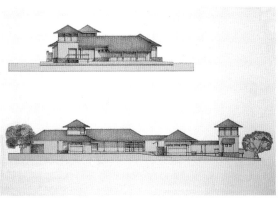

6

Bhd Chedi Bandung

Location: Bandung
Architect: Kerry Hill Architects
Year of Completion: 1993

1

1
**East elevation behind the
swimming pool**

2
Site plan

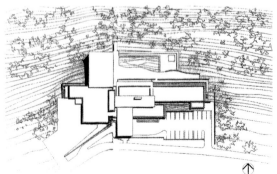

2

The building is situated in the northern and secluded part of Bandung, the villa area of the Dutch ruling elite during the colonial period. The site is dramatic indeed: a small piece of land (8400 m²) on the brink of a richly forested and fairly steep valley (the other side of the valley, forested as densely, was also acquired so as not to be disturbed). The rooms directly face the other side of the valley, endowing them with a scenery of a vast and colorful foliage, which changes with the sun's orbit. It has 44 standard guest–rooms and 7 large suites. The public areas consist of a small reception lobby and a lobby lounge, business center, two meeting rooms, a restaurant, a 25m swimming pool with an elongated side annexed to a pool–side lounge. The other side of the pool just vanishes in mid–air, making the valley even more dramatic.

De Stijl and Art Deco were among the most popular styles in the 1930s. It is indeed fortunate that this heritage has been preserved in Bandung, and wise policy for such styles to be incorporated, in the case of kerry h Hill, into Chedy elements. Chedy could instantly serve as a classic example of how an architect, modernist at heart, has interpreted the legacy of pioneering work and adapted it to contemporary needs and demands.

The color scheme chosen for the interior was appropriately a subdued wooden color, although here and there one may have eye–catching elements, be it a free-standing piece of furniture, the clouds above the seating arrangement of the restaurant, or even just a pot of brightly coloured flowers. The side lamps of the lobby are decidedly art deco style, a sleek iron rod articulated to match the canopy.

The geometry of the fenestration is that of the early modernist style, square and bare, unhesitatingly straightforward, even in the dominating natural environment. Although natural stone finishing is profusely used in a thoughtful manner and measured composition, the shades of contrast are not to be concealed. The inter-penetration of planes and masses, basic to the new modernist lexicon derived from de Stijl, is made possible by stepped flat concrete roofs, following the contour of the sloping valley. Flat concrete roofs with a wide overhang and the appropriately molded eaves, emphasize the horizontalism. (Yuswadi Saliya)

3

3
Interior of lobby lounge

4
Flat concrete roofs following the contour

5
Site and ground floor plan

6
Bird's–eye view from northwest

4

5

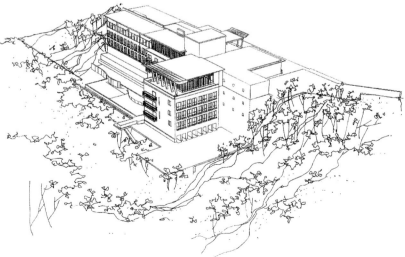

6

The Datai

Location: Langkawi Island
Architect: Akitiek Jururancang (M) Sdn Bhd & Kerry Hill Architects
Year of Completion: 1993

1
Exterior view

2
Site plan

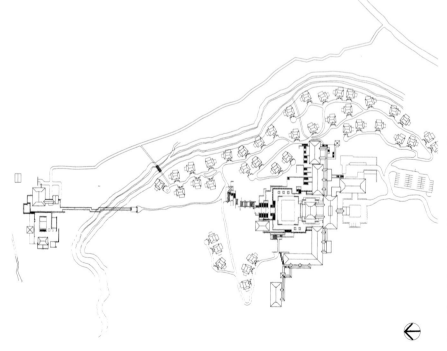

The Datai resort hotel complex is sited on a hill slope amidst undisturbed tall trees of an old tropical rain forest, on the isolated northwestern point of Langkawi Island off the coast of Kedah State in Malaysia. The planning has carefully integrated with the natural terrain and vegetation, choreographing the stunning views of distant western hills and the sea to north and east, even 'borrowing' the Thai island of Tarautao.

At the top of a series of descending platform, the forecourt leads directly to the entrance lobby, traversing past a lotus pool to the lounge which overlooks the main swimming pool on the deck below. Open-sided walkways lead via short bridges to the four floors of rooms and suites arranged L-shaped on both sides of the entrance lobby. An even closer touch of nature is experienced in forty pavilion suites informally scattered along a stream on the east.

The main restaurant opens onto the pool deck while another open-sided restaurant is half-perched on huge jungle trees providing dining among the tree tops. From the pool deck a flight of grand stairs descends to the Beach Club pavilions set on the white sands of the beach.

The Datai fulfills the ultimate 5-star escape holiday's experience of the jungle without its risk and discomfort. (Chen Voon Fee)

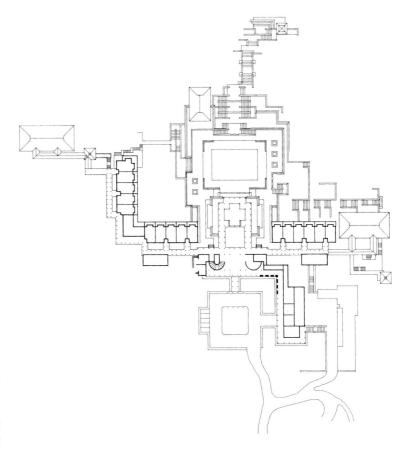

3

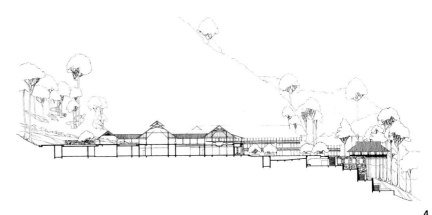

4

3
Entrance level plan

4
Section through entrance and public areas

5
Exterior view

5

6
Water courtyard

7
gallery

8
Restaurant

6

7

8

9

11

10

12

9
Exterior view of Restaurant

10
Courtyard

11
Exterior view of Restaurant

12
Guest room

127

Floirendo Family Villas

Location: Samai Island, Davao
Architect: Francisco Mañosa and Partners
Year of Completion: 1994

1
View of the satellite villas
from the sea

2

Built in 1994, the Floreindo Family Villas is but part of a growing repertoire of Filipino Houses by Architect Francisco "Bobby" Mañosa. The villas are situated a small island that overlooks the Pearl Farm Resort, also designed by the same architect in Samai Island. The villas are a new expression of neo–vernacular architecture that has been the hallmark of the practice of Francisco Mañosa and Partners in exploring articulation of new forms based on traditional indigenous architecture and materials.

The Floreindo Villas were designed as a family retreat. The overall design called for six satellite villas which did not include any kitchen or dining facilities and a main Villa perched on top of a rock at the highest point of a small island. Renamed the Eagle's Nest, the main villa includes staff area, bedrooms, living room, kitchen and dining facilities, which were purposely excluded from the satellite villas. This was seen as a response to the cultural characteristics of the Filipino family in which it is seen advantageous and desirable for the grandparents to be in constant contact with their children and grandchildren. These inherent cultural traits become part of the design logic which transforms the architecture into a culturally sensitive structure that embodies the characteristics and ideals of the Filipino.

With regard to architectural form, the main villa is a series of three linked octagons with a fourth octagon in the second floor as the bedroom space. This design is repeated at a smaller scale in the satellite villas. The octagonal shapes result in an interesting interplay of roof forms that are reminiscent of the native gourd hut, the salakot. The main villa is perched on the rock with extended balconies and decks that cantilever over the Davao Gulf. It includes an entrance foyer, living room, dining room, kitchen and guest rooms on the main floor. The second floor includes the masters bedroom suite. The services and servants quarters are located at a basement level.

The villas express a unique approach to the development of Filipino architecture. The forms, novel and innovative are rooted in the traditional forms found in the island of Davao. The pitched roofs and wide overhangs are characteristic of the region and efficient in protection from the sun and the rain. Built with shingles made with

2
View of the main villa from the sea
3
On the balcony overlooking the sea
4
Interior

3

4

5
View of the satellite villas
from the beach

6
Main villa from the beach

5

6

bamboo halves, the villas explore the use of a whole range of indigenous materials processed both in the traditional and technologically modern manner. The split bamboo roof shingles were cut and treated according to practice handed down from generations. The bamboo was harvested at the proper time of the year when insects have left the bamboo and soaked in sea water for preservation. Anahaw leaves and woven bamboo were used for the eaves, adding a rich texture to the interior of the villas. Other materlais like wall panels made out of Plyboo, an innovative process of venneering bamboo into boards similar to plywood. These panels were used in the bedrooms and guest rooms. Yakal hardwood posts and ipil ipil planks continue the tradition of the use of sustainable materials that express an environmentally friendly and responsive architecture.

On the exterior, the strong geometric shapes and horizontal lines of the roof shingles contrast with the organic and natural forms of the rock and surrounding landscape. This contrast however is down-played with the use of color, texture and materials that begin the blend with the surroundings. The result is a harmonious relationship between natural and man-made forms, each distinct in its own right but not competing for visual dominance. The composition of forms and materials result in an understated elegance in continuous and seamless blends with nature and opposed to working against it.

The Floreindo Family Villas are a result of a design philosophy that explores the development of a regional identity in architecture, in this case of neo-vernacular architecture whose ideas germinate from traditional Filipino form. In their reference to local tradition, its use of indigenous and sustainable materials, they create an architecture that is modern and yet with strong ties to the past, fusing the best of both worlds.
(Francisco "Bobby" Mañosa)

7

7
Interior

8
View of the main villa perched on top of a rock

9
Cantilevered balcony of the main villa

Illustrations courtesy of the Architect

8

9

Balina Serai

Location: Candi Desa, Bali
Architect: Kerry Hill Architects
Year of Completion: 1994

1

1
Exterior view
2
Bird's eye view

2

This supposedly three–star hotel was designed by the well–known Australian Architect Kerry Hill. The site is small, just a 2 ha piece of land, situated in the east coast of Bali, at some distance from Candi Desa, a rather secluded outpost with beautiful secluded beaches. The policy of making small outpost resorts in the northern part of Denpasar was actually the result of the SCETO REPORT. The objective is clear: not to disturb the rural panorama in northern part of Denpasar with huge and dominating buildings.

The site plan is simple and straightforward. Most striking is the masses of simple hipped roof, arranged perpendicular to each other in a Cartesian sort of way –a truly modernist way of composition, with the exactly 20 x 20m size swimming pool as its foci, about 40m off the beach in the center of the compound, separated by a lawn of grass and pillars of coconut trees. The restaurant, the only building with a huge pyramidal roof, is commanding the high ground. It has all the vista of the compound, the pool and the beach.

The thatched roofs (elephant grass/*Typha elephantina*) are truly Balinese in form and technique, and it seems that it is the only Balinese character left.

The rest are geometric games, choice of soft and benign materials and textures, plasticity of light and shadow, of solid and void. The spatial plasticity and the planar rhythm of walls and oblongs will be much more enhanced during the night,due to the lighting arrangements, the night–time architecture will speak for itself in showing a blurred demarcation between interior and exterior, which is also a main feature in Balinese traditional architecture.

All of the joinery details, between horizontal and vertical members, between two different materials, between two different heights, look to be so austere and yet so controlled. The use of panels or components of fine craftsmanship, be it as a divider or lamp fixtures, altogether produce a superb architectural atmosphere still maintaining the Balinese spirit yet far removed from the ordinary romantic *pastiche*. Mies van der Rohe is right all along: that God lies in the details. (Yuswadi Saliya)

3
Detail
4
Plan of a typical room
5
Section across the typical block
6
Axonometric view of site

Drawings and photographs provided by Yuswadi Saliya

3

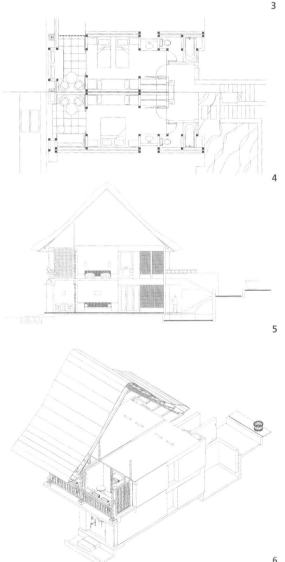

4

5

6

133

Tan House

Location: Bandung
Architect: Tan Tjiang Ay
Year of Completion: 1993

1

1
Contrast between manmade
building and landscape

2
Site and ground floor
plan

3
Axonometric view

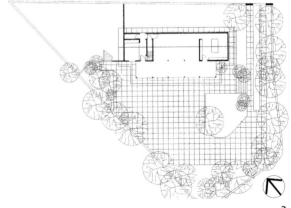

2

3

4

The house is located next to Taman National Djuanda (Djuanda National Park) with a kite-shaped lot of about 2000m², in remote northern Bandung highlands, which the architect-owner acquired a decade ago in 1988. The area has relatively high humidity, monsoon rains, high winds in certain months and cool temperature of 18–25°C throughout the year.

The initial intention was to provide a penny-wise and efficient dwelling space for the architect and his wife, a son and one staff. The architect has never shared the contemporary Indonesian laymen's ideas of an ideal house. More important to him was the intelligent utilization of the site, the climate, the appropriate building materials, a refined structure, etc. In his own words: "A good building first while the house will come later."

True to his functional principles, he contends that the building and site should complement each other to form the house, i.e. in harmony of contrasts. Beauty will come out of this harmony, not from ornamentation. The architectural experiences of the house are to start right at the main gate of the compound, so that a front porch into the house proper was simply not required.

The building mass is pushed toward the northeastern border of the site to enable the creation of a central open space to accommodate various outdoor activities. The open space also allows a longer and gentler-sloped driveway to the garage and provides at the same time a processional entry into the site leading to the house itself. The humidity of the region dictates a slender building, consisting of just 2 bays, so as the cool wind which blows up and down the bordering valley could waft the humid air out of the building easily. In addition, to keep the building high and dry, a local tradition of living on stilts is duly employed. Conceptually, however, the architect believes that one should build in conformity with one's own time and place, one should be truthful to history, that is to say that one should not blindly copy from the past nor rashly follow technology too far ahead.

The house consists of two floors, with the main living area on the upper level, arranged in a linear manner along

a 3 by 15 m glazed serambi or verandah. The serambi overlooks the central open space mentioned previously towards a magnificent panoramic forest beyond. Beneath the serambi is an equally sized sitting area for various purposes, one could imagine garden parties being held there, overflowing into the stone-paved open space at the center of the site. There is no totally enclosed rooms in this house, except of course for the bedrooms. Even the kitchen and the living room are directly connected to the serambi by open doorways. Again, the simple lifestyle of the architect and his family is clearly expressed in the simplicity of the plan.

The architect did not refrain from using unconventional concrete block to build the house, even though this material is generally used for industrial buildings throughout Indonesia. Unrendered it blends well into the surrounding landscape. On the other hand it also provides the necessary contrast between 'man made building versus nature' which were pursued by the architect in the first place. For the roof structure, instead of intricately constructed roof trusses, a commonly known rafters on roof and ridge beam are used. The geometries of the facades are all clearly defined and easily delineated. The fenestration, the square and slender post and lintel structure, the plasticity of solid and void, the playful light and shadow, are all of the dionysian character, well proportioned and thus easy to remember. It is worth noting that the local workers were given free reign to do the plastered ceiling soffits and monolithic cement finish for the floors, since all the details are cleanly straightforward and functionally simple without being naive and plain.

As simple as it is, the house has sufficient solid and void contrast. The private and semi-private parts are housed in a solid concrete block structure, while the public serambi is transparently glazed. The square shaped windows on the solid plane provide the necessary vistas: acting as paintings on the walls throughout the house. Seated at dusk in the subdued light in the living room, one can see through the doorway to the brighter lit serambi, unto the brightly sunlit central open space, and eventually unto the pine-trees veiled sunset way beyond. (Yuswadi Saliya)

5

6

7

4
Sitting area

5
Entrance

6
The serambi

7
Interior

Drawings and photographs provided by Yuswadi Saliya

Abelia Apartments

Location: Singapore
Architect: TangGuanBee Architects
Year of Completion: 1994

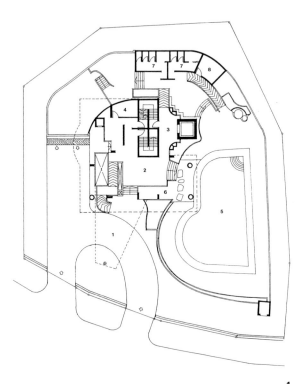

1

1
First story plan
(1. Porch; 2. Entrance lobby;
3. Lift lobby; 4. Maintenance
office; 5. Swimming pool;
6. pond; 7. Changing room;
8. Pumproom)

2
Exterior view

2

This Project consists of a tower block made up of 5 maisonettes set amidst a lush, landscaped garden with a swimming pool. The main intention in the design was to reinterpret the traditional responses to our tropical climate in a manner compatible with high–rise living and in line with contemporary architectural discourse. The result is an architecture of layers, realized both on plan and in the fenestration. For the latter, screens shade glazed openings and recessed planes and curves play against the main building surfaces while planter boxes create yet another layer in the elevations. On plan, voids and double–voume garden terraces connect levels spatially while a concrete pergola adds another intermediary layer to the last, upper–most units. The idea of layering is of course, not new. It has long been a part of the local vernacular in this part of the world.

The design approach is to reconcile prevalent aspects of modern high–rise living with the need to respond to our tropical climate. The extensive use of glass to capture panoramic views, a response that is practically the norm in high–rise design, and to be tempered with the need for shade and shelter from the elements. Layering offered us the opportunity to accommodate what at first appeared to be conflicting and unresolvable demands.

On a subtler level, the architect also questioned some of the entrenched attitudes concerning the styling of high–rise architecture. While diversity and experimentation in the permutations of proportion and form appears to be the norm, the architect chose to temper innovation with a return to the tradition of the tripartite composition. Instead of a uniform treatment for all the units, the 5 maisonettes were broken up to create 3 types of dwelling, each with its own identity, Thus the units are seen first, physically as individual entities, supporting the architectís belief that each home should be seen as an individual domain, and yet, as a result of their common vocabulary, they also form part of a cohesive whole.

The result is a building of parts in proportion to each other, in effect, with a base, body and capital. Carrying the idea of differentiation further, each elevation is treated differently, reflecting the internal arrangement within each dwelling. Some are playful, others restrained. Together, they offer alternatives to the conventional treatment of high–rises as uniform slab–blocks. (Richard K. F. Ho)

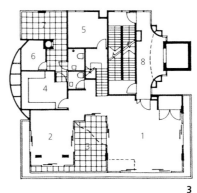

3
Section
(1. living; 2. dining;
3. terrace; 4. kitchen;
5. games room; 6. utility;
7. yard; 8. lift lobby)

4
Typical upper story plan

Drawings and photographs provided by Richard K. F. Ho

3

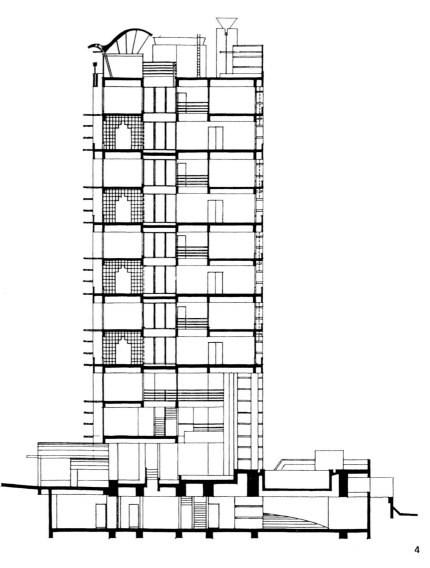

4

Boat Quay Conservation Area

Location: Singapore
Architect: Various
Date of Completion: 1994

1

1
Boat quay in front of
skyscrapers (Courtesy:
Richard K. F. Ho)

2
Artist's impression of
the overall development
(from Mimar 12/1984)

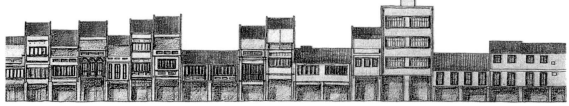

2

Boat Quay, stretching from the mouth of the Singapore River to Elgin Bridge, has played a major role in the history of Singapore. When Sir Stamford Raffles of the British East India Company arrived in 1819, both banks of the Singapore River were lined with mangrove swamps. Once he decided where the commercial center should be, he ordered that earth from a hill at the site of Commercial Square, now Raffles Place, be used to fill up the swamps. That was in 1822 and the first reclamation project in Singapore. The whole operation took about three months and when completed, was named Boat Quay, Parceled and auctioned, by 1842 it was totally developed. On the north bank stood government buildings while on the south bank wealthy merchants built two or three story shop–houses (buildings with the ground floor for commercial use and the upper floors as residences or coolie quarters). The Singapore River became the economic lifeline as more junks used the river for transporting goods and Boat Quay was congested with river traffic. In the 1850's when a new harbor, Keppel Harbour was built to cater to larger ships, Boat Quay became a predominantly Chinese domain. A typical scene of the quay featured cargo–laden tongkangs (flat-bottomed boats) loading or unloading with the help of Chinese coolies heaving and balancing precariously on planks over a filthy river choked with rubbish.

In the early 1980's, the Singapore government decided to clean up the River. The River was dredged and rubbish removed. Squatters and existing polluting industries further upstream were relocated and the tongkangs were moved to Pasir Panjang. The days when boat quay was alive with activity both day and night seemed over. The buildings fell into disrepair and became dilapidated. There were plans for the entire area to be demolished with new high–rise commercial developments taking its place. Boat Quay, permanently etched in the collective memory of the Singapore populace as the symbol of their forefathers of toil and hard work, seemed doomed.

A group of concerned citizens, among them Dr. Goh Poh Seng and William S. W. Lim, decided to form Bu Ye Tian enterprises to present and unsolicited report to the government which outlined a scheme to retain the existing buildings and redevelop boat Quay as a local cultural and recreational complex. 'Bu Ye Tian' was the traditional name for this area along the Singapore River and loosely translated means a place of ceaseless activity. The group was comprised mostly of local professionals, A series of presentations was then made to various government departments.

Although the government did not accept the Bu Ye Tien proposal, it understood the need for the conservation of Singapores valuable and fast–disappearing heritage. Boat Quay was saved from demolition and declared a Conservation Area by the authorities. Beginning in 1989, one by one of the shop–houses has been restored and as investors realized what an asset a conserved shop-house along a river promenade can be, conservation of the shop–houses took on a frenzy and by 1994, all those facing the river have been renovated. Life is coming back to Boat Quay both day and night, albeit of a different kind than in its past.

The conserved shop–houses which were of commercial use before have now taken on another commercial use and have managed to extend their relevance in the collective memory of Singaporeans. What is particularly successful and unique about the conservation effort in boat Quay is that it is done entirely by individual private investors–each renovating his property in his own way and having to find its own equilibrium in the market. Today Boat Quay is a major attraction for both locals and tourists alike due to its wide range of dining and entertainment facilities. There is a vibrancy and energy in Boat Quay not found in other conservation areas in Singapore where one developer takes over the whole conservation area resulting in monotony or contrived variety. (Richard K. F. Ho)

Reference:
Adaptive Reuse: "Singapore River" Mimar 12, 1984.

3

3
Riverside view (from Mimar 12/1984)

Vol. **10** Oceania

1900–1919

Cathedral of the Blessed Sacrament

Location: Christchurch
Architect: Francis William Petre
Year of Design/Construction: 1899–1900/1901–1905

1

1
Exterior

2

Although Francis William Petre (1847–1918) was an admirer of Pugin and a product of the Romantic movement, ironically he did his most convincing architecture within the classical tradition. The Cathedral of the Blessed Sacrament is the outstanding example, demonstrating a sense of European order, classical grandeur and Catholic obedience. The interior, a geometrically–ordered grand gesture of Catholic aspiration and spatial intensity, is particularly fine. The central nave is defined by a two–storied colonnade of Ionic and Corinthian columns. A balustraded gallery over the aisles is supported by an entablature, directing the eye to the free–standing altar within the sanctuary. The nave ceiling is zinc with three coffered domes. Interestingly, the main dome sits above the sanctuary rather than above the crossing. It is a majestic statement, especially when viewed from the rear. Indeed, it might be described as Christchurch's Duomo.

(Russell Walden /Julia Gatley)

References:
McCoy, EJ, "Petre's Churches" in Porter, Frances (Ed), *Historic Buildings of New Zealand: South Island,* Auckland, New Zealand: Methuen, 1983: 150–159.
Stacpoole, John, and Beaven, Peter, *New Zealand Art: Architecture 1820–1970*, Wellington, New Zealand: AH & AW Reed, 1972: 50–51.

2
Floor plan (1. Apse; 2. Bishops' chair; 3. Altar; 4. Sanctuary; 5. Bishop's sacristy 6; Sacristy; 7.Chapel of unity; 8; Holy souls chapel; 9. Lady chapel; 10. Lectern; 11.Blessed sacrament chapel; 12. Spiral staircase; 13. Baptistery; 14. Reconciliation room; 15. Ambulatory)

3
Interior showing the mahogany cross

4
Interior showing the columns and coffered domes

Drawings and photographs courtesy of the Catholic Presbytery, Christchurch, New Zealand

3

4

Main Reading Room, State Library of Victoria

Location: Melbourne
Architects: Bates Peebles and Smart
Engineer: John Monash
Years of Design/Construction: 1906–11/1909–11

1

1
**Swanston Street view of the
State Library of Victoria with
the Dome**

2
Site plan (1. Library;
2. Museum; 3. McCoy Hall;
4. Museum Forecourt)

Drawing taken from J. Taylor:
Australian Architecture Since
1960 (2nd Ed.)

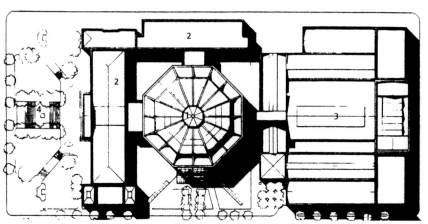

2

Located behind Joseph Reed's 1854 Roman Revival State Library of Victoria, the addition in 1911 of a Main Reading Room designed by Bates Peebles and Smart resulted in the world's largest reinforced concrete dome at that time. Engineer John Monash initially designed the dome and frame to be in Monier concrete. But with the building contract opened to competition, the builders Swanson Brothers proposed the reinforced concrete to follow another overseas patent, that of the Trussed Concrete Steel Company of England (Truscon) while retaining Monash's overall dimensions. The Truscon company used the system of steel bar (Kahn bar) reinforcing developed by American Albert W. Kahn in 1902. The shallow dome roofs a panoptic layout of reading tables and an overseeing librarian and sits on a classical composed polygonal drum which rises over four levels punctuated by arched openings. When complete, the dome was 35 meters in diameter and originally there were 371 square meters of glazing between the massive ribs. Due to roof leakage, eventually all natural light was excluded. The dome was lined internally with fibrous plaster and roofed externally with copper sheet. (Phillip James Goad)

References:
Lewis, Miles (ed.), *Two Hundred Years of Concrete in Australia*, Concrete Institute of Australia, North Sydney, 1988.
Wilson, Granville and Sands, Peter, *Building a City: 100 Years of Melbourne Architecture*, Oxford University Press, Melbourne, 1981.

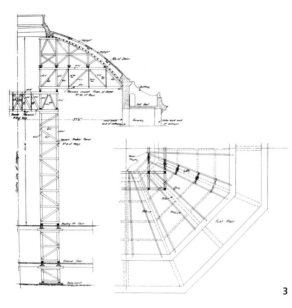

3
Drawing of the dome centering for the main reading room

4
Interior of the domed reading room

Photographs and drawings courtesy of the Trobe Picture Collection, State Library of Victoria, Australia

3

4

"Eryldene"

Location: Gordon, Sydney
Architect: William Hardy Wilson (1881–1955)
Year of completion: 1914

1

1
The front facade and garden
(Photo by Harold Cazeneaux,
1924)

2
Site plan

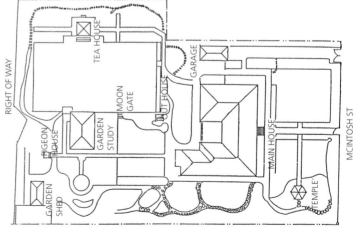

2

William Hardy Wilson (1881–1955), architect, polemicist, artist and orientalist, was an influential figure in Sydney in the early 20th century culture. In 1914 he finished "Eryldene" for EG Waterhouse, a languages professor at Sydney University and a world renowned camellia cultivator, and his family at Gordon a northern Sydney suburb. Like other Wilson houses of the period, notably his own (not far away), the new house was a simple, elegiac domestic interpretation of colonial Georgian, the style Wilson so admired. At "Eryldene" Wilson refers, not only to the colonial past of Sydney but also to the elegant wood architecture of colonial Maryland and Virginia which he had seen first hand on a study trip. An interest in Chinese architecture manifests itself most directly in Eryldene's tea–house.

In 1919 Wilson declared that he would "... carry on the tradition laid by Greenway (the best known architect of colonial Australia) instead of hopping from fashion to fashion." Traces of the understated quality endemic to Georgian architecture show up in the dignified and severe timber facade of "Eryldene" which is composed of regularly spaced verandah columns with matching sleepouts like book–ends at each end. In contrast to the wood facade, the remainder of the house is built in soft, lime–washed brickwork. The interior planning is axial with balanced primary rooms to either side of a central hall.

Wilson's work is a paradigm of simplicity and restraint, which perhaps, like the modern architecture that was to soon surface in Europe, looks with disdain at 19th century eclecticism. Wilson's gaze was, however, atavistic while that of the modernists embraced anteriority.
(Andrew Metcalf)

References:
(Eds) Smith,Ure, Sydney and Stevens, Bertram , "Domestic Architecture in Australia" Special Number of *Art in Australia,* Sydney, 1919.
Indyk, Ivor , "William Hardy Wilson and the Eloquence of Restraint" , *Transition* (Melbourne), Vol 2 No 2 , 1981, pp 11–17.
Edwards, Zeny, *The Grecian Pagoda and the Architecture of Eryldene*, ZED, Sydney, 1995.

3

3
The Loggia (Photo by Harold Cazeneaux, 1924)

4
Floor plan

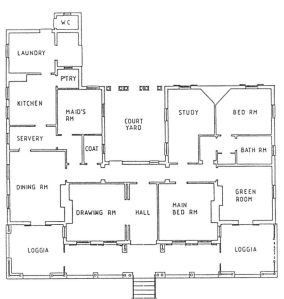

4

5
Looking through the Moon–gate (design by R. Keuth Harris in 1936)
to the Tea House
(Photo by Zeny Edwards)

6
The dining room (Photo by Harold Cazeneaux, 1924)

7
Drawings by Richard Appely

8
Measured drawing of the front entrance
(by Robert Staas, 1991)

9
Drawings by Richard Appely

Drawings and photographs courtesy of Zeny Edwards, taken from *The Grecian Pagoda and the Architecture of the Eryldene*, by Zeny Edwards, 1995, except for the drawings by Richard Appely.

6

'Chinese' Tea House

Study (west)

Pigeon House

Study (east)

8

'The Temple'

NORTH ELEVATION

7

9

Tauroa Homestead

Location: Havelock North, Hawkes Bay
Architect: William Henry Gummer
Years of Design/Construction:1914–1915/1915–1916

1

1
Exterior view (Photo by
Robin Morrison)

2
Ground floor plan (drawn by
Chris Cochran, courtesy of
Alister Taylor)

3
First floor plan (drawn by
Chris Cochran, courtesy of
Alister Taylor)

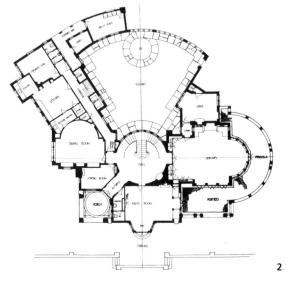

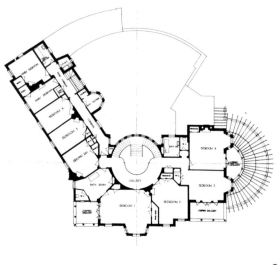

2

3

Tauroa Homestead, designed by William Henry Gummer (1884–1966), a two–storied house built of cavity brick with reinforced concrete columns and beams, has no precedent in domestic design in New Zealand and defies stylistic categorization. Indeed, with its flat roofs, stuccoed exterior, rear courtyard and attention to indoor–outdoor living, it anticipates some of the themes that would be more fully explored by modernist architects in the 1940s windows. Central to the planning of Tauroa is a circular hallway that provides access to a "music room", a sizable library and the splayed rear wing that houses the dining room and the kitchen and other service areas. The hallway also has a magnificent sweeping stairway that leads to the second story. With its two wings, the floor plan can be read as one half of the butterfly plan being used by turn–of–the–century English architects such as Edwin Lutyens, for whom Gummer had worked in England. (Russell Walden/Julia Gatley)

References:
Morrison, Robin, *Images of a House*, Waiura, Martinborough, New Zealand: Alister Taylor, 1978.
New Zealand Historic Places Trust, "Proposal for Classification, Buildings Classification Committee Report: Tauroa", Wellington: Not published, compiled 1989.

4

4
The Library (Photo by Robin Morrison)

5
The dining room (Photo by Robin Morrison)

6
The stairs

Photographs courtesy of the Estate of Robin Morrison, Auckland War Memorial Museum

5

6

Newman College,
University of Melbourne

Location: Melbourne
Architects: Walter Burley Griffin & Marion Mahony
Year of Design: 1915
Year of Completion: 1917

1

1
Interior view of the dome
(Photo by James Birrell)

2
Exterior view of the rotunda
(Photo by Wolfgang Sievers)

2

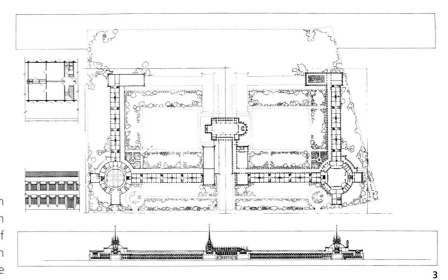

Part of a much larger complex designed by American architects Walter Burley Griffin (1876–1937) and Marion Mahony (1871–1962), the L–shaped northern wing of Newman College is the second largest building in Australia completed by the gifted husband and wife design partnership. The Griffins came to Australia after winning the 1911 competition for the design of Canberra, the nation's new capital city. The Catholic men's residential college was designed to relate geometrically to the center of the University of Melbourne campus. Two embracing L–shaped arms of student rooms over two stories defined two quadrangles. Between these two spaces on axis and at the center of the composition was intended to be a chapel with its nave oriented north–south. At each corner of the L–shapes was a rotunda, one a dining room, the other a library. Of the Griffins'design, only the north wing was built. But the dramatically low and long cloister, the walls faced in Barrabool sandstone, the pointed voussoirs and battered walls, climaxed by the dining room rotunda with its exterior of pinnacles and concrete fleche and its interior of expressed ribs and central highlight structure forming a cross over its center combines at once a mysterious medieval romanticism, innovative reinforced concrete construction, and a symbology that transcended the known Christian imagery to provide a universally applicable language of knowledge and faith.
(Philip James Goad)

References:
Duncan, Jenepher and Gates, Merryn (eds.), *Walter Burley Griffin: a Re–view*, Monash University Gallery, Clayton 1981.
Johnson, Donald Leslie, *The Architecture of Walter Burley Griffin*, Macmillan, South Melbourne, 1977.

3
Site plan/floor plan/ elevation (courtesy of the Art Institute of Chicago)

4
Exterior view of the L–shaped arm with pointed voussoirs and battered walls (Photo: Wolf–gang Sievers)

5
Interior view of the corridor (Photo Wolfgang Sievers)

4

5

"Belvedere" (Stephens House)

Location: Cremorne, Sydney
Architect: Alexander Stewart Jolly
Year of Completion: 1919

1

1
Verandah detail
(Photo: Max Dupain)

2

The (bungalow) style, which developed many variations internationally, was derived by European colonists in India from the local vernacular, then made more compatible with expatriate tastes by incorporating nuances from both Georgian and Arts and Crafts predilections. Architectural examples emerged in Australia both as a post–colonial idiom and later, as deliberately adoptive elements of the so–called California bungalow style, which itself had roots in the Swiss chalet and the Japanese house as well as the Indian source. The exemplar became a hybrid. "Belvedere", a house for F. C. Stephens, demonstrates the Australian version, with overtones of the architecture of Walter Burley Griffin: a spreading low pitched gable major roof, with three subsidiary gabled projections, wide eaves with exposed rafters and inclined brackets, above heavy roughcast brick pylons which emphasize the entry porch and verandahs. The dwelling–rooms could be linked to each other through large door openings so that there would be available a continuity of generous interior space, and this informal arrangement of interior space is expressed externally. The materials were unelaborate: plastered brick and dark stained timber fascias, window frames and joinery. (Neville Quarry)

References:
Johnson, Donald J. *Australian Architecture 1901–51*. Sydney University Press, 1980.
Irving, Robert and Kinstler, John. *Fine Houses of Sydney*. Methuen Australia, Sydney 1982.

3

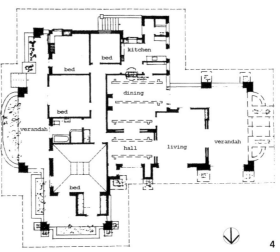

4

2
Exterior view (Photo by Max Dupain, provided by Jennifer Taylor)

3
Dining room (Photo by Max Dupain)

4
The original floor plan (redrawn from Irving, R. and Kinstler, J., *Fine Houses of Sydney*, Sydney, 1982, courtesy of Robert Irving)

Photographs courtesy of Max Dupain & Associates

1920–1939

"Greenway" (Wilkinson House)

Location: Vaucluse, Sydney
Architect: Leslie Wilkinson
Year of Completion: 1923

1

1
Front elevation (Photo by
Max Dupain)

2
The house seen through an
arcade (Photo by
Max Dupain)

3
The site and ground floor
plan (1. living Room; 2. Gallery;
3. Hall; 4. Laundry;
5. KitchenPantry; 6. Dining Room;
7. Pantry; 8. Study; 9. Verandah;
10. Garage)

2

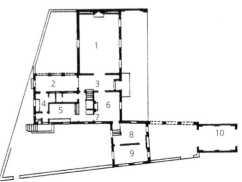

3

In 1919 English born and educated Leslie Wilkinson (1882–1973) reached Australia to head the School of Architecture at the University of Sydney. An enthusiasm for Italian classical and vernacular architecture which informed his own work became fashionable in Sydney after he completed "Greenway", his own house, in 1923. The widespread Wilkinsonian style which held sway in the interwar years has been variously dubbed "Spanish Mission"and "Mediterranean–cum–Georgian". Never–theless, the new professor's teaching, writing and designs urged restraint. He had an interest in, and advocated a sensitive observance of, the indigenous context for architectural work, particularly the flora, climate and built history of Sydney.

Like Hardy Wilson, his exact contemporary, Wilkinson also respected simplicity: "The value of simplicity has been urged and, were examples needed, there stand in all the older settlements ... airy, roomy, comfortable houses, full of dignity and tasteful charm."

At "Greenway" these ideas are demonstrable. Located on the back of the site in order to forge a large sunny garden, the simple two–story house encloses living rooms on the ground floor and bedrooms on the first. These latter include sleepouts, which along with those Hardy Wilson built at "Eryldene", predate the more famous examples of Schindler and Neutra in Los Angeles. (Andrew Metcalf)

References:
(Eds) Smith Ure , Sydney and Stevens, Bertram , "Domestic Architecture in Australia"; Special Number of *Art in Australia*. Sydney, 1919.
(Ed) Falkiner, S, *Leslie Wilkinson, a Practical Idealist*. Valadon Press, Sydney, 1982.

4

4
Main living room (Photo by Anthony Boswell)

5
The Loggia
(Photo: Max Dupain)

6
Front elevation (Photo: Max Dupain)

Drawings (redrawn) and photograph (by Anthony Boswell) from *Leslie Wilkinson, A Practical Idealist*, Valadon Press, 1982, courtesy of David Wilkinson. Photographs courtesy of Max Dupain & Associates.

5

6

Civic Theatre

Location: Auckland
Architects: Bohringer, Taylor and Johnson
Year of Completion: 1929

1

1
Exterior view
(courtesy of Alexander
Turnbull Library, Wellington,
N. Z)

Designed by Sydney architects and specialist cinema designers Bohringer Taylor and Johnson, the Civic Theatre in Auckland, New Zealand is one of the most extravagant and exotic atmospheric cinemas built in Australasia in the 1920s. Substantially intact and one of the last remaining of its type in the region, the Civic's interior design is remarkable for its departure from the more common tendency to follow flamboyant Spanish or decadent classical scenography in its interior decoration. The Civic instead combines a foyer ornamented in the ancient Hindu style and an auditorium modeled on an Indian Moghul palace garden. The decorative program is lavish and extensive. In the foyer, designed as a reproduction of an Indian rock–hewn temple, rampant elephants adorn balcony balustrades and flank niches housing Indian gods. Richly carved plaster brackets conceal colored lights setting the exotic ambiance before entry to the auditorium where inside, the proscenium is flanked by domed minarets and at stage level by golden lionesses with light bulbs as eyes. Overhead, the auditorium ceiling becomes a deep blue night sky complete with twinkling stars once the lights are dimmed. Externally, the Civic Theatre is treated in a stripped classical mode with large fretwork screens between stylized pilasters with a corner tower of skyscraper aspirations. A cornice decorated with sunbursts, dancing maidens, floral spirals, volutes and swags was designed by Arnold Zimmerman, a Swiss scenic artist who had studied at the Ecole des Beaux Arts in Geneva before moving to Sydney. It is the final eclectic touch in this exuberant tribute to the influence of Hollywood and the movies in Australasia.
(Phillip James Goad)

Reference:
Shaw, Peter, *New Zealand Architecture from Polynesian Beginnings to 1980*, Hodder and Stoughton, Auckland, 1991.
Thorne, Ross, *Picture Palace Architecture in Australia,* Sun Books, South Melbourne, 1976.

2

3

2
Exterior view
(Photo: Robin Morrison)

3
Interior
(Photo: Robin Morrison)

Photographs courtesy of The Estate of Robin Morrison, Auckland War Memorial Museum

Macpherson Robertson's Girls High School

Location: Albent Park, Melbourne
Architects: Seabrook and Fildes
Date of Design: 1933
Year of Completion: 1934

1

1
Exterior

2
Perspective drawing (from
*Australian Architecture,
1901–1951,* courtesy of
Donald Leslie Johnson)

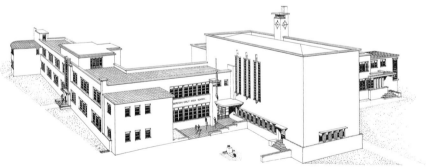

2

Macpherson Robertson's Girls High School is the first convincing large scale example of Dutch–inspired functionalist architecture in Australia. The De Stijl plan and cubistic composition of mainly two storey flat roofed forms is an inventive interpretation of Willem Dudok's Hilversum Town Hall (1928–32), a building much admired by young Australian architects traveling in Europe during the Great Depression. The materials used also reflect this close interest in contermporany Dutch work: cream bricks with highlights of glazed blue bricks and vermilion steel framed windows. The dominant feature of the complex is the projecting three story block containing the school hall with a clock tower rising above it on one side and on the other, an abstract composition of terraced steps, flagpole and cantilevered concrete entrance canopy delineating the main entry. The design by Norman Seabrook (1905–1979) was the winning entry in a competition sponsored by chocolate manufacturer and philanthropist Macpherson Robertson. Construction was completed to mark the 1934 centenary of Melbourne's settlement and signaled a new and enlightened phase of school building design in the state of Victoria.
(Phillip James Goad)

Reference:
Boyd, Robin, *Victorian Modern*, Victorian Architectural Students Society, Melbourne, 1947.
Johnson, Donald Leslie, *Australian Architecture* 1901–51; *Sources of Modernism,* Sydney University Press, Sydney, 1980.

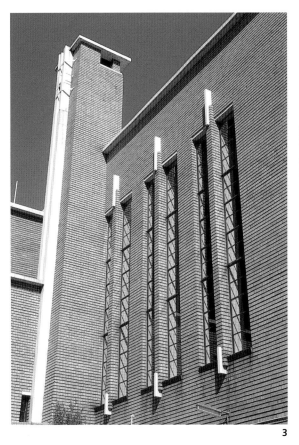

3
Clock Tower

4
Entry

3

4

Wellington Railway Station

Location: Wellington
Architect: William Gray Young of the firm Gray Young, Morton and Young
Years of Design/Construction: 1929–1933/1933–1937

1

1
Exterior view

2
Site and ground floor plan
(Courtesy: Kevin Hishop)

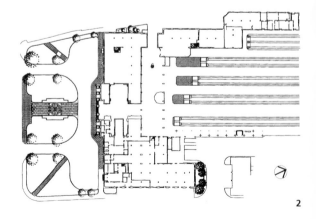

2

Designed by William Gray Young (1885–1962) of the firm Gray Young, Morton and Young, Wellington Railway Station is a fine example of Beaux Arts classicism and a major concrete building, reinforced with a steel frame and clad in a skin of brown–red brickwork. The building is U–shaped in plan and consists of a six–storied central block with a four–storied wing on either side. The wings open outwards to reveal a five–fingered platform arrangement which serves nine railway tracks. The front facade of the building is distinguished by eight round Doric columns, 42 feet high and 5 feet 3 inches wide. The Doric portico becomes the center of a Palladian equation, played out with consummate skill. The main entrance is centrally located, admitting the public to a high–vaulted booking hall, and then to the public concourse, which opens directly onto the railway platforms. Conceptually, the building is a very direct statement of people on the move. It celebrates the mystique of travel by rail. (Russell Walden/Julia Gatley)

References:
Mahoney, JD, *Down at the Station: A Study of the New Zealand Railway Station,* Palmerston North, New Zealand: The Dunmore Press, 1987.
New Zealand Historic Places Trust, 'Registered Historic Places: Category I, Wellington City', Wellington, New Zealand: Not published, compiled 1996.

3

3
The vaulted Booking Hall

4
The Concourse

Photographs courtesy: National Archive of New Zealand

4

1940–1959

Berhampore Flats

Location: Wellington
Architect: Francis Gordon Wilson
Years of Design/Construction: 1938/1939–1940

1

The Berhampore Flats, designed by Francis Gordon Wilson (1900–59), were constructed of loadbearing reinforced concrete and provided medium density state rental accommodation about a central green space and circular community hall. The scheme demonstrates that the International Style was fully established in New Zealand by the late 1930s: roofs are flat; exterior wall surfaces are plastered; and the exterior is generally devoid of elements other than those of a functional nature such as balconies, windows and doors. The scheme does, however, incorporate brick architraves on either side of the front doors to ground floor flats, brick–edged flower beds, port–hole windows and mesh balustrading to the rear balconies. The stairwell on the three–storied portion of the east block is given vertical expression. Of the 50 flats in the complex, 12 were bed–sits, 10 had one bedroom, 26 had two bedrooms, and two had three bedrooms. In the late 1980s, the community hall was adapted for reuse as additional flats and individual laundries were added to the units.

(Russell Walden/Julia Gatley)

References:
Gatley, Julia, 'For Modern Living: Government Blocks of Flats', in Wilson, John (Ed), *Zeal and Crusade: The Modern Movement in Wellington*, Christchurch, New Zealand: The Waihora Press, 1996: 53–60.
Gatley, Julia, 'Labour Takes Command: A History and Analysis of State Rental Flats in New Zealand 1935–49', Wellington, New Zealand: Master of Architecture thesis, Victoria University of Wellington, 1997.

2

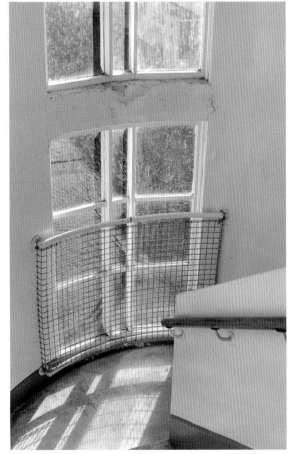

2
A scale model of Berhampore Flats (Courtesy of Tourist Department Collection, Alexander Turnbull Library, Wellington, NZ)

3
Stairwell of east block (Photo: Julia Gatley)

3

Hamill House

Location: Killara, Sydney
Architect: Sydney Ancher
Year of completion: 1949

1

1
The exterior view
(Photo: Max Dupain)

2
Site plan

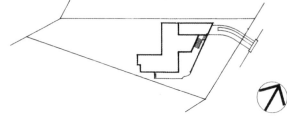

2

Sydney Ancher's (1904–1979) place as a key figure in 20th century Australian architecture is secured by a relatively small number of modest projects which, taken together, formed a threshold for the introduction of modernism, particularly in Sydney, in the twenty years from 1940 to1960. His successful pioneering of red–banner modernist motifs such as the flat roof, undertaken in the face of reactionary responses from the local media and approval authorities, has helped to make his reputation in the eyes of subsequent generations. The Hamill house was one of four, including his own, that Ancher built from 1945 to 1951 on the same street in Killara, one of Sydneyís bushland northern suburbs. They all manage to be stridently modern but regional at the same time.

One finds the living room occupying the bend in an L–shaped plan with all the house's major spaces sharing a sunny orientation but sensibly overlain with generous terraces and deeply shaded verandahs. Hard–edged geometry and light colored masonry surfaces support the architectural framework here, and with the site itself left as undisturbed bushland, this whole tableau stands for the dialectic between nature and culture.
(Andrew Metcalf)

References:
Johnson, D.L., *Australian Architecture 1901–51: Sources of Modernism.* Sydney University Press, Sydney, 1980.
Murray, S., 'Obituary', *Architecture Australia.* March 1980, pp 67–69.

3
First floor plan

4
The exterior view
(Photo: Max Dupain)

Drawings and photographs courtesy: Ancher/Mortlock/Woolley

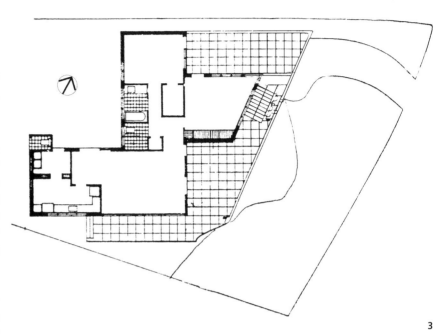

3

4

Rose Seidler House

Location: Turramurra, Sydney
Architect: Harry Seidler
Year of completion: 1950

1

1
Front exterior view
(Photo: Max Dupain)

2
Site plan

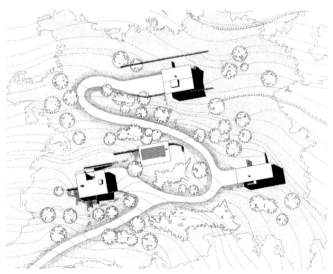

2

3

The Rose Seidler house is an illustration of cultural transfer and transformation. The architect Harry Seidler could be considered as the medium who carried the message. Seidler was born in Vienna, became a refugee during World War II , first in London, then Canada. After gaining a degree in architecture from the University of Manitoba he attended Harvard Graduate School of Design, under the direction of Walter Gropius and Marcel Breuer, and then attending Josef Albers' Design course at Black Mountain College, North Carolina. Seidler worked with Breuer and briefly with Oscar Niemeyer. In 1948, he rejoined the Seidler family, now in Australia.

Thus Seidler carried with him the design paradigms of the Bauhaus pioneers and a cosmopolitan recognition of the architectural attitudes of leading practitioners in Europe and the Americas.

His first house in Australia, for his parents, reflected all these influences, beautifully resolved in a small but dramatic building. The house is a crisp white rectangular prism, with a re-entrant terrace to engage the northern sun and view. The main living floor is raised off the ground on stone walls in a pin-wheel dispersal. Glazing is divided in Mondrianesque patterns and an almost flat roof is clipped neatly to the wall edges. From this archetypical and powerful form, Seidler was to extend his concepts in many larger and significant contributions to Australian architecture. (Neville Quarry)

Award: Sir John Sulman Medal, RAIA NSW Chapter 1951

References:
Taylor, Jennifer. *Australian Architecture Since 1960*. The Law Book Company Ltd, Sydney, 1986.
Frampton, Kenneth and Drew, Philip. *Harry Seidler, Four Decades of Architecture*. Thames and Hudson, London, 1992.

3
Interior (Photo: Max Dupain)
4
**Exterior view from rear
(Photo: Max Dupain)**
5
Floor plan
Drawings and photographs courtesy of the Architect

4

5

Stanhill Flats

Location: Melbourne
Architect: Frederick Romberg
Year of Design: 1942
Year of Completion: 1950

1

1
Exterior view (south)

Stanhill is a masterpiece of free and complex architectural composition designed by German emigré architect Frederick Romberg (1913–1992) who had arrived in Australia in 1939 having been trained in Zurich under Professor Otto Salvisberg, the Swiss expert in off–form reinforced concrete construction. Financed by Jewish businessman Stanley Korman, the construction of the ten story block of flats designed in 1942 was postponed due to World War II. When complete in 1950, the linear bulk of Stanhill defied conventional description. To the north, it resembled a giant ship with its streamlined cantilevered concrete balconies. To the west, the vertical lines of concrete glazing bars indicated an escape stair graphically displayed. While to the south, the most dramatic elevation, a taut glazed skin stepped back at each flat and rose higher and higher to terminate in an east elevation of wide eaves, a corkscrew stair, and a skin of concrete with punched out openings, and a final lower corner of diminutive curved balconies. This was a fluid, additive and hybrid composition more expres- sionistic than functionalist, and unique in Australia. (Phillip James Goad)

References:
Hamann, Conrad,'Early Romberg', *Architecture in Australia*, April/ May 1977, pp 68–75.
Hamann, Conrad,'Frederick Romberg and the Problem of European Authenticity', in Roger, Butler (ed.), *The Europeans: Emigré Artists in Australia 1930–1960,* National Gallery of Australia, Canberra, 1997, pp 37–58.

2

2
Canopy view from above

All photographs taken by and courtesy of Wolfgang Sievers

Grounds House

Location: Toorak, Melbourne
Architect: Roy Grounds (Grounds Romberg & Boyd)
Year of Completion: 1953

1

1
External view
(source: Phillip Goad)

2
Night view of the internal
courtyard looking through
the glass wall into the
illuminated living area

2

3

Designed by the architect for his own use, the Grounds House has a plan that is a perfect square with a circular courtyard as its center. Maximizing a relatively narrow site so as to fit four flats at the rear of the site, the two bedroom house was built close to the street. It is an urbane townhouse, prim and formal. By concealing the circular court within and providing externally only clerestory windows at eaves level, Roy Grounds (1905–1981) created a totally inward looking composition, almost Oriental in its introspective retreat from the outside world. The hovering roof with its upturned eaves, oversized front door with vast ring knocker and perfect symmetry evoke images of Frank Lloyd Wright's Winslow House, Chinese courtyard houses, even a tiny Palladian villa. But the materials suggest Grounds's personal architectural interests: the modest material palette of William Wurster; the refined simplicity of Scandinavia and the shibui of Japan. In the courtyard, Grounds planted black bamboo and a persimmon, further allusions to the Far East. One of a series of geometric plan shape houses and the formal model for Grounds's later and much larger National Gallery of Victoria (1961–68), this house demonstrates Grounds searching for an Australian architecture that blended East and West: it is an ideal villa for the Antipodes. (Phillip James Goad)

Award: RVIA Victorian Architecture Medal (1954)

Reference:
Clerehan, Neil, "The Home of Roy Grounds", *Architecture and Arts*, October 1954, pp. 14–19.
Goad, Philip, *The Modern House in Melbourne* 1945–1975, PhD Dissertation, University of Melbourne, 1992.

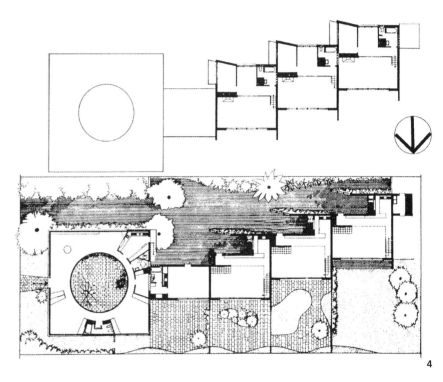

4

3
Daytime view showing side elevation of the maisonette and ti–tree fence screening (source: Phillip Goad)

4
Site and floor plan (courtesy of Neil Clerehan)

5
Living room (source: Phillip Goad)

Photographs (except otherwise noted) provided by the State Library of Victoria courtesy of Lady Grounds

5

Muller House

Location: Whale Beach, Sydney
Architect: Peter Muller
Year of Completion: 1955

1

1
Roof of marine ply with
rolled zinc on top

2
Exterior view showing site

2

The Muller House at Whale Beach is remarkably precocious for 1955 in Australia, and perhaps anywhere. It displays a raw but powerful tectonic quality mixed with a modicum of ideas sourced from Asia, Frank Lloyd Wright and abstract painting. The plan, which looks quite abstract, is composed by selectively securing different parts of the rough, rocky, bush site for various functions such as office, living room, bedrooms and so on, but only just domesticating these natural patches with floors, walls and roof, leaving literal nature largely intact. Such is the case with the fireplace which is fashioned around a large outcrop of rock, or where the building steps around and encloses the extant trees.

Muller questions, even interrogates foundational architectural agendas such as shelter and site, inside and outside and refreshes them in this building. His subsequent career has taken him to Asia, particularly Bali, to undertake research and practice.
(Andrew Metcalf)

References:
'House at Whale Beach', *Architecture Australia*, Jan–March,1956.
Taylor, J., *An Australian Identity: Houses for Sydney 1953–63*. Department of Architecture, University of Sydney, 1972.

3
3
Interior

4
Covered walk and roof

5
Site and ground floor plan
(1. Office; 2. Covered wall; 3. Entry; 4. Living room; 5. Fireplace; 6. Dining; 7. Kitchen; 8. Bed room; 9.Utility)

6
Cross section

Drawing and photographs courtesy of the Architect

4

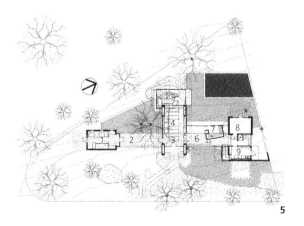

5

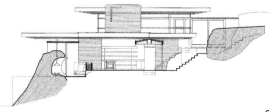

6

Olympic Swimming Stadium

Location: Melbourne
Architects: Kevin Borland, Peter McIntyre, John and Phyllis Murphy
Engineer: W.L. Irwin
Years of Design/Construction: 1952/1953–56

1
Batman Avenue view

The architectural highlight of the 1956 Melbourne Olympic Games was the Olympic Swimming Stadium designed by a team of four young Melbourne architects and their engineer Bill Irwin. Their 1952 competition winning entry was a brilliantly clear structural solution for supporting tiered seating for and a roof over 5500 spectators on either side of a main swimming pool and diving pool. The building was simply tied together with giant roof trusses and the forces were left to balance. The reinforced concrete seating on either side of the pools sat on 14 angled steel girders which were held in place by the roof trusses. The top chords of the trusses took most of the outward thrust of the girders so that the span–depth ratio of each truss was extremely economical. Pin joints were then used to give a determinate structure and vertical ties stabilized the building against eccentric wind and live loads. The huge glass wall at either end of the stadium graphically revealed the building's section suggesting infinite spatial extension. The Olympic Swimming Stadium was and remains, despite alterations and a change in function, a tour–de–force of postwar structural rationalism. In 1956, it signaled Melbourne as Australia's cradle of postwar modernity. (Phillip James Goad)

References:
Butler, Graeme, 'Melbourne Olympics 1956: Swimming Pool', *Architect*, June 1980, pp. 16–20.
Goad, Philip, 'Optimism and Experiment: the early works of Peter McIntyre 1950–1961', *Architecture Australia*, June 1990, pp. 34–53.

2
Western approach view

Photographs taken by and courtesy of Wolfgang Sievers

2

Boyd House

Location: South Yarra, Melbourne
Architect: Robin Boyd (Grounds Romberg & Boyd)
Year of Design: 1957
Year of Completion: 1958

1

1
Courtyard view

2
View from
courtyard

2

Designed by Robin Boyd (1919–1971), Australia's most prominent postwar architectural writer (Australia's Home [1952]; The Australian Ugliness (1960]), this second house for himself and his family demonstrates his consistent attempt to blend complex sources in a single building. The plan of the inner suburban townhouse is a long rectangle roofed by a sweeping catenary of planks suspended on wire cables. Beneath the all-encompassing roof, there are not rooms but platforms. The catenary sweeps the length of the sloping site containing beneath it a central courtyard, a living and parent's zone at one end and the children's block at the other. The horizontal break–up of the window mullions, the subdued natural finishes of the interior, the refined built–in timber furniture and the obscure glass screen walls of the courtyard suggest a pre–existing interest in contemporary Japanese architectural design which would be developed in greater depth following Boyd's trip to Japan in 1961 to write *Kenzo Tange* (1962) and subsequent trips to Japan researching *New Directions in Japanese Architecture* [1968] and as design consultant to the Australian Pavilion at Expo 70 at Osaka. The Boyd House is one of a series of his structurally rational house designs aimed at providing a private, sheltered and self–contained living–garden environment.
(Phillip James Goad)

Reference:
Serle, Geoffrey, *Robin Boyd: a Life*, Melbourne University Press, Melbourne, 1995.
Goad, Philip, *The Modern House in Melbourne 1945–1975*, PhD Dissertation, University of Melbourne, 1992.

3
View of courtyard from the family living room

4
Living room

5
Ground/first floor plans / section (from George Serle, *Robin Boyd: a life, Melbourne*, 1995)

Photographs by Marc Strizic, courtesy of Vi$copy Ltd.

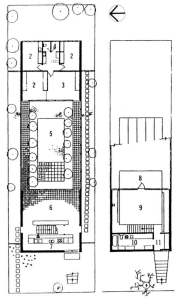

1 car port
2 children's bedrooms
3 children's sitting room
4 children's shower
5 courtyard
6 family living room
7 kitchen
8 balcony
9 parents' bed–sitting room
10 bathroom
11 entrance

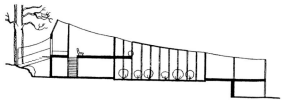

5

ICI House

Location: East Melbourne
Architects: Bates, Smart and McCutcheon
Year of Design: 1956
Year of Completion: 1959

1
Exterior view (Photo by
Wolfgang Sievers)

1

Designed as the national headquarters for the British firm Imperial Chemical Industries, ICI House in Melbourne is the first free-standing fully glazed curtain wall commercial skyscraper in Australia. Raised on pilotis, the blue glazed linear slab of offices with its lift core expressed as clearly separate, broke the city's 132 foot height limit and changed irrevocably central Melbourne is consistent skyline. On the north face, aluminum sunshades provide the only surface modulation to a sheer wall of glass and blue glazed spandrel panels. The height exemption was based on the provision of a public garden plaza at ground level. Designed collaboratively by the architects, sculptor Gerald Lewers and landscape architect John Stevens, the garden contained succulents, massive boulders and a biomorphic shaped bronze fountain. Recent renovations and additions at ground level by the original architects have been sympathetic though none of the original upper floor office interiors remain. (Phillip James Goad)

2

References:
Goad, Philip, "Monuments at Risk", *Transition,* 24, Autumn 1988, pp. 50–51.
Special Issue on ICI House, *Architecture Today*, December 1958.

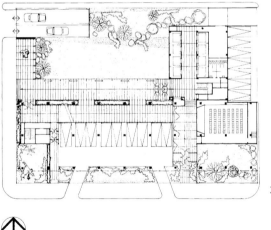

3

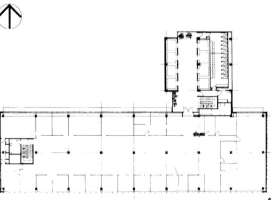

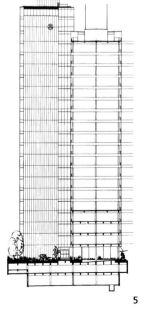

2
Courtyard view
(Photo: Wolfgang Sievers)

3
Site and ground floor plan

4
Typical floor plan

5
North–south cross section

Drawings and photographs courtesy of Bates, Smart & McCutcheon

4   **5**

1960–1979

War Memorial Hall

Location: Wanganui
Architect: Newman, Smith and Greenhough
Years of Design/Construction: 1956–1957/1958–1960

1
Exterior view

2
Site plan (1. War Memorial
Hall; 2. Museum; 3. Library;
4. Art Gallery; 5. Saverge Club)

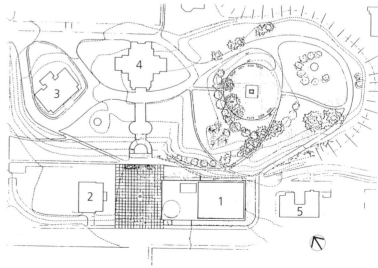

The War Memorial Hall is a clean, white, modernist block floating on piloti. It has a flat roof and is distinguished by an open concrete grille that wraps around the north corner. About 1500 mm inside the grille is a glass curtain wall. The main entrance to the building is located under the bulk of the upper level. Glass doors lead to an entrance foyer. An open staircase rises to the main foyer at first floor level, spacious with its 5.5 m stud height. From there, access is gained to the principal spaces: the main hall, with its sprung floor, raised ceiling supported on exposed trusses, and clerestory windows; the concert chamber, with tiered seating for 400 people; and the Pioneer Room, a room which could be used as an adjunct to the two main spaces, or separately for meetings or receptions. It is the Pioneer Room that is located inside the north corner of the building and, consequently, within the concrete grilles. Though a public building, the War Memorial Hall is simple in plan and detail, and honest in its expression of materials. It is an outstanding example of 1950s New Zealand modernism.
(Russell Walden/Julia Gatley)

Award: New Zealand Institute of Architects Gold Medal for 1961

References:
Journal of the New Zealand Institute of Architects: Vol 22 No 6 (July 1955: 127–128); Vol 23 No 2 (March 1956: 33–37); Vol 23 No 3 (April 1956: 61–67); Vol 27 No 7 (August 1960: 167–180); Vol 29 No 3 (April 1962: 71).

3
Pioneer room

4
Ground floor plan

5
Main floor plan

Drawings and photographs courtesy of Gordon Smith

3

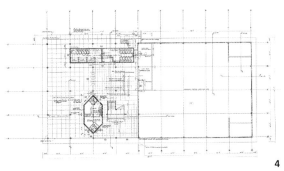

4

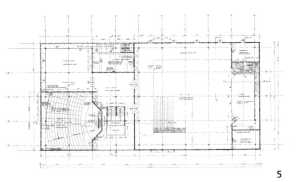

5

Chapel of Futuna

Location: Wellington
Architect: John Scott
Sculptor: Jim Allen
Years of Design/Construction: 1958–1959/1959–1961

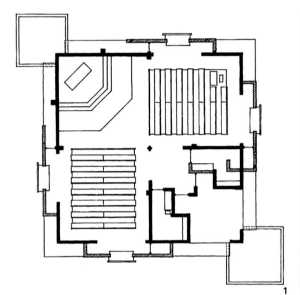

1
Floor plan of the building as built

2
Hewn pole with branches supporting the roof structure
(Photo: Gavin Woodward)

3
Interior. The windows and the crucifix were designed by sculptor Jim Allen
(Photo: Robin Morrison)

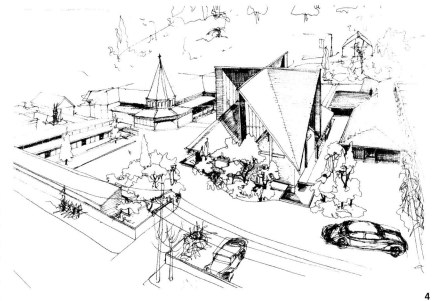

Futuna Chapel is a Catholic retreat chapel and, as far as religious architecture in the Pacific is concerned, a rare synthesis by architect John Scott (1924–1992), sculptor and brother–builders. Indeed, it has been described as a ìNew Zealand architecture ... a rich characterisation of Maori and Pakeha values in a natural settingî .The building is square in plan. It is divided into four quarters. This division is expressed in the steeply pitched roof: two opposing quarters are hipped and the other two are adjacent half–gables. One of the four quarters is given over to the entrance, resulting in an L–shaped interior. The plan arranges retreatants into two banks of Ronchamp–inspired pews. Both face the raised slab of red granite that is the altar. Central to the building is a hewn pole with branches supporting the exposed timber roof structure. Walls are rough–textured and the floor, serpentine marble. Though small in scale, this building is rich in theological and architectural references: it captures the verticality and luminosity of the Gothic and, on a clear sunny day, has a unique capacity for metaphysical transformation in colored light.
(Russell Walden/Julia Gatley)

Award: New Zealand Institute of Architects Gold Medal for 1968

References:
Walden, Russell, *Voices of Silence: New Zealand's Chapel of Futuna*, Wellington, New Zealand: Victoria University Press, 1987.

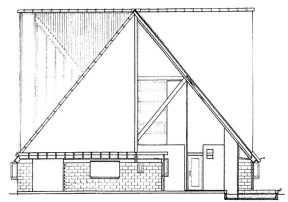

4

4
Bird's eye view of the design solution

5
Cross section of the chapel shows the manner in which the roof is supported

6
Northwest elevation

5

6

Rickard House

Location: Wahroonga, Sydney
Architect: Bruce Rickard
Year of completion: 1961

1
Exterior view of northern elevation
(pool added in1975)

2
Site plan

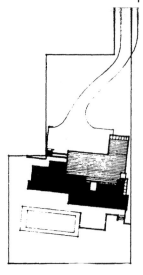

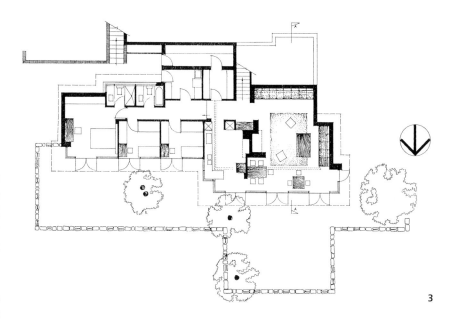

3

There is a high level of family home ownership in Australia and many architect's early domestic commissions are generated by their immediate families or themselves, and often architect's own houses are an opportunity for complex statements of local context merged with personal influences from architectural heroes.

Certain attributes of the work of Frank Lloyd Wright were particularly suited to the family life styles and suburban bush landscape sites around Sydney–the sense of a sweeping sheltering roof, the merging of interior and exterior spaces, the overlapping of architectural sequences and the exploitation of the natural beauty of Australian hardwood timber and recycled sandstock bricks. Bruce Rickard's own house confidently manages the disposition of these attributes, in a manner that is distinctive and relaxed, with a sensitivity to site specificity, scale and spatial graciousness, that is simultaneously secure and expansive. Born and educated in Australia, obtaining a Master of Landscape Architecture Degree at the University of Pennsylvania, and highly appreciative of Wright's buildings, Rickard continues his own architectural practice in Sydney in a singularly Australian interpretation of organic architecture. (Neville Quarry)

Reference:
Taylor, Jennifer. *Australian Architecture Since 1960*. The Law Book Company Ltd, Sydney, 1986.

4

5

3
Upper floor plan

4
Living room

5
Study room

Photographs by
Max Dupain. Drawings and
photographs courtesy of
the Architect.

Woolley House

Location: Mosman, Sydney
Architect: Ken Woolley
Year of completion: 1962

1

1
Interior

2
Axonometric view

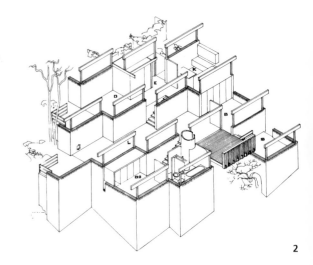

2

Ken Woolley's own house in Sydney's inner northern suburbs was seminal and iconoclastic for its time and has become something of a historical signpost for the direction of Australian residential design in the years since.

Woolley planned the house as a series of 3.6 m square modules, each under a simple raked roof. The modules step and stagger horizontally and vertically in relation to one another creating an open interior which follows the steep site. As he said at the time , "the design derives from an idea that the floors would be garden terraces stepping down the hillside, part of which would be covered by a massive timber roof…"

With its honest, forthright palette of raw, unfinished materials and a base of solid masonry crowned by a floating roof, the Woolley house is an example par excellence of 1960's and 70's values associated with the "Sydney School" which constituted an emergent regional opposition to abstract international style modernism.

Award: Wilkinson Award, 1962

References:
Taylor, J., *An Australian Identity: Houses for Sydney 1953–63.* Department of Architecture, University of Sydney,1972.
Architect's Own House *Architecture Australia,* December, 1963, pp 76–79.

3

3
Southwest aspect of the House (Photo: David Moore)

4
Southeast aspect of the House (Photo: David Moore)

5
Section

Drawings and photographs courtesy of the Architect

4

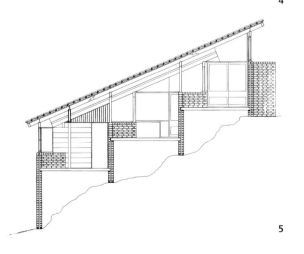

5

C.B. Alexander Agricultural College

Location: Tocal
Architects: Philip Cox and Ian McKay
Years of Construction: 1963–1964

1

1
The chapel spire

2
Site plan

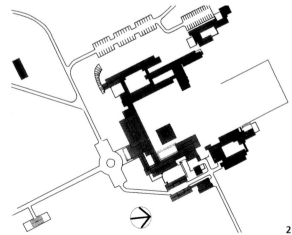

2

The C.B. Alexander Agricultural College at Tocal, NSW, Australia accommodates 150 students and 40 staff, on a hill–crest site overlooking a river valley. The complex was built by the Presbyterian Church as an independent residential college to train young men in land use techniques. The many functions of this group of buildings– chapel, assembly hall, dining room, classrooms, dormitories and machinery sheds, have separate expression (like the chapel spire and the basilica–like assembly hall), yet each integrates into a harmonious complex, arranged in a number of sheltered courtyards, altogether fitting gently into the pastoral landscape. A few robust materials are used consistently inside and out: load bearing salmon pink bricks, dark brown stained sawn trusses of intricate construction, plank ceilings, concrete tile roofs and peeled log colonnades. The near–vernacular monastic–rustic form – simple rectangular buildings with wide overhangs and strong recesses casting deep shade–follows a rich elaboration of traditional craftsmanship which although faintly nostalgic, has evolved into a vocabulary which is both contemporary and satisfying. (Neville Quarry).

Award: Sir John Sulman and Blackett Awards, RAIA NSW Chapter, 1965

References:
Dobney, Stephen (ed.). *Cox Architects. Selected and Current Works*. The Images Publishing Group, Mulgrave, Australia, 1994.
Taylor, Jennifer. *Australian Architecture Since 1960*. The Law Book Company Ltd, Sydney, 1986.

3

3
Covered way in courtyard

4
Chapel spire structure

Photgraphs by
Patrick Bingham Hall. Drawings and photographs courtesy of Cox, Richardson, Taylor and Partners

4

Wentworth Memorial Church

Location: Vaucluse, Sydney
Architect: Clarke Gazzard, design architect: Don Gazzard
Year of Completion: 1965

1

1
General view of back

2
Internal space

2

The church tower, atop a hill, is spectacularly visible from the surrounding suburbs. The tower has not the conventional identification of an ecclesiastical spire, but is a more mundane shape, like a theater fly tower, but nonetheless a marker of spiritual speciality. From the roadway, pedestrians take a path which meanders around the hillside, past rock outcrops and remnant bush, all the while catching glimpses of the church from different oblique angles and vantage points, before arriving, via a lychgate, at a brick paved forecourt and then ultimately to the interior– natural finish timber floors and ceiling, white walls and from a discreet clerestory, daylight washes onto the sanctuary.

The church is the epitome of an architectural experience– a distant prospect, gradually revealed in a journey through space, culminating in the contemplation, closely from the outside and then from within, of an interior enclosure suffused by dramatic light. The construction materials are conventional: white bagged brickwork, terra cotta tile, dark brown stained timber; the composition dynamic–simple skewed planes, and the total sensory experience of exploration and arrival is extraordinary. (Neville Quarry)

Reference:
Freeland, John Maxwell. *Architecture in Australia: A History*. Cheshire, Melbourne, 1968.

3

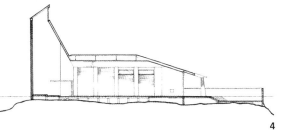

4

3
General view

4
Section

5
Site diagram

Photographs by David Moore
Drawings and photographs
courtesy of the Architect

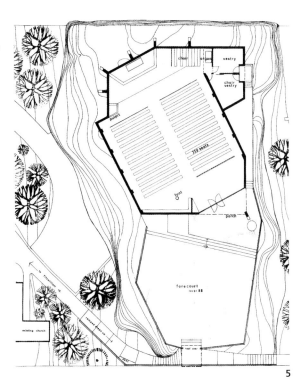

5

Union College Halls of Residence, University of Queensland

Location: Brisbane
Architect: James Birrell
Years of Construction: 1961–1965

1

1
Exterior view
2
Plan

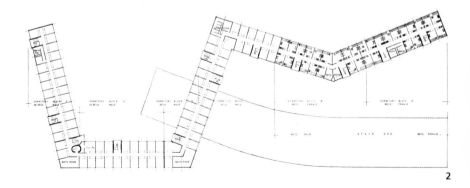

2

In Australia, prior to the end of World War 2, University college buildings tended to reflect in their architecture, the traditions of Oxford and Cambridge. Post–war, various modes of modernism were invoked, ranging from the cosmetic international to the deliberately tough and direct expression of materials and functions.

This University College for 200 students is built with an uncompromising palette of materials: off–form concrete, and manganese bricks in direct, almost diagrammatic, column and beam construction. To preserve mature eucalyptus trees on a narrow site, the buildings are dispersed in a casual and loose arrangement of winding three story dormitory wings, partly raised on reinforced concrete pilotis, in scale quite like the English cloistered tradition, but the abstract composition of cranked bars is topographically unique. Two asymmetrical courtyards are generated, one of which is not entirely enclosed. Dining, leisure and staff quarters are located at ground level. For the sub–tropical climate, the window system incorporates hoppers at a lower level and above, center pivoted metal framed double glazed windows with internal venetian blinds. The rather spare use of architectural elements and forceful interiors combine to produce a powerful, ascetic aesthetic. (Neville Quarry)

References:
Taylor, Jennifer. *Australian Architecture Since 1960*. The Law Book Company Ltd, Sydney, 1986.
Wilson, Andrew & Macarthur, John, eds. *Birrell: Work from the Office of James Birrell*. NMBW Publications, Melbourne, Australia 1997.

3
Exterior view
4
Courtyard
5
Interior
6
Elevation

Photographs courtesy of the Architect

3

4

5

6

Athfield House

Location: Wellington
Architect: Ian Athfield
Years of Design/Construction: From 1965
Year of Completion: Not Applicable

1

1
Exterior

Ian Athfield does not think of architecture as being 'fixed' –as being an end–point–but prefers to think of it as 'having no beginning and no end'. Nowhere is this more evident than in the appearance of his own home. With its white–plastered masses perching precariously on a steep hillside overlooking Wellington city, the Athfield House exploits the local topography and has become a well–known landmark. It began as a social nucleus (1965–66), to which Athfield added a bedroom wing (1969), a studio and observation tower (1972), and then a swimming pool and an architect's office (1980–82). The resulting roofscape is that of a Mediterranean village. Appropriately, the house provides for living, working and building. To view the agglomerate plan is to see the many levels and oddly–shaped rooms to which Athfield continues to add. Beneath the extroverted dynamism of the exterior, however, the interior is cave–like and the mood is one of withdrawal: the house is private, warm and relaxed. Walls are white; and floors are brick. Non–conformist in many ways, the Athfield House testifies to the earthy directness and casual demeanor of its architect–owner. (Russell Walden/Julia Gatley)

Reference:
Stacpoole, John, and Beaven, Peter, *New Zealand Art: Architecture 1820–1970*, Wellington, New Zealand: AH & AW Reed, 1972.
Walden, Russell, Two Houses in New Zealand–Architect: Ian Athfield, *Architectural Review* Vol CLXXI No 1023 (May 1982: 48–52).

2

**2
Partial
exterior**

**3
Interior**

3

4
Detail

5
Exterior

6
Site plan

7
Section

Drawings and photographs
courtesy of the Architect

5

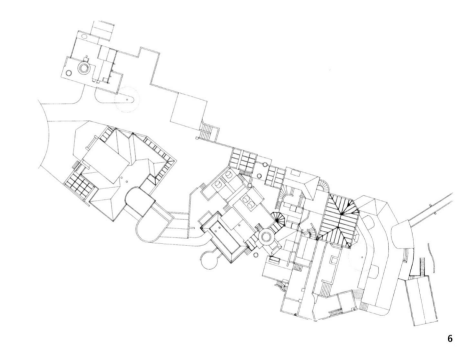

6

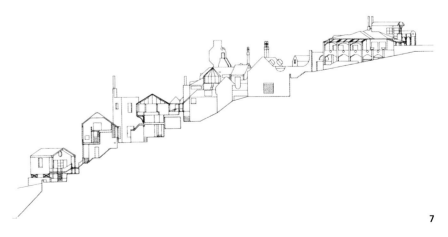

7

Australia Square

Location: Sydney
Architect: Harry Seidler
Structural Engineer: P. C. Nervi
Years of Construction: 1961–1967

1

1
Executive reception room

The major elements which constitute Australia Square are quite elementary architectural forms. The most dominant is the 50 story tower: a tall white cylinder, articulated vertically by ribs and banded horizontally by strips of dark windows, deep green spandrel panels and white quartz faced edge beams at each story, with two recessed equipment floors at levels 19 and 35, and a louvered screen at the topmost level. From a distance, the dark glass and spandrel panels visually merge, so that the exterior reads as simply a vertical and horizontal grid, wrapped around a tube.

Bordering the eastern edge of the site the 13 story Plaza Building is a simple rectangular prism, raised above the ground on seven clusters of four columns, splayed like waiters' fingers bearing trays. The west and east facades of the Plaza Building have aluminum sun screens at each level of windows, a single layer on the east and where there is no shading from neighboring buildings on the west, a double set, one fixed and one adjustable layer of screening. The virtues of Australia Square are not merely dependent however on its splendid architectural form. Through the successful sociability of its plaza spaces, Australia Square established a major modern civic place for Sydney. (Neville Quarry)

Award: Sir John Sulman Medal and Civic Design Award, RAIA NSW Chapter 1967

Reference:
Frampton, Kenneth and Drew, Philip. *Harry Seidler, Four Decades of Architecture*. Thames and Hudson, London, 1992.
Seidler, H. *Australia Square*. Horwitz, Sydney 1969.

2

2
Exterior

3
Upper and lower plaza plan
(1. Upper plaza; 2. Calder Stabile;
3. Steps down to shopping Circle;
4. Entrance lobby; 5. Tapestry by
Le Corbusier; 6. Tapestry by
Vasarely; 7. Low rise lifts;
8. Medium-rise lifts; 9. High rise
lifts; 10. Express lift;
11. Vent shaft; 12. Lower plaza;
13. Fountain;
14. Outdoor restaurant;
15. Ramp down to parking)

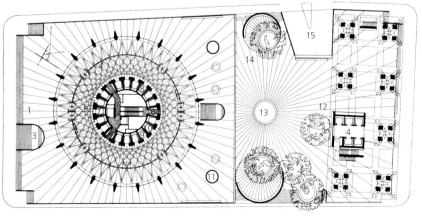

3

4
Outdoor public space

5
Interior showing exposed
structure on ceiling

4

5

6
Exterior view of the Tower
showing reducing projecting
exterior columns and
exposed structure on
ceilings

7
Ground floor structure

8
Typical floor structure

All photographs by
Max Dupain. Drawings and
photographs courtesy of the
Architect.

6

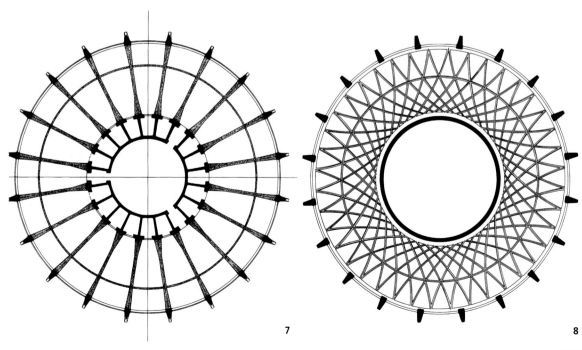

7

8

Seidler House

Location: Killara, Sydney
Architect: Harry Seidler
Years of Construction: 1966–1967

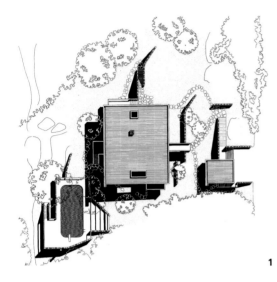

1
Site plan

2
Exterior view from rear

3
Front view

This house is sumptuous, in terms of quality of materials, of size, of architectural experience and of generous responsiveness, on a large site, to a suburban bush environment. The strong structural theme is of concrete block piers supporting concrete slab floors at many different levels, clear of the natural ground. Essentially the plan is rectangular, but planar spatial divisions, both horizontal and vertical, animate the interior by conjuring a series of areas flowing apart and yet still retaining a sense of continuity. The inclined plane of the concrete roof has downturn edge beams and overhangs which provide sun screening. Off-form concrete and blockwork are exposed externally and internally, ceilings are timber boarding and there is a large stone fireplace which has a strong sculptural presence. (Neville Quarry)

Award: Wilkinson Award RAIA NSW Chapter 1967

Reference:
Frampton, Kenneth and Drew, Philip. *Harry Seidler, Four Decades of Architecture*. Thames and Hudson, London, 1992.
Taylor, Jennifer. *Australian Architecture Since 1960*. The Law Book Company Ltd, Sydney, 1986.

4

4
Interior

5
Sculpture

6
Floor plan and section

Photographs by Max Dupain. Drawings and photographs courtesy of the Architect

5

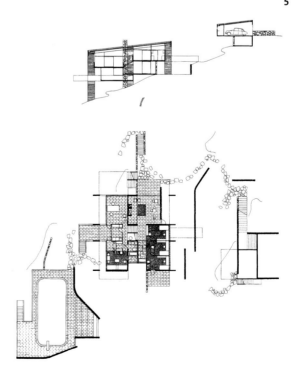

6

Christchurch Town Hall

Location: Christchurch
Architect: Warren and Mahoney Architects Ltd
Years of Design/Construction: 1965–1968/1968–1972

1
Ferrier Fountain and Limes Room

2
Exterior view of the auditorium

3
First floor plan

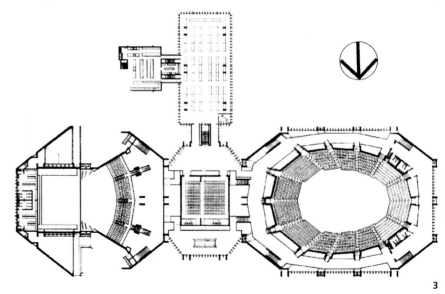

Christchurch Town Hall is a comprehensive and dignified civic complex. The major elements are treated separately and expressed individually. In this way, we see the oval drum of the main auditorium, the fan of the concert chamber, and the box of the stage tower. The exterior is irregular and informal, lively and exciting. It is complemented by the park and river of its surrounds. Internally, a central foyer provides access to the main spaces without confusion and also allows the crowds to promenade during intervals. The main auditorium achieved an international reputation as a result of its acoustics. Large sound reflectors float above the gallery seating which is divided into blocks that step back from the stage. Further, the height of the auditorium and the form of the ceiling were determined by the reverberation time selected for the space. Throughout the complex, finishes are simple: concrete plastered white cement and quartz to walls and columns, in-situ fairfaced beams, quartz chips, limited marble facing, meranti timber precast concrete trough units, and concrete block wall panels. Paired columns appear throughout and act as a unifying element. This was an early major project for an architectural partnership that would become one of New Zealand's best known. (Russell Walden/Julia Gatley)

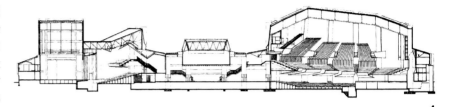

4

5

References:
Journal of the New Zealand Institute of Architects: Vol 31 No 7 (August 1964: 227); Vol 33 No 3 (March 1966: 94); Vol 33 No 10 (October 1966: 292–326); Vol 36 No 10 (October 1969: 325); Vol 39 No 10 (October 1972: 292–303); Vol 40 No 6 (June 1973: 156–159).

4
Longitudinal section

5
**Convention Center
(completed 1997)**

6
Interior

Drawings and photographs
courtesy of the Architect

6

Sydney Opera House

Location: Sydney
Architect: Jorn Utzon and Hall, Todd and Littlemore
Years of Construction: 1957–1973

1

1
General view from the
Sydney Harbor (Photo:
Luo Xiaowei)

2
The opera Hall

2

Jorn Utzon won the 1956 Sydney Opera House competition with a memorable concept of two great halls cut into a massive plinth and roofed with a set of light concrete shells. This binary opposition of heavy and light emerged from the architect's study of Incan stepped-platform temples and Gothic cathedral roofs, and showed him to be capable of an uncanny synthesis of cross-cultural sources. The work of design development which followed showed Utzon to be an obsessive tectonic researcher looking for techniques that would reconcile sculptural expressiveness with the sort of standardization that is required for rational building construction.

After a protracted struggle with the government client over cost, architectural documentation and deadlines, Utzon resigned as architect at the stage where the exterior shell was complete. The Sydney consortium of Hall, Todd and Littlemore were then engaged as architects until the project's completion. While there is some similarity between Utzon's concepts for the interior and the work executed, it should be noted that the interior work is that of the Sydney architects.

At the Opera House a grand plinth grounds the building decisively and thereby declares a solidarity with the earth. The shells on the other hand are of the sky: ignoring gravity they seem to touch the ground at a very few points and never seem to appear unstable. Utzon's Sydney Opera House implicates us and tenders clues about our own metaphysical place, clinging to a lineament between topographic surface and infinite space. (Andrew Metcalf)

Award: Commemorative Sulman Medal, 1992.

References:
Giedion, S., *Space Time and Architecture. The Growth of a New Tradition.* Cambridge Mass., 1967, 5th ed.
Kerr, J.S., *The Sydney Opera House Interim Conservation Plan.* Sydney Opera House Trust, Sydney, 1993.
Junz, Jack, Sydney Revisited *The Arup Journal,* vol.23, no.1, Spring, 1988, Ove Arup Partnership, London

3
Main Auditorium plan (1. concert hall; 2. concert hall foyer; 3. opera theater; 4. opera theater foyer; 5. main restaurant)

4
Concert Hall axial section (1. car concourse; 2. staircase to foyer; 3. foyer, box office, cloak rooms; 4. concert hall foyer; 4a. promenade lounge; 5. organ loft; 6. concert hall; 7. rehearsal room; 8. drama theater; 9. drama theater stage; 10. rehearsal/ recording hall; 11. cinema/ chamber music hall and exhibition hall foyer)

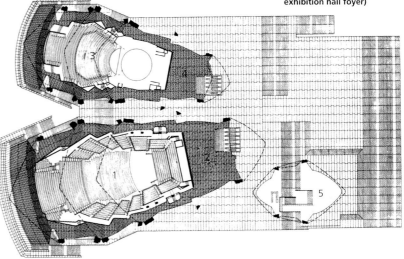

3

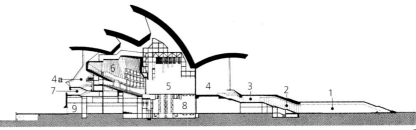

4

5

5
Opera Theater axial section
(1. car concourse ;
2. staircase to foyer ;
3. foyer, box office, cloak rooms;
4. opera theater foger;
4a. promenade lounge; 5. opera theater stage; 6.opera theater.
7. opera theatre lounge;
8. below stage area;
9. restaurant)

6
The Orchestral Hall

7
Night view

8
Roof structure

9
Axonometric view of the tower crane system of structural assembly

Drawings provided by Jennifer Taylor.
All photographs (except otherwise noted) taken from and by Permission of *The Arup Journal*, (Spring, 1988)

7

8

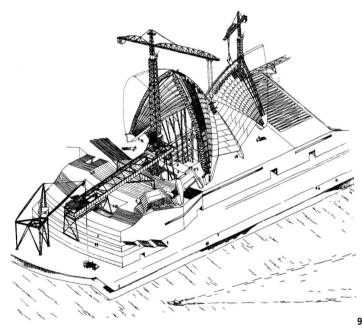

9

Cameron Offices

Location: Belconnen, Canberra
Architect: John Andrews
Years of Construction: 1971–1976

1
Exterior
(Photo: David Moore)

2
Site plan

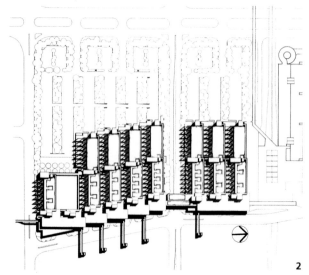

In the early 1970s John Andrews returned to Australia from a career in Canada which produced the well known Scarborough College in Toronto and Gund Hall for the Graduate School of Design in Harvard. He had been commissioned by the Australian government to undertake the Cameron Offices project, the first stage of Belconnen town center 20 kilometers from Canberra, the nation's capital.

Still occupied by its original tenant, the Department of Census and Statistics, Cameron Offices is a controversial alternative model for satellite city office building. The built design emerged from Andrews' questioning of the original brief for five high rise towers and proposing instead, that they be laid on the side in the form of low rise accommodation. Andrews construed the project as seven wings or fingers of office space alternating with landscaped courts and a lateral circulation spine bridging across one end of the fingers creating a point of address and executive offices for all the departments housed in the finger blocks.

Wrought on a heroic scale, in abstract forms built from insitu concrete and glass, the Cameron Offices project has a commanding presence, both as a form in the Belconnen Town Centre which has grown up around it, and as an historic emblem of the 1970s city planning and architectural boom in Canberra. (Andrew Metcalf)

References:
Taylor, J. and Andrews J., *John Andrews: Architecture a Performing Art.* Oxford University Press, Melbourne, 1982.
Taylor, J., *Australian Architecture Since 1960.* Law Book Company, Sydney, 1986.

3

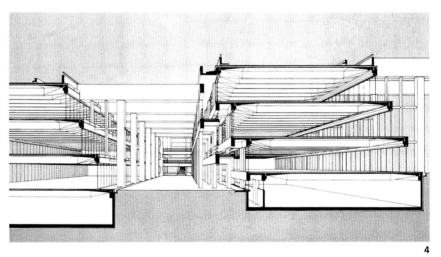

4

3
**General view from north
(Photo: David Moore)**

4
Section

5
Partial exterior
(Photo: David Moore)

6

7

8

National Athletics Stadium

Location: Bruce, Canberra
Architect: Philip Cox
Years of Construction: 1975–1977

1

1
Exterior view
2
Site plan

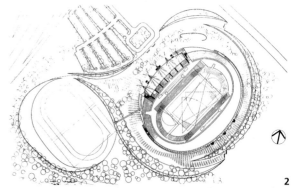

2

On the part of its government sponsor the National Athletic Stadium in Canberra was an exploratory foray into new ground: it was the first purpose–built athletic stadium of any size in Australia, and the first component of the Australian Institute of Sport which has since become a national center for all sports.

Philip Cox's design, however, was remarkably assured in its handling of the site and the architectural technology of tension structures. Working with a low budget, Cox, who had no previous experience with this sort of large scale architectural engineering, ingeniously spread the available resources by building the covered grandstand contiguous with an extensive earth berm which encompasses the stadium perimeter and a warm–up track, thus establishing a monumental scale of operations for the whole project. To support the roof he added an imposing five–masted cable–stayed suspension structure, positioning the masts like a set of triumphal markers to announce the building and its entry points.

For Philip Cox the National Athletic stadium proclaimed an undoubted talent for a building type which, for the rest of the century, was to become the staple diet of his architectural office. (Andrew Metcalf)

Award: Merit Award, NSW Chapter, RAIA, 1977.

References:
(Australian Architects Series) *Philip Cox, Richardson Taylor and Partners.* RAIA, Canberra,1988.
Taylor, J., *Australian Architecture Since 1960.* Law Book Company, Sydney,1986.

3

3
Stadium seen from inside
4
Detail of anchor
5
Side view of the Stadium roof

Drawings and photographs courtesy of Cox, Richardson, Taylor

4

5

Air Niugini Staff Housing

Location: Korobosea
Architect: Russell Hall with Desmond Collins, then with National
        Housing Commission in Port Moresby
Year of Completion: 1978

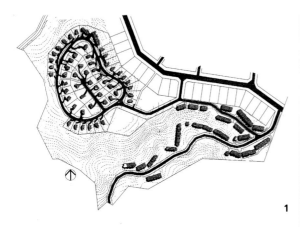

1
Site plan

2
Exterior view

3
Detached houses

1

2

3

224

This housing complex is located in Korobesa, National Capital District of Papua New Guinea, with 102 townhouses in blocks of 3 to 7 units with 2 or 3 bedrooms each and 50 detached houses with 2 or 3 bedrooms.

The design, siting of buildings, and choice of building materials respond particularly well to the challenging hillside site, the tropical climate with an extended dry season and periods of intense tropical rains, and the increasing security requirements in the capital city of Papua New Guinea. Careful design and siting of buildings along the contours of the site's steep escarpments maximize natural ventilation and optimal views. Deep overhangs ensure sun control and protection from tropical rains. Shaded outdoor spaces and pedestrian circulation contribute to the comfort of the residents and correspond to the customary outdoor lifestyle. Vehicular access is limited to one ring road and great care was taken to maintain existing trees and ground cover. Treated timber walls blend harmoniously with the natural environment. Security measures are tastefully incorporated into the design. (Rahim B. Milani)

Reference:
Australian Architects: Rex Addison, Lindsay Clare & Russell Hall, Royal Australian Institute of Architects, Education Division, Manuka, A.C.T., 1990

4

4
Townhouse

5
Floor plans and sections of detached houses

6
sections of townhouses

Drawings and photographs courtesy of Russell Hall Architects

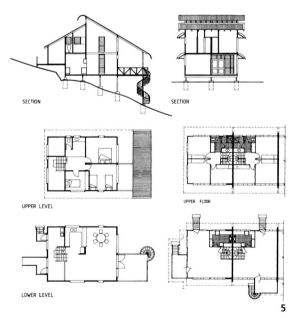

SECTION   SECTION

UPPER LEVEL   UPPER FLOOR

LOWER LEVEL

5

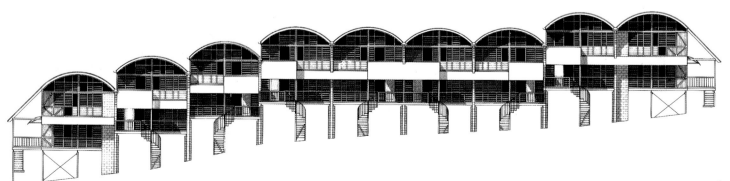

6

1980–1999

Jackson House

Location: Shoreham
Architect: Daryl Jackson
Years of Construction: 1979–1980

1

1
Hillside view
2
Site plan

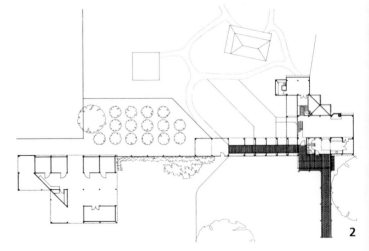

2

3
Interior

4
Garden

5
Axonometric view

Drawings and photographs
courtesy of the Architect

4

Daryl Jackson's family farm at Shoreham, Victoria, Australia on the Mornington Peninsular south of Melbourne is an interesting exercise in Australian 'bush carpentry' inspired by an existing vernacular farm building on the site and by reference to the angular cut wood forms of US architecture in the 1960s and 1970s. Out of this blending of sources Jackson designed a house and a barn building joined by an open timber pergola. Both of these structures have sloping corrugated metal roofs pitched to reflect the slope of the site. The house is clad in rough timber planks and the barn in the corrugated metal.

Internally the house ambles informally over four levels which have the generous dimensions of a barn. A series of lattice screens, which were common on the architect's other buildings of the time, shade the large areas of window glass. The Jackson house is an historically informed observance of the Australian vernacular architectural tradition and a contribution to the development of that tradition at the same time.
(Andrew Metcalf)

Award: National Timber in Architecture Award, 1982.

Reference:
Taylor, J., *Australian Architecture Since 1960.* Law Book Company, Sydney, 1986.

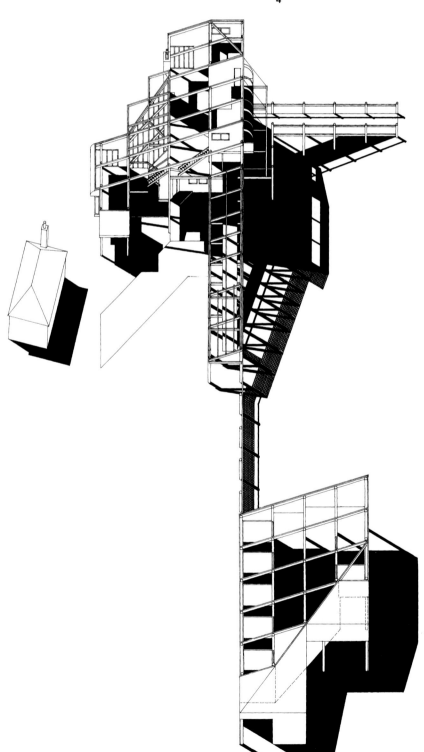

3

5

Nicholas and Carruthers Houses

Location: Mt. Irvine
Architect: Glenn Murcutt
Year of Completion: 1980

1

1
Exterior of Nicholas House

2
First plan

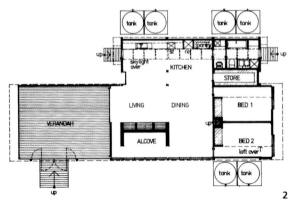

2

3

These two houses on a secluded mountain farm near Sydney are sited carefully to allow both contact and privacy in relation to each other and to foster an awareness of the genius of the site itself. The Mt Irvine houses testify to Glenn Murcutt's skill at adapting Australian archetypes–in this case the vernacular farm building and some received wisdom about climate control –to a contemporary programmme without sliding into parody or kitsch in the process.

Designed with a balance of open planned living areas and private bedrooms, and built using timber frames and cladding with a corrugated metal roof, the two houses induce us to think of the traditional house but, on balance, infer a future when low–impact buildings made from renewable materials will no doubt be more common than they were in the late 1970s when these houses were designed. They were an important keystone in Murcutt's career and the establishment of his international reputation. Within a dozen years of their completion he won the Alvar Aalto Medal.
(Andrew Metcalf)

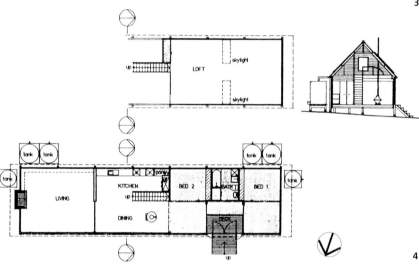

4

Award: Robin Boyd Award, 1981

Reference:
Metcalf. A., Flashing Forms of Corrugated Steel for Weekend Farmers, AIA Journal. August 1982, pp. 62–64.
Fromonot, F., Glenn Murcutt Works and Projects, Thames & Hudson, London, 1992.

5

3
Exterior of Carruthers House

4
Plan and section

5
Interior of Carruthers House

Drawings provided by the Image Library, and photographs by Max Dupain, by courtesy of the Architect

Raun Raun Theatre

Location: Goroka
Architect: Paul Frame of Frameworks Architects Pty.
Ltd., in association with Rex Addison
Engineer: John Ryder of Ove Arup and Partners
Pacific Pty. Ltd.
Year of Completion: 1982

1
Exterior

2
General plan

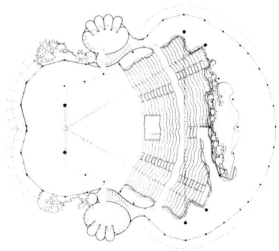

Raun Raun Theater, built in Goroka, Eastern Highlands Province of Papua New Guinea, is the home base of a touring theater group established by the National Cultural Council of Papua New Guinea to promote a national cultural identity. The theater building design draws on traditional architectural forms and materials, creating a welcoming environment for both village and urban audiences.

The distinctive roof form, a soaring pyramid of timber and *kunai* (swordgrass) thatch evokes strong connections with the typical Highlands round houses, though on a much larger scale. Spanning up to 20 meters and rising some 18 meters in height, the roof is supported by three intersecting parallel chord timber trusses as well as finer braces and ties.

No formal seats or flooring are used in the theater; instead tiers of timber posts driven into the ground follow the natural rise of the land and create seating on the compacted ground. The stage is at the lowest level, framed by the dominant elements of the roof and the floor. (Rahim B. Milani)

Award: PNG Institute of Architects Merit Award, 1986

3

3
The timber construction of the theatre

4
Interior

5
Longitudinal section

Drawings and photographs courtesy of the Architect

4

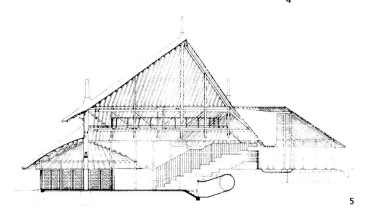

5

233

Yulara Tourist Resort

Location: Northern Territory, Australia
Architects: Philip Cox & Partners
Years of Construction: 1981–1984

1

1
Sail structure

2
Site plan (1. Resort rooms;
2. Resort 1 , Central facilities;
3. Visitor centre; 4. Flats and
mall; 5. Shopping square;
6. Tavern 7. Community Hall;
8. Resort 2, Central facilities;
9. Resort 2 rooms;
10. Detached houses;
11. School;
12. Police station; 13. Camp
grounds; 14. Camp control;
15. Service station;
16. Aboriginal housing)

2

3

Ayers Rock, 'Uluru', is a great geological monolith a thousand feet high in the center of Australia. To build a tourist resort near this mighty rock, which holds the double significance of being an item of geological uniqueness and an icon of aboriginal legend, requires some bravado and much sensitivity. Uluru is the prime object of attention.This resort, 'Yulara', is far enough away not to defile Uluru and close enough to be able to see it across the relentless landscape of red earth and spinifex. Actually a small village, the planning spine wanders loosely across the plain, with short axial vistas and a sequence of defined public outdoor gathering places, all accessed via shaded pedestrian routes. The buildings and spaces provide relief from the severe climate and terse natural domain, but in color and organization do not ignore it–the sense of adjacent harshness, just beyond the artifice, is always evident. The resort is also an early attempt at using ecologically sustainable principles, with banks of solar collectors, double skin roofs, fabric shades to shelter outdoor places and an on–site sewage treatment plant. Construction is steel roof framing on load bearing concrete block, bagged and washed with the desert sand.
(Neville Quarry)

Awards: BHP Australian Steel Award, 1985
Tracey Memorial Award, RAIA NT Chapter, 1985
Sir Zelman Cowen Award, RAIA, 1985.

Reference:
Quarry, N. *Award Winning Australian Architecture*. Craftsman House, Sydney, Australia 1997
Dobney, Stephen (ed.). *Cox Architects. Selected and Current Works*. The Images Publishing Group, Mulgrave, Australia, 1994.

4

3
Aerial view from northwest with Ayers Rock in background

4
View of the Complex

5
Main entrance to the Visitors' Center

5

6
Sail structure

6

236

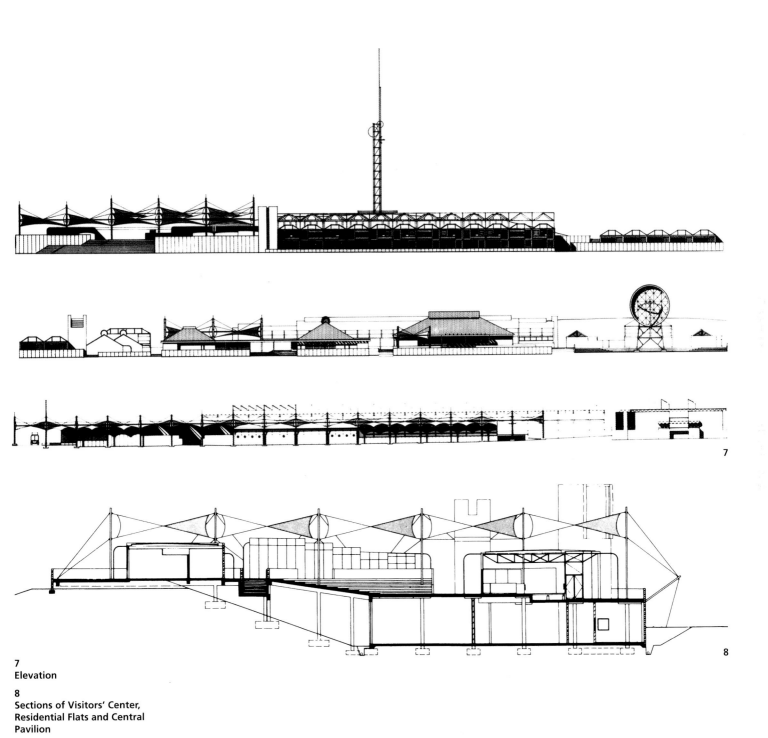

7
Elevation

8
**Sections of Visitors' Center,
Residential Flats and Central
Pavilion**

Drawings and photographs
Courtesy of the Architect

Papua New Guinea National Parliament Building

Location: Waigani
Architect: Cecil Hogan, then of PNG Department of Works and Supply, and Peddle Thorp PNG Pty. Ltd.
Year of Completion: 1984

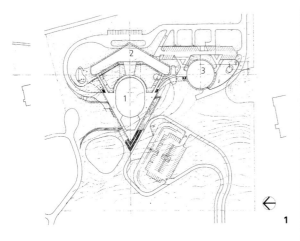

1
Site plan (1. Block A; 2. Block B;
3. Block C)
(courtesy of Rahim Milani)

2
Exterior view of the
Parliament Building
(courtesy of Rahim Milani)

Traditional designs, indigenous art forms and native timbers of Papua New Guinea are carefully integrated into the design of the National Parliament Building(floor area: 20,000m²) located in Waigani, Nationalí Capital District of Papua New Guinea.

The complex is comprised of three separate buildings under a single expansive roof, some two hectares in area, which is reminiscent of the monumental roof style of traditional spirit houses (*Haus Tambaran*) of the Sepik River area of Papua New Guinea.

The first building encompasses the Grand Hall, the Parliament Chamber and the Gallery. Leading into the Grand Hall one passes under a huge triangular entrance facade, ornamented with mosaics constructed by local Papua New Guinean craftsmen, again inspired by the *Haus Tambaran*. Inside, the Grand Hall is adorned with finely carved poles and walls made of rosewood carved with designs representative of different provinces of Papua New Guinea. Also within this first building in the complex is a huge ceiling mural overlooking both the Parliament Chamber and the Gallery.

A separate building houses the Prime Minister's suites and administrative offices.

Recreational areas are modeled on the traditional highlands roundhouses of Papua New Guinea. Facilities include dining rooms for parliament members and their guests, a swimming pool, barbecue area, squash courts, sauna, staff cafeteria and theater. (Rahim B. Milani)

Reference:
Destination Papua New Guinea, produced and copyright by Destination Papua New Guinea Pty. Ltd., Port Moresby, Papua New Guinea, pp. 26–27, 1995.
Briggs, Mike. *Parliament House Papua New Guinea*. Independent Books (P.O. Box 168, Port Moresby, PNG) 1989.

3

3
View from above

4
Exterior view of the Parliament Building (courtesy Rahim Milani)

5
Floor plan (courtesy of Rahim Milani) Architect's concept sketches

4

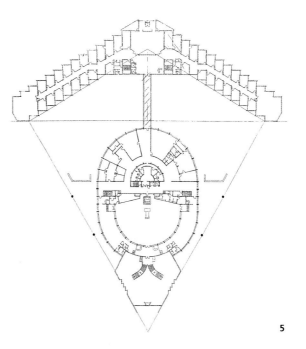

5

6
Interior

7

7
C block

8
Speaker's Chair and carvings above

9
Detail from carved lintel above main door

All photographs (unless specified) taken from Mike Briggs' *Parliament House Papua New Guinea*, 1989 courtesy of the Independent Group Ltd, Port Moresby, (Photographer: Rocky Roe Photographics) by kind permission of the Papua New Guinea National Parliament

8

9

241

Riverside Center

Location: Brisbane
Architect: Harry Seidler
Years of Construction: 1983–1986

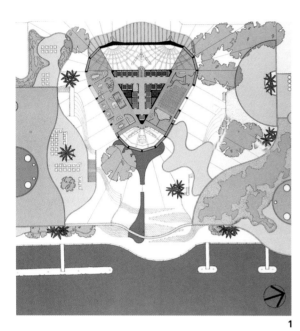

1

1
Plaza plan

2
Aerial view from the east
above the river

2

Brisbane's Riverside Center, at one end of the sub–tropical city's central business district, occupies a two hectare site on the banks of the Brisbane River and is home to the Stock Exchange and 40 floors of office space.

By dent of its carefully considered triangular plan, two thirds of the building's windows share views up and down the river. The other major architectural determinant is sun control: it takes the form of fixed aluminum awnings across the head of each window on the north and west facades, whilst the shady south facade has no protection at all, revealing the grey Sardinian granite cladding of the tower. At street level a site plan, which evokes the curvilinear landscape compositions of the Brazilian landscape architect Roberto Burle Marx, is arranged to include an amenable environment with changes of level, retail, terraces, fountains, landscaping and a ferry terminal. From an urban design standpoint, Seidler's Riverside project showed the way for the extensive regeneration of the Brisbane River banks which followed.

With its clever, rational planning, natural sun control and sophisticated construction, Riverside Center is one of several late 20th century Seidler commercial projects that have set a framework for commercial architecture in the region. (Andrew Metcalf)

Reference:
Riverside Centre , *Constructional Review,* Vol 61 No 1, February 1988. Frampton, K. and Drew, P., *Harry Seidler – Four Decades of Architecture.* Thames & Hudson, London, 1994.

3
Tower floor structure
4
Section through base of Tower and Plaza

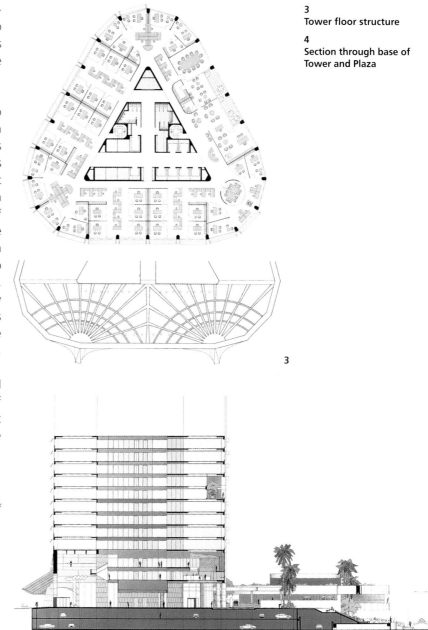

3

4

5
Lobby space
surrounding the core
showing the sculpture

6

7

6
View of the Plaza and waterfront promenade from top of the Tower

7
Looking through the Lobby sculpture at ceiling rib

Photographs by John Gollings. Drawings and photographs courtesy of the Architect

245

Parliament House of Australia

Location: Canberra
Architects: Mitchell/Giurgola & Thorp
Years of Construction:1981–1988

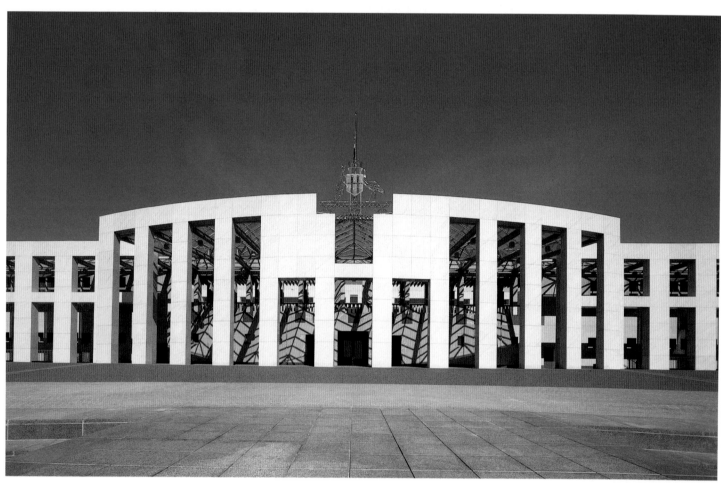

1

1
The Great Verandah and public entry to Parliament House, where the monumental rhythm of the white marble–clad piers forms the backdrop to the open, sun–drenched, red–granite–paved public forecourt to the building.

2
Parti diagram

3
The Australian Coat of Arms at the Public Entry to Parliament House, specially designed and fabricated in tubular stainless steel by Australian sculptor Robin Blau, working in close collaboration with the architectural design team.

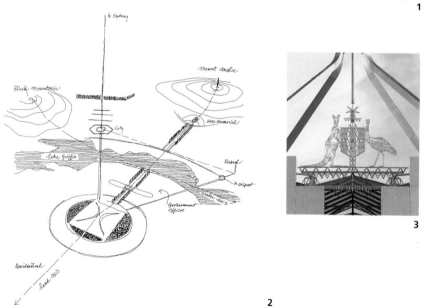

3

2

246

The architects were chosen in 1980 by an international competition and their initial design concepts–a cross axial plan within a circle, overlaid by two complimentarily–curving stepped walls to define a low ziggurat cross section–survived the intricate brief development and the constructional realities. The Capital Hill location was envisaged by Walter Burley Griffin, who produced the original master plan for Canberra, as a people's place, to be more dominant than the parliamentary buildings. The Mitchell/Giurgola Thorp design is characterized by a great grass–ramped roof, accessible to the public. Above the summit, the national flag is borne upon huge stainless steel quadripod legs. The roof form is held between grand curving stone walls, which subtend four enclosures of accommodation–one for each parliamentary chamber, another for politiciansí special access, the fourth for the public entrance, great verandah and forecourt. Thus the hierarchical symbolism is established: national emblem surmounting the populace, who are in turn, underpinned by their elected representatives. The interiors, particularly the Senate and the House of Representatives, show meticulous craftsmanship, carefully considered materials and finishes and sensitive incorporation of art works purposely made for locations within the building complex. (Neville Quarry)

Award: Sir Zelman Cowen Award, RAIA 1989

References:
Quarry, N. *Award Winning Australian Architecture*, Craftsman House, Sydney 1997
Jahn, Graham. *Contemporary Australian Architecture*. G+B Arts International, Switzerland, 1994

4
View to the north along the Land Axis from the Public Entry, Parliament House, with the Provisional Parliament House (completed in 1927) and the War Memorial (completed in 1941) visible along the wide panorama characterizing the city's central urban design axis.

5
Landscape/ground floor plan

6
Site elevation from Lake Burley Griffin, competition stage

4

5

6

7

7
Looking north within the Parliament House's Great Verandah, where natural finishes in timeless materials such as granite, marble, precast concrete, and bronze were utilized in keeping with the Parliament's brief for a 200–year minimum lifespan.

8
The Public Foyer, entered from the building's forecourt, is the first monumental interior space at Parliament House; accessed by means of the monumental stairs and lifts is provided to the first floor, where the public has free passage throughout the major spaces of the building.

8

9
In the House Chamber at Parliament House, open public galleries for spectators form an essential part of the Chamber's space at the first floor level, while glazed sound-proof galleries at the second floor allow teachers to explain the proceedings to visiting schoolchildren, or for voice-over translation to be provided to visiting delegations.

10
The Senate Chamber at Parliament House, whose rich, vibrant red-ochre tones were part of the Architect's design in modulating the traditional British colors of the two Houses of Parliament to the natural colors inherent in the Australian landscape. Movable louvers in the skylight, which are operable both manually and automatically, allow the enlivening qualities of changing natural light to enter the Chamber.

11
The Great Hall in Parliament House was created to accommodate Parliamentary dinners, formal functions, and other State occasions, and can seat over 700 people for banquets. A monumental tapestry designed by Australian painter Arthur Boyd for the hall in collaboration with the Architect and hand-woven by Victorian Tapestry Workshop in Melbourne creates the visual focus on the speaker's dais at the south end of the room.

All photographs taken by John Gollings. Drawings, photographs and captions courtesy of the Architect

9

10

11

Sydney Football Stadium

Location: Sydney
Architects: Cox, Richardson & Taylor
Years of Construction: 1985–1988

1

1
Aerial view

2
Site plan (1. Sports stadium;
2. Tennis courts; 3. Swimming
pool; 4. Practice field; 5.Practice
cricket nets; 6. On-groun carpark;
7. Entry; 8.Exit; 9. S. C. G. Entry/
Exit)

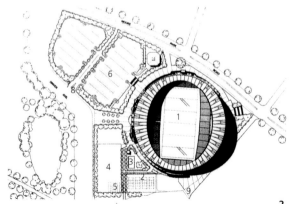

2

Encompassing a rectangular playing field, over the concrete framed grandstands of the Sydney Football Stadium the perimeter roof is steel framed, propped and cable stayed, forming an elliptical band which soars and dips with quiet sculptural vivacity. The sensuous rationale of its shape and variable width (30 meters at the halfway line where most people like to congregate, to 10 meters at the goal ends) was generated partly in response to the sightlines and preferences (increased seating towards the middle of the field) of the spectators, and as an effort to keep the scale low in the suburban neighborhood. Television aerial shots at night are breathtaking and by day the swooping roof gives lively promise of the sport spectacles that are about to be encountered within. The Stadium holds 40,000 spectators, with 25,000 under cover. Floors are concrete framed, superstructure steel. The Stadium was designed for Rugby League play, but Rugby Union and soccer also utilize the arena.
(Neville Quarry)

Award: Engineering Excellence Award 1988

References:
Dobney, Stephen (ed.). *Cox Architects. Selected and Current Works.* The Images Publishing Group, Mulgrave, Australia, 1994.
Jahn, Graham. *Contemporary Australian Architecture.* G+B Arts International, Switzerland, 1994

3
Roof structure

4
Real view of stand

5
Section

6
Computer designed elevation

Photographs by Patrick Bingham–Hall. Drawing and photographs courtesy of Cox, Richardson & Taylor

3

4

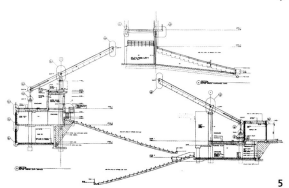

5

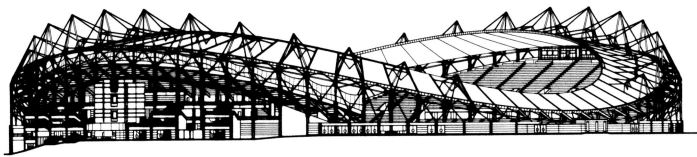

6

Brambuk Living Cultural Centre

Location: Halls Gap
Architect: Gregory Burgess
Years of Design: 1986–1988
Year of Completion: 1990

1

1
Interior
2
Site plan

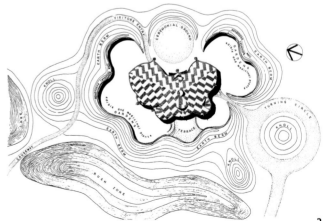

2

Located within the Grampians National Park in Western Victoria, Australia, the Brambuk Living Cultural Centre is an Aboriginal owned and managed facility that provides historic and contemporary insight into the Aboriginal people and culture of Victoria. Designed by Melbourne architect Gregory Burgess (1945–) in close consultation with local Aboriginal groups, the center is part museum, part meeting place and part information center. With its roof form suggesting an Emperor Moth or a White Cockatoo ('Brambuk' in local dialect) as well as the mound and hut shelters once typical of Aboriginal structures in Western Victoria, the building sits within curved dance and garden enclosures formed by earth berms. The building's plan contains similarly curved spaces formed by overlapping geometries and at the center there is a massive brick and stone chimney. A kidney–shaped ramp snakes its way behind this chimney and around a shop leading upwards to a first floor cafe. There are views to the peak on the other side of the valley providing yet another evocation of the undulating form of the center's striped corrugated iron roof. The base walls are of local sandstone and the vertebral roof structure is organized about a massive laminated timber beam, the giant spine of this almost living piece of architecture. (Phillip James Goad)

Award: Sir Zelman Cowen National RAIA Award (1990); and RAIA (Victorian Chapter) Award-Institutional Buildings Category (1990).

3

3
Exterior

4
Interior

5
Sections

Drawings and photographs courtesy of the Architect

4

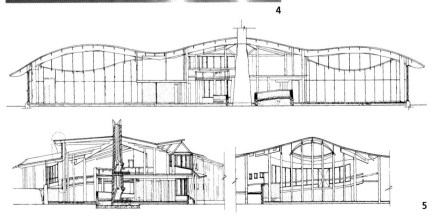

5

Beach House

Location: St Andrews Beach
Architect: Nonda Katsalidis
Year of Completion: 1991

1

1
Exterior elevation of
the bedroom wing

2
Floor plan

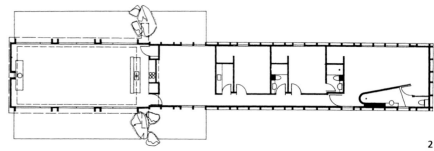

2

The beach house Nonda Katsalidis built for himself in the early 1990s in the dunes at St Andrews Beach, Victoria, Australia, is notable for a rhetorical use of archetypes, powerful binary oppositions and raw materials. The house sealed "Katsaldis' reputation as one of Australia's leading designers at the end of the century."

An elongated plan of Georgian simplicity and Miesian directness apportions dwelling space into separate living and sleeping compartments which are infused differently with distinct forms and materials. The bedrooms are housed in a modest wooden "crate" that appears like flotsam on the sand, and the living spaces are located in a taller, glass walled and steel roofed pavilion which suggests an instrument–such as a camera–obscura–for viewing the landscape.

Rusting steel panels, unfinished hardwood planks, large rocks and a sand terrace levelled out of the dune itself seem instantly old and already accelerated into the weathered condition any material would eventually depict on such an exposed seaside. (Andrew Metcalf)

Award: Robin Boyd Award (Commendation), 1992

References:
Two Beach Houses,*Architecture Australia*, May/June 1992, pp 38–41.
St. Andrews Beach House,*Domus,* April 1996, pp 36–39.

3

3
Exterior view of the Beach House

4
Detail of junction between living areas and the bedroom wing

5
Elevation

6
Sectional perspective

Drawings and photographs courtesy of the Architect

4

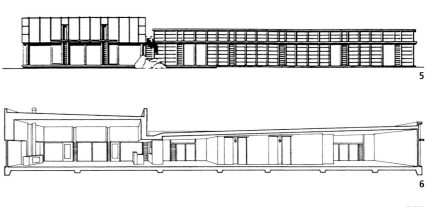

5

6

Parliament of Fiji

Location: Suva
Architect: Vitia Architects and Fijian Government Architects
Year of Completion: 1992

1

1
Parliament House entrance

2
Master plan
(courtesy of Vitia Architects)

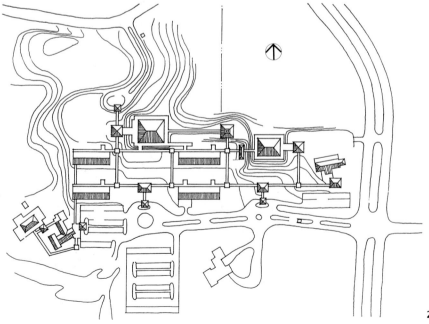

2

The Parliament of Fiji was completed in 1992 just before an election and, with its celebration of Fijian traditions, it clearly reflects the Government's policy of reinforcing the indigenous culture within this multicultural community. The complex is located on elevated ground overlooking, and symbolically linking, the sea on one side and the land on the other. The site planning is intended to relate to that of a traditional village with an arrangement of buildings around courtyards and linked by landscaping and covered walkways.

The office buildings are narrow, of low scale and conventional design, and naturally lit and ventilated with walkways for shading on the north side. Landscaping has been specifically designed for its shading properties. The composition is focused on the landmark of the Parliament House, the Vale ni Bose Lawa, which is elevated on a stone base serving as the traditional "yavu". The building is based on the "bure kalou" with a dominating shingle–clad steeply pitched roof. In the interior round concrete columns refer to timber poles, and furniture is of craft production. Decoration comes primarily from "lalawa–magimagi" weaving, pennants of bark cloth, and "masi" (tapa cloth). (Jennifer Taylor)

References:
Ansell, Rob, Cultural confidence in Fijian architecture. *Architecture New Zealand*, September/October, 1992, pp.68–69
Fiji: Our National Heritage: Parliament of Fiji, (poster produced by Justin Francis), Department of Town and Country Planning and the Ministry for Commerce, Industry and Tourism, Fiji, c.1992

3

4

5

3
Ramped covered linkways

4
Aerial view

5
Interior: Parliament Chambers

All photographs taken from Parliament of Fiji poster (Photographer: Justin Francis) produced by Justin Francis for the Department of Town and County Planning and the Ministry for Commerce, Industry and Tourism, Fiji, by kind permission of the Parliament of Fiji.

Great Southern Stand, Melbourne Cricket Ground

Location: Melbourne
Architects: Tompkins Shaw & Evans/Daryl Jackson Pty Ltd
Years of Design/Construction: 1989–1990/1990–1992

1

1
Arrival

2
Design sketch: section
through Grandstand

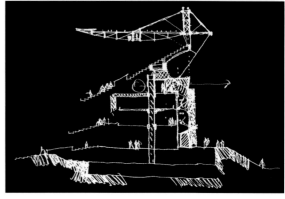

2

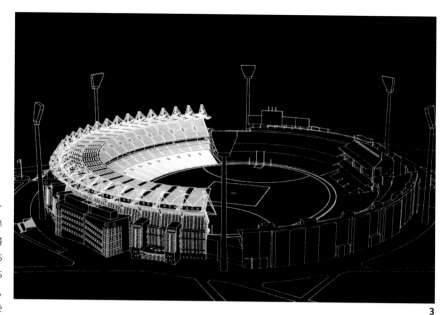

Built to replace the 1937 Southern Stand of the world-famous Melbourne Cricket Ground, the Great Southern Stand is a grandstand of three upper galleries housing 46,500 spectators. A total of 60,000 spectators is accommodated within its precinct which also includes seven restaurants, twenty-five bars and food outlets, seventy-five sponsor suites, offices, four team change rooms and parking for 250 cars. Externally the articulation of spectator movement by inclined ramps with lines of porthole windows and angled glazed stair bays is crowned by a dramatic half-ring of steel roof stays, masts and cantilever truss supports for the grandstand roof recalling the kinetic engineering aesthetic of Constructivist stadia designs of the 1920's. Each of the elevated seating galleries has uninterrupted column-free views with corporate boxes stacked neatly between and above the two lower level galleries. Unprotected steel box girders cantilever to support the upper galleries and provide a full length sloping support to the top gallery. These girders carry pre-stressed concrete seating plats and the concrete frames beneath are connected longitudinally with precast post-tensioned beams. The vigorous and structurally expressive design reflects the involvement of Daryl Jackson [1937-] renowned in Australia for his expertise in sporting structures and stadium design. Described by awards juries as heroic, the Great Southern Stand is a monument to Australia's love of sport and to a local tradition of structural expressionism.(Phillip James Goad)

Award: Sir Zelman Cowen National RAIA Award 1992
RAIA Victorian Architecture Medal 1992
RAIA (Victorian Chapter) Award- Institutional Buildings Category, 1992

Reference:

MCG Southern Stand, *Architect*, July 1992, pp16-17.
Jackson Daryl, *Daryl Jackson: selected and Current Works*, Images Publishing, Mulgrave, Victoria, 1996.

3

3
Axonometric view

4
Top deck

5
Circulation ramps

Drawings and photographs courtesy of Daryl Jackson Pty. Ltd.

4

5

Governor Phillip and Governor Macquarie Towers

Location: Sydney
Architect: Denton Corker Marshall
Year of Completion: 1994

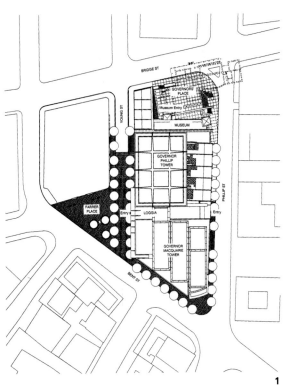

1

1
Site plan

2
Governor Phillip Tower
foyer

3
Exterior view of the
Governor Phillip Tower

2

3

Governor Phillip Tower is built over the site of Australia's first official government residence and is a neighbor to a group of Victorian terraces. In order to clear these historical objects the tower's first office floor is 40 meters above the street. A stone–lined and glass–roofed lobby is created in this tall space. Inside, a pervasive gridding and paneling breaks these monumental surfaces down into smaller units of visual information so that the giant scale is overlain with a smaller, manageable one.

The tower makes a distinctive profile on Sydney's skyline, particularly at night. Its facade is also made up of a gridded system using polished black granite, glass panels and stainless steel fins and inlays. Such careful integration of different scales, the expression of structure and industrialized building plus the resolution of the many difficult issues at street level make Denton Corker and Marshall's tower a paradigm of architecture and urbanism. (Andrew Metcalf)

Award: Sulman Medal, 1994

Note: The two towers were parts of one development and built at the same time. Governor Phillip Tower was the first stage of the development and was awarded the Sulman Medal on its own merits even though the whole developments was not completed at the time. Governor Macquarie Tower was completed within the same year. (Susan Clarke)

5

References:
Thomas, B. and McClelland, N., 'Governor Phillip Tower, Sydney', *Arup Journal,* 3/1994, pp. 15–18.
(Australian Architects Series) *Denton Corker Marshall.* RAIA, Canberra, 1988.

4
Entrance to Governor Phillip Tower
5
Governor Macquarie Tower
6
Section of Governor Phillip Tower

Photographs by John Gollings. Drawings and photographs courtesy of the Architect

4

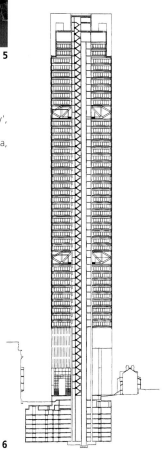

6

Headquarters for the South Pacific Commission

Location: Anse Vata, Noumea
Architect: Architects Pacific
Years of Construction: 1993–1994

1

1
Southern elevation of the
Conference Center

2
Site plan

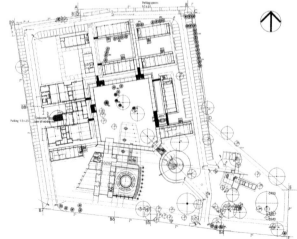

2

The 1992 competition for the Headquarters for the South Pacific Commission in Noumea, New Caledonia was won by Architects Pacific with an imaginative, practical and symbolic proposal conceived around a Micronesian navigational chart seen as representing communication, knowledge and culture and so serving as a fitting symbol for the activities of the Commission, and the Pacific Islands in general. Further nautical metaphors can be found in the roof forms, referring to canoes, and in the timber joinery employing traditional canoe building techniques. Flora from the various Pacific islands forms a critical part in unifying the composition and making reference to the paths of the navigators.

The principal building consists of the Conference Center and the elevated library which provides cover for an open gathering space below. In the Conference Center large vertical louvers of 'masi' tapa cloth control light, and external reflecting pools bring patterned light to the interior making further metaphoric statements about the ocean location. The Pacific theme continues with a stitched coconut wood wall and Kohu wood from the Solomon Islands and Vanuatu lining the ceiling.

The site–planning provides for a vertical ring road with landscaped parking bays between the buildings, and serviced by an inner circulation tier of a double height walkway enclosing a central open space. The individual buildings are narrow for cross–ventilation, with the long sides to the north and south and provide open–sided access along one edge. (Jennifer Taylor)

References:
Keith-Reid, Robert, "The Best Little Boathouse In Noumea", *Islands Business*, Vol.21, No. 12, December 1995, pp.36-27
"Pacific Metaphor for Headquarters", *Architecture New Zealand*, November/ December 1992, pp.22-23

3

3
East–west elevation of the Conference Center

4
Exterior view from north

5
Conference Center floor plan

Drawings and photographs courtesy of the Architect

4

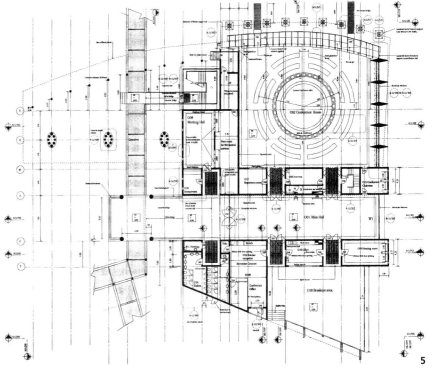

5

Melbourne Exhibition Centre

Location: Melbourne
Architects: Denton Corker Marshall
Years of Design/Construction: 1995/1995–1996

1

1
Aerial view
2
Entrance

2

Designed for temporary commercial exhibitions, the Melbourne Exhibition Centre is a dramatic linear building containing all–purpose large span spaces gained by a structural system of giant curved steel–framed bow–trusses. With a cross–section that resembles a modern airport with carparking underneath and multiple entry points along a linear circulation spine, the center has Melbourne's Yarra River as its giant urban tarmac. Instead of a transit hall, the exhibition area –as either one large flexible space of 30,000 m^2 or subdivided into a series of smaller exhibition halls–owes its internal inspiration to the artificially–lit black–box spaces of the art gallery. Instead of the exhibition building as naturally–lit specimen glass–house, it is endowed with the status of hangar–as–gallery. On the river side of the building a glazed verandah acts as circulation spine running for over half a kilometer with a generous expanse of landscaped foreground before the river and the visual counterpoint of a historic 19th century baroque. A forest of stick–like steel columns supports this verandah's gently curved roof. Internally and externally, the building is clad in thin veneers of grey, silver and black metallic and fiber–cement panels evocative of the sheath–like cladding of aircraft. The aerofoil edge to the building's eaves reinforces this reference. At its eastern end, a giant angled blade announces the building's presence on the riverbank–a giant signpost to the gleaming shed that emerges from a disparate collection of box forms concealing the concrete frame of an unfinished building beneath. (Phillip James Goad)

Award: Sir Zelman Cowen National RAIA Award 1996 Sir Osborn McCutcheon RAIA (Victorian Chapter) Award– Commercial Buildings Category, 1996

References:
Denton Corker Marshall: "Ehibition Centre, Melbourne"and Philip Goad: "Reinventing Typologies: the Melbourne Exhibition Centre" *UME 2*,1996,pp 18–27 & 28–29.
"Exhibit One: the Melbourne Exhibition Centre" *Architecture Australia*, May/June 1996, pp46–51.

3

3
Interior

4
Interior

5
Floor plan

6
North–South section

Photographs by John Gollings. Drawings and photographs courtesy of the Architect

4

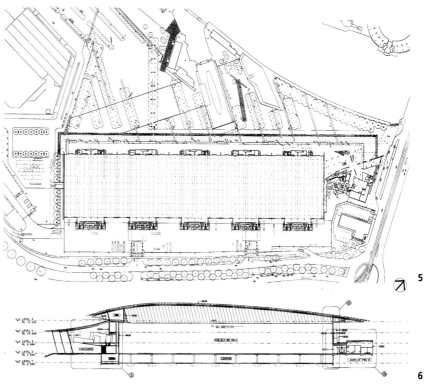

5

6

Pugh House

Location: Wellington
Architect: Melling: Morse Architects
Years of Design/Construction: 1995/1995–1996

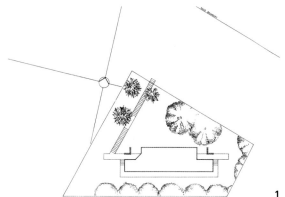

1

1
Site plan

2
Exterior view

3
Ground floor plan

4
First floor plan

2

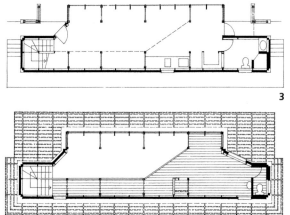

3

4

The Pugh House, wedged securely into the slope of a hill behind mature stands of cypress trees and native bush, reveals itself only in glimpses. It is two-storied but only one-bedroomed and, built to a rigorously tight budget, is necessarily small in area. The house is a narrow rectangle in plan. Its north wall is completely glazed and its roof, flat, giving it the appearance of a giant speaker-box and providing a sharp contrast to the restless hips and gables of its suburban neighbors. The client's distaste for sheet lining materials provided the inspiration to expose every component of the timber framing internally. The frames are repeated externally at either end of the house, the exterior members distinguished from the interior ones by weathering. The exterior framing also serves to identify the two entrances to the house, located as they are at either end. Recycled timber doors provide access to an open living space with a double-height ceiling. A mezzanine sleeping loft at one end is accessed by a staircase at the other. A narrow gallery links the two. Whilst the house carries no overt Polynesian signals, it offers the gift of human identity and the calm of deep consideration.
(Russell Walden/Julia Gatley)

Reference:
Walden, Russell, *Manufactured Trees: The Bronwyn Pugh House*, Forthcoming book.

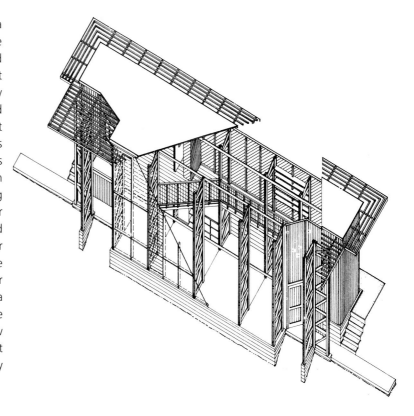

5

5
Axonometric view from northwest

6
Interior

Drawings and photographs courtesy of the Architects

6

Jean-Marie Tjibaou Cultural Centre

Location: Noumea
Architect: Renzo Piano Workshop
Year of Completion: 1998

1

1
Exterior view from the sea
2
Site plan

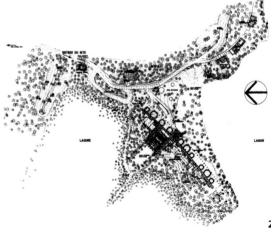

2

The Jean Marie Tjibaou Cultural Centre in Noumea, New Caledonia, is a potent gesture from the French Government to the Karnak people. The project pays homage to Jean Marie Tjibaou, the Karnak pro–independence leader who was assassinated during the conflicts of the 1980s. An outcome of the Matigon Accord for Peace was the proposal to conduct an international competition for the building of a cultural center.

The Italian architect, Renzo Piano, was one of the 170 entrants to the competition. Renzo Piano is renown not only for the innovative qualities of his buildings which often incorporate a technical response to environmental concerns, but also for the exhaustive studies which form the basis of his work. In preparing for the competition and in developing his winning scheme, he worked closely with Alban Bensa, eminent anthropologist and specialist in the culture of the South Pacific. Through this collaboration he was able to draw upon the indigenous culture and provide new directions for cultural expression.

The building form has a particularly strong and moving relationship to its site. It responds to the peninsula location by turning its back to the strong winds and rough sea and opening itself up to the gentleness of the protected lagoon. A succession of three groups of 'houses' address the main circulation spine and open onto gardens which are rich in character. His use of modern technology to extend traditional forms produces an environment with plays of shadow and light, captured gentle breezes and a natural, organic sense. Pianos understanding of the site characteristics, position and climate, the potential of materials and technology, and the marriage between past and future give birth to a new model for Pacific architecture.

This building, which grew from a complex and passionate political background, responds to the issues and context in a deeply meaningful way. The buildings significance lies in the provision of a strong symbol of peace, the affirmation of Karnak culture and the opening of doors for future developments. (Deborah Dearing)

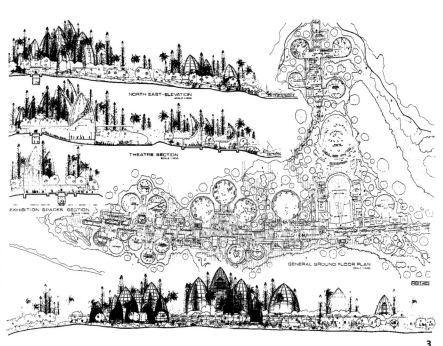

3

3
Ground floor plan and sections

4
Village 1: Reception, Exposition, Cafeteria and Spectacle

5
Village 2: media, offices

6
Village 3: Thematic workshops (music, dance, patrimonies)

Dr. Deborah Dearing is the Director of Urban Design Advisory Service, Pymont, NSW, Australia

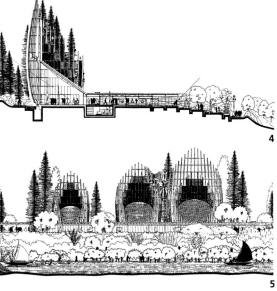

4

5

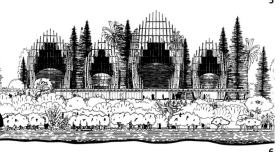

6

7

7
Aerial view

8
Typical section

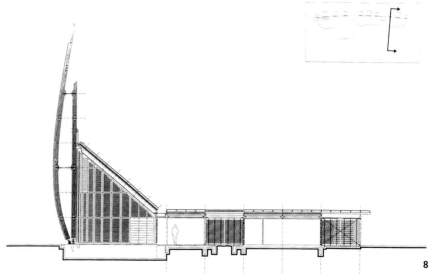

8

9

9
Exterior view from the sea

10
The Shield

11
Indigenous houses

All drawing and photographs
courtesy of the Arcthitect. All
photographs by John Gollings.

10

11

Nominators' Statements

Southeast Asia

Chen Voon Fee
Richard K. F. Ho
Sumet Jumsai
Duangrit Bunnag
Francisco "Bobby" Mañosa
Yuswadi Saliya
Brian Brace Taylor

Oceania

Phillip James Goad
Andrew Metcalf
Rahim B. Milani
Neville Quarry
Russell Walden
Julia Gatley

SOUTHEAST ASIA

Chen Voon Fee

Mr. Chen Voon Fee, A.A. Dipl., A.P.A.M., specialized in architectural research, writing and documentation and conservation planning and development. He had been in private practice in partnerships from 1960–1970s, and in a 1-man consultancy firm since 1982. His design projects include: Singapore Conference Hall/Trade Union Congress (1961–63), Negeri Sembilan State Mosque (1963–67), Perak Turf Club sports Club (1965–68), Geology Building (1966–68) and Faculty of Arts Extension (1969–71) of the University of Malaya and the Great Hall, Library & Lecture Halls, University Science Malaysia, Penang (1972–78).

He co-founded Malaysia's conservation group: The Heritage of Malaysia Trust in 1982, was its Council Member and Deputy President till 1995. He was awarded PAM Jurors Prize for Conservation of Bamboo House, Kuala Kansar in 1995. His other conservation/adaptive re-use projects include: Central Market & Central Square (with William Lim Associates), Creative Centre, National Art Gallery (1987–98) and ex Anglo-Oriental Building to Mahkota College (1986–88), all winning different awards. He was Architectural Consultant to National Museum and Selangor State Museum on conservation projects in 1990s.

He was Editor of *Architecture, Encyclopedia of Malaysia* and Writer of *Kuala Lumpur – A Sketchbook* (with Artist Chin Kon Yit).

He also taught in the University of Strathclyde, Dept. of Architecture & Building Science (4th year lecturer) 1971–72, and University Technology Malaysia, Faculty of Built Environment (External Tutor and Examiner) 1970–80s.

Nomination Criteria

Outstanding examples of: the vernacular architecture in timber construction and rich craft tradition; of imported architectural styles from both East and West showing creative interpretation and adaptation to local climate, materials and building technology; of the application of Modern styles from the International Style to contemporary architectural trends showing innovation, successful adaptation to local conditions and expressions of different stages of the country's history and development.

The nominations were considered significant built expressions of the country's traditions, cultural diversity, nationalism and modern aspirations.

Richard K. F. Ho

Born in 1956, he graduated from the National   University of Singapore in 1981 with Honors. He then worked with William Lim (Singapore) and Kerry Hill (Singapore) before venturing to Austria in 1985 where he worked with Helmut Schimek. In 1989, he moved to Milan where he worked with Aldo Rossi. He returned to Singapore in November 1991 and set up his own studio, which won the Singapore Institute of

Architects Design Award in 1995.

Besides practicing architecture, Richard Ho is also Adjunct Senior Lecturer in the Master of Architecture course at the National University of Singapore. He is one of the Asian visual artists, film directors and architects invited to exhibit his works at the "Cities on the Move" exhibition at the Secession Museum in Vienna in November 1997, which has since moved to Bordeaux, France and New York City, USA.

Sumet Jumsai

Dr. Sumet Jumsai is a faculty member at the Department of Architecture at Cambridge University where he was a student and where he also taught briefly. His works have appeared in various international publications and exhibitions, including the Venice Biennale 1996. He is possibly known best for the design of the Robot Building in Bangkok (1986) which is selected by the Museum of Contemporary Art, Los Angeles as one of the 50 seminal buildings of the century, and which forms part of the Museum's permanent collection after a world-wide traveling exhibition beginning in 1998 called "End of the Century".

He is also painter, social worker, conservationist and author. His best known book *NAGA*, Oxford University Press, 1988, deals with the origin of civilization in the Asia-Pacific Region.

Duangrit Bunnag

Graduated with Honor from the Faculty of Architecture, Chulalongkorn University, Bangkok in 1989, he further studied in the School of Architecture, University of Southern California in Los Angeles in 1989 and the Architectural Association School of Architecture in London with GradDiplDes-AA in 1995. He worked in ARCHITECTS 49 LIMITED since 1989 and became its Senior Architect 1995-96 and Junior Associate in 1996. He is presently Director of Duangrit Bunnag Architect limited partnership, Bangkok and Editor of the art4d magazine where he has published many articles and papers .

He has been involved in many project designs, city planning, competition, project management as well as design collaboration with foreign architects. In 1990 he won a second place award in the ASA Experimental Design Bangkok in the Next Decade.

He has also been thesis adviser and studio critic at the Chulalongkorn University, gaveing and host lectures at various universities.

Nomination Criteria

The nomination is, somehow, similar to the selection of proper species for Noah's Ark of architecture. It is a commission requiring the more logical sense of preservation and conservation rather than personal attitude of nominator towards each project. The selection was considered as the best representatives from each period of decades that mark the great shift of architectural development of their time. More or less like the selection of best samples of their species or breeds to join the eternal trip on the biggest ark of architecture ever.

Some of the projects are not the best samples of good design from architectural aspect, but did make a polemic statement in the region and move the architectural development of the region to the next level. Some very well recognized at their time, but surprisingly remembered by generations of architects later. Among those, most of them are the best of projects had not been kind and widely respected as masterpiece architecture of the period, both by architects and other academics. A wide range of criteria produced an interesting wide range of nomination and selection that might effect architecture of newer generations, millenniums to come.

Francisco "Bobby" Mañosa

Born in 1931, he studied at the University of Santo Tomas in Manila where he completed his Bachelor of Architecture in 1953. Named as one of the seven visionary architects in Asia by Asiaweek in 1982, he has led the move in Philippines the towards the development of a Philippine architectural identity and has been consistent in this pursuit throughout his practice. He is well known for his work in the Tahanan Philipino, also known as the Coconut Palaces which explored the use of indigenous architecture and form as well as the design of the San Miguel Building, which he worked on with his brothers.

He is Honorary Fellow of the Philippine Institute of Architects and Fellow of United Architects of the Philippines. He was awarded Most Outstanding Professional of the Year by the Philippine Regulation Commission in 1994; First Recipient of Golden Award in the Field of Philippine Architecture by the United Architects of the Philippines in 1989; chosen as one of the Seven Visionary Architects of Asia by the Asia Week Magazine in 1983, and awarded Knight of the Order of St. Gregory by Pope Paul II in 1982.

Nomination Criteria

The criteria for the selection of the structures to represent Philippine architecture was based on the structure's ability to express a character that is uniquely Filipino. The structures represent a combination, adaptation or creation of an architecture that can be identified predominantly as Filipino. In the early structures, those built between 1900 to 1940, the architecture can be seen as a combination of colonial, classical architecture with the castilian and native (Bahay Kubo) house. This character changed in the succeeding buildings that are a willful adaptation of western styles with local motifs and decorative patterns as in the Metropolitan Theater. This led to a more representational architecture that infused Philippine culture with predominantly modernist attitudes. The more recent buildings can be seen as a shift wherein the expression of Philippine culture is clearer and strongly associated with traditional forms and motifs. These criteria set the basis wherein the structures were chosen for their ability to tell the story of the development of Philippine architecture.

Yuswadi Saliya

Born 1938 in Bandung, Indonesia. Garjana Arsitek (Ir.) from the Department of Architecture, Faculty of Engineering and Planning, Institut Teknologi Bandung (ITB) in 1966, Master of Architecture from the University of Hawaii 1975 and Ph.D. candidate ITB in 1997. He has been lecturer in the Department of Architecture at ITB from 1967 and also in practice at Atelier–6, Bandung/Jakart completing numerous projects such as the Master Plan for Tourism Dept. of Nusa Tenggara Timur (team) and Chief Architect of the Architectural Dept. Building of ITB. He is Member of the Indonesian Institute of Architects (IAI) and Indonesian Society of Architectural Historian (LSAT) as well as Counseil International des Monuments et des Sites (ICOMOS).

Nomination Criteria

1). Significance in the light of national architectural heritage, its contribution to the national (international) legacy of architectural history.
2). Consensus among the nominators in terms of the typo–morphological variations in SoutheastAsia.

Brian Brace Taylor

Born in the United States of America,Brian Brace Taylor is an architectural historian living in Pari's where he is Professor at the *Ecole d'architecture Paris–Belleville*. After receiving a doctorate from Harvard University, he was a curator of drawings at the *Foundation Le Corbusier* in Paris, before becoming an editor at *L'Architecture d'Aujourdhui* magazine for four years. Subsequently, Professor Taylor was a founder and editor for nearly 10 years of the review *Mimar, Architecture in Development*. During this time, he published several monographs on architects in the developing world, including *Geoffrey Bawa* (Thames & Hudson, 1995) and *Raj Rewal* (Concept Media, 1992). His most recent books include *Pierre Chareau* (Taschen, 1998) and a survey of contemporary Asian architecture. He is Visiting Professor at Bard College in New York.

Nomination Criteria

The criteria for the selection of buildings to represent Cambodia (Kampuchea) in the early–to–mid–20th century was based upon their potentially seminal qualities as unique masterpieces of design. In the case of the Central Market in Phnom Penh, it is an edifice built during the French colonial period, but one whose structure, form, scale and aesthetic restraint represents a fascinating mixture of allusions to antiquity as well as to modern concerns. The Sihanouk housing, also designed by a foreign architect but after Cambodian independence, demonstrates acute sensitivity to the local climate and to issues of high–density urban housing problems then facing the city–for example, adaptability to local cultural needs.

With regard to the grand Lycee A. Yersin in Dalat, Vietnarn, my reasons for proposing its inclusion for the colonial period are that its intrinsic design qualities, and its nonetheless "neutral aesthetic appeal"–rendering no homage to any particular style, Eastern or Western–challenged the mediocre aspects and the attempts to "orientalize" the other colonial buildings in Vietnarn in this period.

In Burma (Myanmar), the Municipal Offices complex near to the sule pagoda is a political statement of peculiar rarity in this country. It represents a turning point–unfortunately not for the better–in the development of Burmese colonial and post–colonial architecture. It should be recognized as both a futile attempt by the British administration to allow "traditional Burmese" architectural decoration to be added to an already well–conceived Western design in order to placate nationalist aspirations, and as an heroic gesture by a Burmese designer to find a modern expression for an architectural heritage nearly obliterated by British vandalism and purposeful destruction for nearly a century.

Oceania

Phillip James Goad

Dr. Phillip James Goad (b. 1961), B.Arch. (Hons),PhD (Melb), is an architectural historian and Senior Lecturer, Deputy Head, Architectural Program, Faculty of Architecture Building & Planning, University of Melbourne. He specialized in theory and history of the 20th century Australian architecture and is the author of the books *Robin Boyd: The Architect as Critic* (1989) and *Melbourne Architecture* (1998) and contributor to *Architecture Australia*, *Architectural Record*, *Architectural Review*, *Casabella*, *L'architecture d'aujourd'hui*, *Spazio e Societa*, *Transition* and *UME*. He is also President of the Society of Architectural Historian, Australia and New Zealand (SAHANZ) and Member of Society of Architectural Historians (USA).

Nomination Criteria

The buildings originally nominated reflected stylistic, structural and regional diversity within the production of architecture in Australia, New Zealand and New Guinea in the 20th century. The selection was not limited to icons of International Modernism nor by the region's urbanity particularly in the late 20th century, its link at certain times to global cultural forces such as 1920s Hollywood, technological progress, and European immigration from the late 1930s. The selection also importantly included buildings that attempt to describe the region itself, its heritage of indigenous culture and hence the invariably hybrid architectural productions of postcolonial cultures.

Andrew Metcalf

Andrew Metcalf is a graduate of the N.S.W. Institute of Technology and The University of Toronto and has operated as an architect, teacher and critic since 1975. Since 1996 he has lived in Canberra where he works in architectural practice and education. Metcalf is the author of three books: *Undesign Your House* (1983), *Thinking Architecture* (1995) and *Architecture in Transition* (1997) and is conducting long-term research into the context in which Renaissance architectural texts were written, published and read. His architectural work has been published in journals such as *Architecture*, *International Architect*, *Domus*, *Ambiente* and *Architecture Australia*.

In 1996 he was a Visiting Fellow at Corpus Christi College in Cambridge and invited to the International Social Sciences Institute, University of Edinburgh as an Honorary Visiting Associate.

Nomination Criteria

In the first instance the Oceania editor asked each nominator to supply a list of 50 buildings. This was the context in which my nominations were made. In so doing I sought to nominate buildings which contained one or more of the following characteristics:
–significant character of regionalism
–new direction for architecture
–building which has been widely influential on subsequent architecture
–building which represents a high point in the development or craft of a particular

type, e.g. office buildings.
–building which is highly regarded and talked about by architects, critics and historians
–key building in an architect's career

Rahim B. Milani

Professor Rahim B. Milani, Diplom Ingenieur of Architecture, FH Regensburg, Germany; Bachelor of Environmental Design and Master of Architecture, University of Minnesota, USA; he is presently Professor and Head of Department of Architecture and Building at the Papua New Guinea University of Technology in Lae, Papua New Guinea. His research and publications on the traditional architecture and settlement patterns of Papua New Guinea, combined with more than 25 years of professional experience, make him well–qualified to nominate outstanding buildings from the Oceania region.

Nomination Criteria

The fundamental basis for selection of the buildings was the degree to which the architect endeavored to interpret the traditional architecture of Papua New Guinea into contemporary urban forms and functions. In the developing urban environment of Papua New Guinea, economy and expediency often overrule cultural sensitivity and appropriate response to the site. I have attempted to identify buildings that avoid such compromises and manifest a clear effort to find an appropriate contemporary response to culture as well as the environment.

Neville Quarry, AM LFRAIA

Neville Quarry holds the title of Emeritus Professor of the University of Technology, Sydney, where he taught architecture for twenty years. During 1997 he was Dean of the Faculty of Architecture, University of Sydney. At the Papua New Guinea University of Technology he was Foundation Professor of Architecture 1971–75. He taught at the School of Architecture, University of Melbourne 1961–78 and has been a visiting professor at many other universities throughout the world.

His major publication is *Award Winning Australian Architecture*, Craftsman House, Sydney 1997. He is a frequent contributor to architecture journals and to architectural conferences and has been a member of the judging panel of many national and international architectural competitions and advisory committees.

The major awards received by Professor Quarry are the Order of Australia AM 1995, the RAIA Gold Medal 1994, the UIA Jean Tschumi Prize 1981, and the Papua New Guinea Independence Medal 1975.

He holds the Degree of Bachelor of Architecture, University of Melbourne and Master of Architecture, Rice University and is a Life Fellow of the Royal Australian Institute of Architects.

Nomination Criteria

Three principles underlie my nominations:

First that the nominated work must have a vivid autonomous architectural presence. Second, that the work must have flourished as a powerful influence upon the form making endeavors of later architects and had an ultimately positive impact upon the architectural perceptions of the community.

Third, that the work of architecture has resonated with the cultural context of its time, and lead that context forward.

Russell Walden

Russell Walden, BArch(NZ), MArch(Dist)(Auckland), PhD(Birm), FNZIA. Associate Professor in the History of Architecture. Previous appointments: Senior Lecturer, The University of Central England in Birmingham, England. Before that in practice as an architect in England and New Zealand. Teaching interests in the history of architecture. Research interests – history of Western architecture. Books: *The Open Hand, Essays on Le Corbusier*, MIT Press, Cambridge, Massachusetts, 1977, pb 1982; *Voices of Silence, New Zealand's Chapel of Futuna*, Victoria University Press, Wellington NZ, 1987; Finnish Harvest, *Chapel in Otaniemi*, Otava Publishing Co. (English and German Editions), Helsinki, 1997. Currently working on a new book called *Exalting Architecture, Sense, Sublimity and Sagacity*. Memberships: Fellow of New Zealand Institute of Architects.

Julia Gatley

B. 1966. Presently employed as a conservation adviser with the New Zealand Historic Places Trust and a part–time lecturer and tutor at the School of Architecture, Victoria University of Wellington, Wellington, New Zealand, in architectural history and heritage conservation. Completed a Master of Architecture at Victoria University of Wellington in 1997. Has a particular interest in Modern Movement architecture and was recognised as a 'de facto' editor in the publication of Wilson, John (Ed), *Zeal and Crusade: The Modern Movement in Wellington*, Christchurch, New Zealand: Te Waihora Press, 1996. Crrently working on a new book which will provide a history of Wellington's Architectural Centre Inc., founded in 1946.

Nomination Criteria

Though New Zealand might be isolated geographically, its architecture cannot be considered in isolation from international influences. What we see is a general trafficking of architectural ideas to this country by a variety of means: New Zealand architects have continued to travel, study and work overseas; architects from other countries (traditionally Britain, Europe, North America and Australia, but increasingly from Asia) have continued to visit and/or immigrate to New Zealand (or at least to have buildings built here); and a large number of books and periodicals have continued to be imported into New Zealand. Further, New Zealand's own architectural press has continued to draw from international sources. Consequently, while Maori motifs and indigenous materials differentiate some, many New Zealand buildings would sit equally well transplanted to other temperate lands.

General Bibliography

Southeast Asia

1. Aasen, Clarence, (1998), Architecture Of Siam: A Cultural History Interpretation, Kuala Lumpur: Oxford University Press
2. Beamish, Jane and Ferguson, Jane, (1985), A History of Singapore Architecture, Singapore: Graham Brash
3. Chan Chee Yoong (ed.), (1987), Post–Merdeka Architecture Malaysia, 1957–1987, Kuala Lumpur: Pertubuhan Akitek Malaysia
4. Chen, Voon Fee (Vol ed.), (1998), The Encyclopedia Of Malaysian Architecture, Singapore: Archipelago Press
5. Chew, Christopher C. W. (ed.), (1988), Contemporary Vernacular: Conceptions and Perceptions–AA Asia Monograph One , Singapore : AA Asia
6. Ching, Nancy , (1977), Questioning Development in the Southeast Asia, Singapore: Select Books
7. Dumarcay, Jacques, (1991), The Palaces of South–East Asia – Architecture and Customs, Singapore: Oxford University Press, (1987).
8. The House in South–East Asia, Singapore: Oxford University Press
9. Eryudhawan, Bambang (ed.), et al.(1995), Arsitek Muda Indonesia: penjelajahan 1990 – 1995, Indonesi: Arsitek Muda Indonesia
10. Falconer, John (ed.) et al. (1998), Myanmar Style – Art, Architecture and Design of Burma, Singapore: Periplus Editions (HK) Pte Ltd
11. Hoskin, John, (1995), Bangkok by Design– Architectural Diversity in the City of Angels, Bangkok: Post Books
12. Inglis, Kim (ed.), (1997), Tropical Asian Style, Singapore: Periplus Editions (HK) Pte Ltd.
13. Iwan Sudradjat, (1991), A Study of Indonesian Architectural History, PhD Thesis, University of Sydney, Department of Architecture
14. Jumsai, Sumet, (1988), NAGA. Cultural Origins in Siam and the West Pacific, Bangkok: Chalermnit Press
15. Klassen, Winand, (1986), Architecture in the Philippines: Filipino Building in a Cross–Cultural Context, Cebu City: University of San Carlos
16. Lee, Kip Lin, (1988), The Singapore House 1819– 1942, Singapore: Times Edition
17. Leerdam, Ben F. van (1995), Architect Henri Maclaine Point: An Intensive Search on the Essence of Javanese Architecture, Doctoral Dissertation, Technische Universiteit Delft, Faculteit der Bouwkunde
18. Lim Jee Yuan, (1987), The Malay House: Rediscovering Malaysia's Indigenous Shelter System, Pulau Pinang: Institut Masyarakat
19. Lim, William S. W., (1998), Asian New Urbanism, Singapore: Select Books
20. (1990), Cities for People: Reflections of a Southeast Asian Architect, Singapore: Select Books 21.
21. (1980), An Alternative Urban Strategy, Singapore: DP Architects (Pte)
22. (1975), Equity and Urban Environment in the Third World: with Special Reference to ASEAN Countries and Singapore, Singapore: DP Consultant Service Pte Ltd.
23. Lim, William S.W. , Mok Wei Wei (et al.), (1982), Singapore River, Bu Ye Tian: A Conservation Proposal for Boat Quay, Singapore: Bu Ye Tian Enterprises Pte Ltd.
24. Lim, William S. W. and Tan, Hock Beng, (1998), Contemporary Vernacular – Evoking Traditions in the Asian Architecture, Singapore: Select Books
25. Naengnoi Suksri and Freeman, Michael, (1996), Palaces of Bangkok – Royal Residences of the Chakri Dynasty, Bangkok: Asia Books Co. Pte Ltd.
26. Nagashima, Koichi (ed.), (1980), Contemporary Asian Architecture: Works of APAC Members, Process Architecture No. 20, Tokyo: Process Architecture Publishing Co. Pte. Ltd.
27. Polites, Nicholas, (1977), The Architecture of Leandro V. Locsin, New York: Weatherhill
28. Powell, Robert, (1994), Living Legacy: Singapore's Architectural Heritage Renewed, Singapore: Singapore Heritage Society
29. (1998), Urban Asian House: Living in Tropical Cities, Singapore: Select Books
30. (1993), The Asian House – Contemporary Houses of South East Asia, Singapore: Select Books
31. (1996), The Tropical Asian House, Singapore: Select Books
32. (1997), Line, Edge & Shade – The Search for a Design Language in Tropical Asia, Singapore: Page One Publishing
33. Pusadee Tiptas, (1989), Design in Thailand in Rattanakosin Period: Two Decades of Architectural Design in Thailand 1968 – 1989, Bangkok: Creative Print
34. (1992), An Architectural Digest From Past to Present, Bangkok: The Association of Siamese Architects Under Royal Patronage(ASA)
35. (1996), Siamese Architect: Principle, Role, Work and Concept 1932–1994 Vol. 2, Bangkok: The Association of Siamese Architects Under Royal Patronage (ASA)

36. Schaik, Leon van (ed.), (1996), Asian Design Forum #7, Asian Design Forum
37. Singapore Planning and Urban Research Group, (1967, 1971), SPUR 1865–1967 and SPUR 1968–1971, Singapore: SPUR
38. Sompop Pirom, (1985), Pyre in Rattanakosin, Bangkok: Amarin Printing
39. Sumalyo, Yulianto, (1995), Dutch Colonial Architecture in Indonesia, Yogjakarta: Gadjah Mada University Press
40. Tan, Hock Beng, 1994, Tropical Architecture and Interiors–Tradition–based Design of Indonesia, Malaysia , Singapore and Thailand, Singapore: Page One Publishing Pte Ltd
41. Tay, Kheng Soon, (1989), Mega–Cities in the Tropics: Towards an Architectural Agenda for the Future, Singapore: Institute of the Southeast Asian Studies
42. Taylor, Brian B. and Hoskin, John, (1996), Sumet Jumsai, Bangkok: The Key Publisher
43. Vlatseas, S., (1990), A History of Malaysian Architecture, Singapore: Longman
44. Waterson, Roxana, (1990), The Living House–An Anthropology of Architecture in South–East Asia, Singapore: Oxford University Press
45. Wyatt, David K., (1984), Thailand: A Short History, Bangkok: Silkworm Books
46. Yeang, Ken, (1996), The Skyscraper – Bioclimatically Considered, London: Academy Editions
47. (1992), The Architecture of Malaysia, Amsterdam: Pepin Press
48. Yeoh, Brenda S. A., (1996), Contesting Spaces : Power Relations and the Urban Built Environment in Colonial Singapore, USA: Oxford University Press

Oceania

General
1. Taylor, Jennifer, "Oceania: Australia, New Zealand, Papua New Guinea and the smaller islands of the South Pacific", Banister Fletcher, History of Architecture, 19th Edition, Butterworths, London, 1987 (20th Edition, London, 1995)

Australia
2. Boyd, Robin ,Australia's Home: its Origins, Builders and Occupiers,Melbourne University Press,Melbourne,1987(First Edition 1952)
3. Freeland, John Maxwell, Architecture in Australia: A History, Cheshire, Melbourne,1968
4. Howells,Trevor, and Michael Nicholson,Towards the Dawn: Federation Architecture in Australia1890–1915, Hale and Iremonger, Sydney, 1989
5. Irving, Robert (Ed.), The History and Design of the Australian House,Oxford University Press, Melbourne,1985
6. Jahn, Graham, Contemporary Australian Architecture, G+ B Arts International Limited, Basel, Switzerland, 1994
7. Johnson, Donald Leslie, Australian Architecture, 1901–1951: Sources of Modernism, Sydney University Press, Sydney, 1980
8. Ogg, Alan, Architecture in Steel: The Australian Context, Royal Australian Institute of Architects, Red Hill, 1987
9. Quarry, Neville, Award Winning Australian Architecture, Craftsman Press: G+B Arts International, Sydney, 1997
10. Taylor, Jennifer,An Australian Identity: Houses for Sydney: 1953–1963, Department of Architecture, University of Sydney, 1984 (First edition 1972)
11. Taylor, Jennifer,Australian Architecture Since 1960, Royal Australian Institute of Architecture, Manuka, ACT, 1990 (First edition 1986)

New Zealand
12. Fowler, Michael,Buildings for New Zealanders, Lansdowne Press, Auckland,1984
13. Hill, Martin, New Zealand Architecture, School Publications Branch, Department of Education, Wellington, 1981
14. Hodgson,Terence,Looking at the Architecture of New Zealand, Grandham House, Wellington, 1990
15. Mitchell, David, and Gillian Chaplin, The Elegant Shed: New Zealand Architecture since 1945, Oxford University Press, Auckland, 1984
16. Shaw, Peter, New Zealand Architecture: From Polynesian Beginnings to 1990, Hodder and Stoughton, Auckland, 1991
17. Stackpoole, John, and Peter Bevan, New Zealand Art: Architecture 1820–1970, A. H. & A. W. Reed, Wellington, 1972
18. Wilson, John (Ed.), Zeal and Crusade; Modern Architecture in Wellington, Te Waihora Press, Wellington, 1996.

Index

This Index contains names of cities, countries, architects, engineers, owners and buildings mentioned in the General Introduction, the Introductory Essay and the Selected Buildings

Part I: General Introduction and Southeast Asia

A

AA Asia (Singapore) XXVIII
AA School of Architecture, London XXI
Aasen, Clarence XIX
Abelia Apartment, Singapore XXV, 136–137
Abhaiwongse, Chitrasen 54
Akitiek Jururancang (M) Sdn Bhd 124
Amorsolo, Fernado 27
Anglo–Oriental Building, Kuala Lumpur 48–49
Antonio, Pablo XX
Arellano, Juan XVIII 26, 27
art4d XXVIII
Arup, Ove XV
Asia Insurance Building, Singapore XIX, 58–59
Asian Planning and Architectural Consultants (APAC) XXIII
Atelier des Batisseurs (ATBAT) XIX, 18–21
Athens Charter XIX
Aula ITB, Bandung XX, 18–21

B

Bali 132
Balina Serai, Bali XXVI, 132–133
Bandung 18, 38, 122, 134
Bangkok 4, 12, 54, 80, 82, 90, 94, 104
Bank of America Building, Bangkok 94–95
Bauhaus XIX
Bawa, Geoffrey XXV
Bedmar, Ernesto 120
Bedmar & Shi Designers Pte Ltd 120
Berrety, W. 39
Bhd Chedi Bandung, Bandung 122–123
Boat Quay Conservation Area, Singapore 138–139
Bodiansky, Vladimir 70
Boulder Dam, Colorado XV
Bray, A. G. 36, 37
British Council, Bangkok XXIII, 82–83
British East India Company 139
Brunei XVIII
Bu Ye Tian enterprises XVIII, 139
Bu Ye Tian Conservation, Singapore XXV
Bund, Shanghai XIX
Bunnag, Duangrit XXIV, 275
Burnham, Daniel 27

C

Cambodia XVIII
Case Study Homes, Los Angeles XV
Central Market, Phnom Penh XIX, 46–47
Central Market & Central Square, Kuala Lumpur, 110–113
Chandigarh XXII, 69
Chapel at Romchamp XXII
Chapel of the Holy Sacrifice (1955) XXIII
Chauchon, Louis XX, 46,47
Chen Voon Fee 67, 69, 110, 274
China XIX

Cité Sihanouk, La, Phnom Penh XVII, 70–71
Clementi, Governor Sir Cecil 31, 35
Clifford, Sir Hugh Charles 31
Clifford Pier, Singapore 30–31
A.O. Coltman, Booty, Edwards & Partners 48
Congrés Internationaux d'Architecture Moderne (CIAM) XIX
Cooke, E. S. 60
Correa, Charles, XXV
Cort Theater, New York 27

D

Dalat 42
The Datai, Langkawi Island XXVI, 124
Davao 128
Francisco Mañosa and Partners 128, 129
Design Forum (Malaysia) XXIV
Design Partnership 84, 86
Desbois, Jean XIX, 46, 47
Dialogue House, Malaysia XXVIII
Dodge House XV
Drew, Jane XXII

E

Eu House, Singapore XXVI, 120–121
Eu Tong Sen 23

F

Far Eastern University, Philippines XIX
Federal House, Kuala Lumpur XIX, 56–57
Fletcher, Banister XVIII
Floirendo Family Villas, Davao XXVI, 128–131
Foster, Norman XXV
Frampton, Kenneth XIV
Francisco Mañosa and Partners 128
Fry, E. Maxwell XXII

G

Geology Building, University of Malaya, Kuala Lumpur XX, 74–75
Gill, Irving XV
Goh, Dr. Poh Seng 139
Golden Mile Complex, (formerly known as Who Hup Complex), Singapore XXIII, 86–87
Grand Lycee Yersin, Dalat 42–45
Gropius, Walter XIX, XX

H

R. Hamzah & Yeang Sdn 116
Hanning, Gerald 70
Helsinki Station 35
Hong Kong XXI, XXIII
Hijjas Kasturi Associates Sdn 108
Hill, Kerry XXIII, 122, 132
Ho, Richard 274
Ho, Tao XXI
Hongsakul, Korn 12
Hotel Indonesia XX
Hubback, Arthur Bennison 15

I

India XVIII
Indonesia XXIII
Institut Teknologi Bandung (ITB) see Aula
International Convention Center, Manila XXIII
Istana Kenangan (now the Perak State Royal Museum), Kuala
Kangsar, Perak XIX, 24–25
Istana Sri Menanti 8–11
Iversen, B. M. 56

J

Jakarta, Cengkareng 100
Johnston, Alexander Laurie ?
Jumsai, Sumet XVIII, XXI, 82, 90, 104, 275

K

Kallang Airport, Singapore XIX
Kampong Bugis Development Project, Singapore XXII
Kasturi, Hijjas XXI, 108,109
Kerry Hill Architects 122, 124, 132
Kesteven, L. 32
King Chulalongkorn (Rama V) 4, 12
Klassen, Winand XVIII
Kuala Kangsar, Perak XIX, 14, 24
Kuala Lumpur 48, 56, 60, 64, 74, 96, 108, 110

L

Lagisquet, J. 42
Laguna de Bay 88, 89
Lamb, Thomas W. 27
Langkawi Island 124
Laos XVIII
Leandro V. Locsin and Associates 76
Le Corbusier XXII 69
Lee Yan Lian Building, Kuala Lumpur XIX, 60–63
Lem House, Singapore XXIV
Lever House 65
Lim, Chong Keat 65
Lim , Jimmy Cheok Siang XXIII, 96
Lim, William XVI, XXI, XXIII, 65, 85, 87, 139
Locsin, Leandro XXIII, 76, 77, 88, 89
Loew's Theater, New York 27
Los Baños 88
Luth Building, Malaysia XXIV

M

Maison Jaoul XXII
Majestic Theatre, Singapore 22–23
Maki, Fumihiko XXI
Malayan Architects Co–partnership 66, 67, 72, 74
Malaysia XVII, XXI, XXIII
Manila 26, 76
Manila Post Office XVIII, 27
Mañosa, Francisco "Bobby" 128, 276
Mapus Institute of Technology, Philippines XX!
Marine Drive, Bombay XIX
Marine Parade Community Club, Singapore XXV
Menara Maybank, Kuala Lumpur XXIV, 108–109
Menara Mesiniaga, Selangor XXV, 116–119
Metropolitan Theater, Manila XVIII, 26–29
Mies van der Rohe XIX, XXI
Molyan, Vann 65

Mt. Makiling 88, 89
Mundhat Ratanaroj Mansion 5
Municipal Offices Building (Now The Rangoon City Development
Corporation or YCDC), Rangoon 36–37
Myanmar XVIII

N

Nagashima, Koichi XXI
Nagoya Tower XXV
Nalbantoglu, Gulsum Baydar XVII
Nation Building, Bangkok XXII
Nation Tower, Bangkok XXII
National Arts Center of the Philippines 88–89
National School of Arts and Crafts, Thailand XXIII
Negri Sembilan 8
Ng, Keng Siang 58

O

Ocampo, H. R. 79
Ongard Architects 80

P

Panabhandhu School, Classroom and Dormitory Building, Bangkok
80–81
Parliament Building, Kuala Lumpur 64–65
People's Park Complex, Singapore XXIII, 84–85
Philippine International Convention Center XXI
Philippine Legislative Building 27
Philippines XVIII
Phnom Penh 46, 70
Phra Thinang Chakri Maha Prasat in the Grand Palace, Thailand XIX
Phraya Rajasongkram 12
Pont, Henri Maclaine XIX, 18,39
Prairie House XV
Prince Narisaranuwatiwong 4
Public Works Department, Singapore 27
Pyre For Rama V, Bangkok 12

Q

R

Rachadamnern Boulevard Row House , Bangkok XX, 54–55
Raffles, Sir Stamford 139
Rahman, Tunku Abdul 65
Rangoon 36
Reuter House, Singapore XXVI, 114
Rivoli Theater 27
Robot Building, Bangkok XXV, 104–107

S

Saarinen Eliel 35
Saliya, Yuswadi 277
Samai Island, Davao 128
Science Museum, Bangkok XXIII, 90
Selangor, Klang 32
Selangor, Subang Jaya 116
Selora Bung Karno Sports Centre XXII
Serembian 8
Shah Alam Palace 33
Shanghai Armory Tower XXII

Shoemaker, Wolff, IEp4, 15
Singapore XvIII, XXI, 22, 30, 34, 52, 58, 66, 84, 86, 136, 138
Singapore Conference Hall, Singapore 66–69
Singapore Improvement Trust XIX, 52
Singapore Railway Station & Hotel XIX, 34–35
Soejano & Rachman 100
Soekarno–Hatta International Airport 100–103
South Korea XXIII
Spooner, C. E. 15
State Mosque, Negri sembilan, Seremban XX, 72–73
Suan Dusit Palace 5
Sultan Sulaiman Mosque, Selangor 32
Swan & MacLaren XX, 34

T

Tampines North Community Club, Singapore XXII
Tan House, Bandung 134–135
Tan Kok–Meng XX
Tan Tjiang Ay 134
Tang C K. XXI
TangGuanBee Architects 136
Tay Kheng Soon 85. 87
Taylor, Brian Brace XIX, 277
Telephone Board Exchange, Singapore XXIII
Tennessee Valley Authority XV
Thailand XXIII
Theater of Performing Arts, Cultural Center of the Philippines 76–79
Tiong Bahru Estate 53
Tiong Bahru Flats, Singapore XIX, 52–53
Tugu Monas National Monument XX
Tukang Kahar 8
Tukang Taib 9

U

U Maung Maung 37
U Maung Tin 36,37
U Tha Tun 37
Ubudiah Mosque, Kuala Kangsar (Perak) XIX, 33–34
Urban Redevelopment Authority (URA) 85

V

Vietnam XVIII
Villa Isola, Bandung XIX, 38–41
Vimanmek Palace, Bangkok 4–7

W

Wagner, Otto 33
Walian House, Kuala Lumpur XXIII, 38–41
William Lim Associates 110,114
Williams, E. Owen XVI
Who Hup 31, 37
Wright, F.L. XV

X

Y

Yeang, Ken,116
Yeoh, Brenda XVI
Yersin, Alexander 43

Z

Part II: Oceania

A

Aalto, Aalto XXIX
Addison, Rex XXXV, 232
Ancher, Sydney, 170, 171
Anse Vata, Noumea 262
Air Niugini Staff Housing, Korobosea 224–225
American Express Tower, Sydney XXXII
Andrews, John XXXIV, 218, 219
Andrew' Farmhouse, Eugowra XXXV
Anzac War Memorial, Sydney XXVIII
Architectural Centre, Wellington XIX
Athfield, Ian, 202, 203
Athfield House 202–205
Architects Pacific 262
Auckland XXVIII
Australasia XXIX
Australia XXVI–XXXIII
Australian Institute of Sport 223
Australia Square, Sydney, 206–209
Ayers Rock,'Uluru' 235

B

Bates Peebles and Smart 144, 145
Bates Smart and McCutcheon, 184
Bauhaus 173
Beach House, St. Andrews 254–255
Behrens, Peter XXIX
'Belvedere' (Stephens House) 154–155
Berhampore Flats XXXII, 168–169
Birrell, James XXXV, 200
Bohringer, Taylor and Johnson XXXII, 160, 161
Borland, Kevin XXXV, 180
Boyd, Robin, 182, 183
Boyd House182–183
Breuer, Marcel, 173
Brambuk Cultural Center XXXVII, 252–253
Britten House XXXII
Burgess, Gregory XXXVII, 253

C

C. B. Alexander Agricultural College, Tocal, XXXIV, 194–195
Cameron Offices, Canberra 218–221
Campbell, John XXXI
Canberra Plan XXVIII
Canberra VI, 246
Belconnen, Canberra 218
Bruce, Canberra 222
Capitol Theatre, Melbourne XXXII
Case Study Homes, Los Angeles XXXV
Cathedral of the Blessed Sacrament 142–143
Centre of Maori Studies, Puukenga XXXVII
Chapel of Futuna XXXV, 190–191
Christchurch XXX, 142, 212
Christchurch Town Hall 212–213
Church of the Resurrection, Keysborough XXXVI
City Mutual Life Assurance Building, Sydney, XXVIII
Civic Theatre XXXII, 160–161
Clarke Gazzrd 198
Collins, Desmond 224

Corrigan, Peter XXXVI
Cox, Philip XXXIV, 196, 222, 223
Cox Richardson & Taylor 250

D

Daryl Jackson Pty Ltd 258
Dalton, John XXXV
Dearing, Deborah 260
Dellit, Bruce XXVIII
Denton Corker Marshall XXXII, XXXIII, 260, 261, 264
Dudok, Willem XXXII, 163

E

'Eryldene' 146–149

F

Fiji XXXVIII
Fijian Government Architects 256
Frame, Paul 232
Frameworks Architects Pty. Ltd. 232

G

Gabriel Poole House, Doonan XXXI
Gatley, Julia 281
Gazzard, Don 198
Gibson, Robin XXXV
Goad, Philip 279
Governor Phillip and Governor Macquarie Tower XXXVI, 260–261
Goroka, Eastern Highlands Province, Papua New Guinea XXXI, 232
Grampians National Park in Western Victoria, Australia 253
Gray Young, Morton and Young 164
Great Southern Stand of Melbourne Cricket Ground 258–259
'Greenway'(Wikinson House) 158–159
Griffin, Walter Burley XXXII, 152, 153, 247
Gropius Walter 173
Grounds, Roy 176, 177
Grounds House 176–177
Grounds Romberg & Boyd 176, 183
Group Architects XXIX
Gummer, William Henry   XXXII, 150, 151
Gummer and Ford and Partners XXXII

H

Hall, Russell 224
Hall, Todd and Littlemore 214, 215
Halls Gap 252
Hamill House 170–171
Hawkes Bay 150
Headquarters South Pacific Commission, Noumea 262–263
Hennessey and Hennessey XXVIII
Hilversum Town Hall 163
Hogan, Cecil 238

I

ICI House 184–185
Irwin, W.L. 180

J

Jackson, Daryl XXXV, 228, 229, 258, 259
Jackson House, Shoreham 228–229
JASMAX XXXVII
Jean Marie Tjibaou Cultural Centre, Noumea, 268–271
John and Phyllis Murphy, Borland and McIntyre 180
Jolly, Alexander Stewart 154

K

Kahn, Albert W. 145
Katsalidis, Nonda 254, 255
Korobosea, National Capital District, Papua New Guinea 224

L

Lewers, Gerald   185
Lutyens, Edwin XXXI, 151

M

Macpherson Robertson Girls' High School 162–163
Macquarie Street Tower, Sydney XXXVI
Mahony, Marion 152
Main Reading Room, State Library of Victoria 144
Marika–Alderton House XXXVII
Marx, Roberto Burle 243
McIntyre Peter 180
McKay Ian XXXIV, 196
Massey House, Wellington XXXIII
Melbourne 144, 152, 174, 180, 258, 264
Albert Park, Melbourne 162
Carlton, Melbourne XXXII
East Melbourne 184
Port Philip Area, Melbourne XXXI
South Yarra, Melbourne 182
Toorak, Melbourne 176
Melbourne Exhibition Center, Melbourne 264–265
Melling: Morse Architects 266
Mendelsohn, Eric XXIX
Metcalf Andrew 279
Milani Rahim 280
Mitchell/Giurgola & Thorp XXXVI, 246, 247
MLC Building XXX
Monash, John 144, 145
Mt. Irvine, NSW, Australia 230
Muller, Peter XXXIV, 178, 179
Muller House 178–179
Murcutt, Glenn XXXVII, 230
Murphy, John and Phyllis 180

N

National Athletic Stadium Canberra XXXIV, 222–223
National Cultural Council of Papua New Guinea 233
National Museum of New Zealand XXXIII
Nervi, Pier Luigi 206
Neutra, Richard 159
New Caledonia XXXIV
New Zealand XXX
Newman, Smith and Greenhough 188
Newman College, University of Melbourne 152–153
Newman, Smith and Greenhough .XXIX
Nicholas and Carruthers House 230–231
Northern Territory, Australia 234

Noumea, New Caledonia 268

O

Olympic Swimming Pool, Melbourne XXX, 180–181
Ove Arup and Partners Pacific Pty. Ltd. 232

P

Paimio Sanitarium XXIX
Palmerston North Public Library XXXVII
Papua New Guinea XXX
Papua New Guinea National Parliament Building 238–241
Parliament Building, Wellington XXVII
Parliament House of Australia XXXVI, 246–249
Parliament of Fiji 256–257
Parliament buildings of Fiji, Papua New Guinea, Vanuatu and Western Samoa XXXIV
Peddle Thorp PNG Pty. Ltd. 238
Petre, Francis William 142, 143
Philip Cox & Partners 234
Piano, Renzo XXXVI, 258, 259
Plishke, Ernst XXIX
Plischke and Firth XXIX
Poole, Gabriel XXXV
PNG Department of Works and Supply 238
Prudential Building, Wellington XXVIII
Pugh House 266–267

Q

Quarry Neville 280
Queensland XXXV
Queensland Art Gallery XXXV

R

Raetihi Ratana Church XXXI
Raun Raun Theater Goroka 232–233
Reed, Joseph 145
Rickard, Bruce XXXIV, 193
Rickard House 192–193
Riverside Center, Brisbane 242–245
Romberg, Frederick 174
Rose Seidler House XXXIII, 172–175

S

Schindler, Rudolf 159
Scott, John XXXV, 190–191
Seabrook and Fildes 162, 163
Seabrook, Norman 162, 163
Seidler, Harry 172, 173, 206, 210, 244
Seidler House 210–211
Shoreham 228
Sodersten, Emil XXVIII
Solomon Islands XVII
South Pacific Commission 263
St Andrew's Beach 254
Stanhill Flats, Melbourne 174–175
State Insurance Building, Wellington, XXXII
State Theatre, Sydney XXVIII
Stephens, F.C. 155
Stephenson and Turner XXIX
Stevens, John 185

Suva 256
Swanson Brothers 145
Sydney XXXVI, 206, 214, 220, 250, 260
Gordon, Sydney 146
Cremorne, Sydney 154
Glebe Sydney XXXVI
Killara, Sydney 210
Mosman, Sydney 194
Paddington, Sydney XXXVI
Turramurra, Sydney 172
Vaucluse, Sydney 158, 198
Woolloomooloo, Sydney XXXVI
Wahroonga, Sydney 192
Whale Beach, Sydney 178
Sydney Football Stadium 250–251
Sydney Opera House 214–217
Sydney School XXXV

T

Tauroa Homestead 150–151
Taylor, Jennifer XXVI
Te Papa Tongarewa, the Museum of New Zealand XXXVII
Thompson, Rewi XXXVII
Tocal 196
Tompkins Shaw & Evans 258
Troppo Architects, Darwin XXXI
Trussed Concrete Steel Company of England (Truscon) 145

U

Union College Hall of Residence, University of Queensland 200–201
Utzon, Jorn 214, 215

V

Venturi, Robert XXXVI
Vitia Architects 256

W

Waigani, National Capital District, Papua New Guinea 238
Walden, Russell 281
Walker, Roger XXXV
Warren, Miles XXXIV
Warren and Peter Bevan XXIX
Wanganui 188–189
War Memorial Hall, Wanganui 188–189
Warren and Mahoney Architects Ltd 212
Waterhouse, E.G. 147
Wellington XXXII, 168, 190, 266
Wellington Library XXXIII
Wellington Railway Station 164–165
Wentworth Memorial Church 198–199
Western Samoa XXVI
White, Henry E. XXXII
Wilkinson, Leslie XXXI,158, 159
Wilson, Francis Gordon XXXII, 168, 169
Wilson, William Hardy XXXII, 146, 147
Wilston House, Brisbane XXXV
Woolley, Ken 194, 195
Woolley House 194–195
Wright, Frank Lloyd 178, 193

X

Y

Young, William Gray 163
Yulara Tourist Resort 234–237

Z